NAKED SPIRITUALITY

'This is a quiet book, a deeply gentle and candid book, that is the distillate of a life-time of belonging to God. It is McLaren, in his maturity and at his pastoral best, bringing a love-song of great intimacy and external beauty.'

Phyllis Tickle, author of *The Great Emergence*

'In our rapidly changing world, Brian McLaren has walked with a generation through the painful and necessary re-examination of the nature of Church and Christianity. This work reveals the struggles and depths of Brian's faith within that exploration, and invites us into a most profound and hopeful consideration of our own.'

Jason Clark, Deep Church

'Medicine for the soul. NAKED SPIRITUALITY is filled with uncommon honesty. It is a tonic for all those who yearn for practical help with the development of rhythms of life – free from the stifling tyranny of legalism – that will foster a depth of Christ-centred spirituality.'

Steve Chalke MBE, Founder of Oasis Global,
Faithworks & Stop The Traffik, UN Special Advisor
on Community Action Against Human Trafficking

'This is one of Brian's greatest hits. It is a book that strips things down to the bare essentials. You will find something on these pages that will help you breathe again.'

Shane Claiborne, author of *The Irresistible Revolution*

NAKED SPIRITUALITY

A Life with God in
Twelve Simple Words

BRIAN D. MCLAREN

HODDER &
STOUGHTON

First published in Great Britain in 2011 by Hodder & Stoughton
An Hachette UK company

1

A CIP catalogue record for this title is available
from the British Library

ISBN 978 0 340 99545 7

Typeset in Monotype Sabon by Ellipsis Books Limited, Glasgow

Printed in Great Britain by Clays Ltd, St Ives plc

Hodder & Stoughton policy is to use papers that are natural,
renewable and recyclable products and made from wood grown
in sustainable forests. The logging and manufacturing processes
are expected to conform to the environmental regulations
of the country of origin.

Hodder & Stoughton Ltd
338 Euston Road
London NW1 3BH

www.hodderfaith.com

Contents

Four: Harmony: The Season of Spiritual Deepening

Acknowledgements

Thanks to pastor and fly fisherman Jeff Petersen for reading an early draft of this book and offering helpful input. Thanks to seasoned editors Mickey Maudlin (from HarperOne in the United States) and Katherine Venn (at Hodder & Stoughton in the United Kingdom) for their sage guidance in shaping this book. Thanks to Ann Moru for her unmatched editorial assistance. Thanks to my talented literary agent Kathryn Helmers for the many ways she helps me navigate the fascinating world of publishing, and to Laci Scott who has deftly and graciously managed my work as a travelling speaker for as long as I can remember. Thanks, as always, to my many mentors and friends whose contributions are woven into every word I write and who have blessed my life beyond words. Deepest thanks to Grace, our kids, and my parents and extended family, in whose love I live. I am blessed indeed.

This book is dedicated to my grandchildren, born and unborn, in hopes that it will someday be a resource for their spiritual journey.

Preface

He was naked.

In broad daylight. In church.

He had taken off all his clothing – in front of the local bishop, in front of his neighbours and peers, and in front of his angry father. He now stood before them all. 'I shall go naked to meet my naked Lord,' he said.

We know him as St Francis, but at that moment he was just Giovanni Francesco di Bernardone, a young man on trial in the portico of the church of Santa Maria Maggiore in Assisi, Italy. Standing there self-exposed, he must have seemed more a candidate for involuntary hospitalisation than elevation to sainthood.

His father was a prosperous merchant of fine fabrics, an appreciating commodity at the beginning of the thirteenth century when dressing *up* was becoming more and more essential for those wishing to ascend the socio-economic ladder. He had accused Francis of selling some of his merchandise to raise money for a church renovation project. Since that fabric had indeed been sold and the proceeds invested in Francis' mission,

Francis had nothing to offer in restitution. So he gave his father everything he had: his money, the shirt off his back, along with the rest of his garments, saying, 'I return not only my money, but also my clothes.' In so doing, Francis stripped off the identity he had acquired from his earthly father and clothed himself in a more primal and primary identity: as God's unclothed creature, God's naked and vulnerable child.

That wasn't Francis' only experience of public nakedness. Once, the story goes, Francis commanded his colleague Friar Ruffino to go preach in the Assisi church 'naked, save only for thy breeches'. When Friar Ruffino complied, Francis felt ashamed for issuing such an extreme command, so he went and joined him in naked preaching (we're not sure whether the 'breeches' were included or not). Years later, he stripped naked again and went out in the snow to make snowmen – this time in an attempt to deal with his sensual desires. One would imagine that the technique worked well enough, at least for the time he was outdoors in the freezing cold.

Francis joined a long tradition of nakedness in the service of spirituality, stretching from the days of Samuel and Saul, through Isaiah's three-year stint preaching nude, to Jesus himself.[1] In the Sermon on the Mount where Jesus talks about turning the other cheek and walking the second mile, he says that if someone takes you to court, suing you for your overcoat, you might as well give them your other clothes as well, implying (I think) that in so doing, your self-exposure will serve to expose the heartless greed of your opponent. Jesus lived out this teaching three years later when, by his exposure on the cross, he exposed the brutality of the occupying Romans and the hypocrisy of the local religious establishment.

In a set of details both strange and poignant, Mark's Gospel tells us that before being crucified, Jesus was stripped of his clothes three times. After the first stripping, he was mockingly clothed in a purple cloak of royalty, in which he was derided, spat upon and beaten. Then he was stripped a second time and re-clothed in his own garment. Finally he was stripped once more, and the soldiers cast lots to see who would take home his outer garment, his inner garment, and maybe his sandals as bonus pay for their day's work. Hanging on that cross, contrary to our discreet religious art, Jesus was exposed. It wasn't until after Jesus was dead that a kind soul, Joseph of Arimathea, covered the naked corpse with a linen cloth.[2]

Naked we came from the womb, Job said, and naked we shall depart this life, but in between, we clothe ourselves in a thousand fascinating ways. Think of the immense variety and meaning of clothing in human society – military uniforms, academic regalia, religious robes; clothing as status symbol, designer labels as the mark of belonging to an in-group, festive costumes to celebrate a holiday or season; a prom dress, a wedding gown, bikini, burka; white lab coat, faded blue jeans; bright green shirts or bold red jerseys to proclaim political protest or team loyalty. We all learn to speak verbal languages – English, Chinese, Spanish, and so on – but we all must become fluent in the finely nuanced languages of dress as well.

If clothing means and expresses so much, then of course so does nakedness.

In his list of things for which there is a time and season, the sage of Ecclesiastes did not say, 'A time to get dressed and a time to get naked,' but there are indeed such times. Without nakedness, for example, you can't go under the bright light of surgery. And without nakedness, you can't enter into the candle-light of intimacy.

This is a book about getting naked ... not physically, but spiritually. It's about stripping away the symbols and status of public religion – the Sunday-dress version people often call 'organised religion'. And it's about attending to the well-being of the soul clothed only in naked human skin. As a result, it must be a vulnerable book, tender in tone, gentle in touch. You won't find much in the way of aggressive arguments here, but rather shy experience daring to step into the light. It's an honest book, and I hope a practical one too, perhaps with some awkward spiritual parallels to what they used to call a 'marital manual'.

You won't need to agree with all the planks of my theological platform; I am a Christian and all I write flows from my experience in that rich tradition, but you may be of another tradition entirely, or of no known tradition at all. Instead of seeking theological agreement, this book invites you to experiment with the naked experience of God that provides the raw material from which all worthwhile theology derives.

There's a lot of dirty theology out there ... the religious counterpart to dirty politics and dirty business, I suppose. You might call it spiritual pornography: a kind of for-profit exploitive nakedness. It's found in many of the same places as physical pornography (the internet and satellite/cable TV for starters), and it promises similar things: instant intimacy, fantasy and make-believe, private voyeurism and vicarious experience, communion without commitment. That's certainly not what we're after in these pages.

No, we're after a lost treasure as old as the story of the Garden of Eden: the possibility of being naked and not ashamed ... naked before God, naked before one another too, so we have no need to cover up, to protect, to posture, to dress to impress, just the freedom to be who we are, what we are, as we are.[3] At their best, religious and spiritual communities help us discover this pure and naked spiritual encounter. At their worst, they simply make us more ashamed, pressuring us to cover up more, pushing us to further enhance our image with the best designer labels and latest spiritual fads, weighing us down with layer upon layer of heavy, uncomfortable, pretentious, well-starched religiosity. As someone who has experienced some of the best and some of the worst of religion and spirituality, I hope this book will help you strip away distractions and discover that precious hidden treasure, that primal gift underneath.

Introduction:

Introduction

'So what do you do for a living?' you might ask if we happened to sit next to each other on a flight, mutually ignoring the flight attendant's spiel about how to turn our seat cushions into a flotation device and what electronic devices we need to turn off before take-off. 'I'm an author,' I might whisper, which might then prompt you to ask what I write books about. I'd probably reply, 'I write books on spirituality, cultural change and social issues,' or something like that. More often than not, we'd end up getting into an interesting conversation that would last until well after we reached our cruising altitude. (Unless you want to take a nap – I promise I wouldn't bother you in that case.)

Since we haven't actually met, I have to imagine what you might tell me about yourself. I was a pastor for over twenty years, so I learned to be a good listener.

If you're like a lot of people I meet, you might describe yourself as 'more spiritual than religious'. You're seeking meaning and depth in your life, maybe even a deeper experience of God, but you don't feel that traditional 'organised religion' helps very much.

Or you may be faithfully religious – a lifelong church-goer, a paid or unpaid minister, a diligent seminarian or theologian, a hard-working pastor, para-church worker, or priest. But you feel you're on autopilot, going through the motions. You're keeping the religious treadmill spinning, but your soul is dry, thirsty, empty, tired. You feel a little toasted, if not fully burned out. Too much guilt. Too many 'should's. Too much pressure. Too much activity and controversy without a clear sense of worthwhile outcomes. You wish you could rediscover the deeper purpose of it all, the point, why you do what you do.

You may have been engaging in some deep questioning and theological rethinking.[1] You can no longer live with the faith you inherited from your parents or constructed earlier in your life. As you sort through your dogma and doctrine, you've found yourself praying less, less thrilled about worship or Scripture or church attendance. You've been so focused on sorting and purging your theological theories that you've lost track of the spiritual practices that sustain an actual relationship with God. You may even wonder if such a thing is possible for someone like you.

You may have come to the point where even the word *God* is problematic for you. You are so dreadfully sick and tired of hearing God's name over-used and abused that you'd rather not add to the commotion. You're tempted to compensate for all the noisy religious overstatement by speaking of God as seldom and softly as possible. As you've been going through this painful process of rethinking both your theology and your practice of faith, your experience of God may have gradually been evaporating from your life. As a result, God may be shrinking from

4

a substantial Someone to a vague something, leaving a thin residue that is next to nothing. All that may remain for you is a theoretical concept, an esoteric principle, a distant abstraction that's eventually not worth talking about ... or to.

You may be spiritually disappointed and wounded; you may feel God has abandoned you, turned on you, left you, and you don't know where to go next. You may be, perhaps without admitting it even to yourself, one of the increasing numbers of theologians, pastors, priests and lifelong Christians who has become an atheist because of longstanding disillusionment, unanswered questions and unresolved pain.

You may have been so sceptical and cynical for so long that now you're sceptical of scepticism and cynical about cynicism. You wonder if there could be a post-sceptical faith, a post-cynical hope, and maybe even a post-atheist love.

You may be rebuilding after a faith collapse, or you may be embarking on your virgin voyage into faith and a spiritual life. Either way, you have no interest in fake spirituality, forced spirituality, hyped spirituality, inflated spirituality. You want to strip away all the layers of pretence and get down to naked reality. You 'get' what Fr Richard Rohr says:

> The goal of all spirituality is to lead the 'naked person' to stand trustfully before the naked God. The important thing is that we're naked; in other words that we come without title, merit, shame, or even demerit. All we can offer to God is who we really are, which to all of us never seems like enough. I am sure this is the way true lovers feel too.[2]

Doctrinal correctness, institutional participation and religious conformity don't suffice any more. You need a life centred on simple, doable, durable practices that will help you begin and sustain a naked encounter with the holy mystery and pure loving presence that people commonly call God.[3]

If we happened to meet – on a plane or train, at a party, or wherever – and if you expressed to me any of these kinds of struggles or needs, this is the book I would want to be able to give you before we say goodbye. I wrote it because it's the kind of book I wish someone had given to me at several points during my own spiritual journey – when I was first getting started, or when I hit some rough patches of doubt or struggle.

All that's required to get started is a little tiny seed of faith – faith that there's something or Someone out there (or 'in here') worth searching for. That might not seem like much, but I know it's enough.

Chapter 1

Spiritual Experiences and Spiritual Experience

> I had been my whole life a bell, and I never knew it until at that moment I was lifted and struck.
>
> Annie Dillard[1]

I grew up in a religious home. A full-dose, hard-core, shaken-together-and-my-cup-runneth-over conservative-Bible-believing-Evangelical-Fundamentalist Christian home. Christmas and Easter? Of course! Every Sunday morning? Obviously! Sunday School? Complete with memorising Bible verses and singing Christian choruses and competing in Bible Olympics! Holidays and Sundays were just the spiritual appetisers. For the main course, there was also church every Sunday night. And there was Wednesday night prayer meeting too. And in the summer, Vacation Bible School and Christian summer camp. There were even occasional revival meetings that required attendance every night for a week – or two weeks, God help us. Then there were special kids and youth programmes on top of everything else. If that weren't sufficient to save our souls from secularism, at every meal we bowed our heads for prayer – including when we went out to restaurants, which always made me squirm and then feel guilty for squirming.[2] And after dinner on most nights

– a kind of spiritual dessert – my dad would have us read a daily devotional guide. And I haven't even mentioned prayers and Bible stories at bedtime.

You'd think with all that religion, I might have overdosed and become an atheist. Or at least an agnostic. And maybe I would have, except that underneath all the layers upon layers of religion, I discovered a living, breathing, naked spirituality.

For you, the discovery may have occurred in a Twelve-Step meeting. When you found yourself fighting for survival against a raging addiction, suddenly faith in higher power really mattered. You needed more than a dressed-up Sunday religion; you needed a naked spirituality that would help you get sane again.

Or it may have happened in a small fellowship group on a college campus, or on a retreat, or in a time of illness or bereavement, in the middle of a divorce, or maybe walking along a path in a forest. Maybe someone close to you was transformed before your eyes and it turned out that their spiritual conversion was contagious. However it happened, what had been a concept or theory got translated into naked experience and real-life practice. You felt something. You knew something. You changed.

I think there is a kind of innate spirituality in young children; the primal connection of child to parent translates naturally into trust in God. But as we mature, our spirituality must mature too. Otherwise, that child-like connection will be lost along with childhood innocence. In my case, a more robust spirituality started sneaking up on me in my early teens. I had learned hundreds of Bible stories, memorised dozens of Bible verses, said thousands of prayers – including one called 'the sinner's prayer', important to all fundamentalists. But around puberty, there were little inklings of a new space opening up in my psyche, a capacity for doubt and a capacity for a kind of experience that I had never had before. (It's interesting how intellectual and spiritual capacities seem to develop along with sexual ones.) I wasn't sure what I was looking for, but by the time I was sixteen, I was on the path of passionate spirituality.

I think I was fifteen when a seventeen-year-old fellow I met at summer camp told me the story of his dramatic conversion several months earlier. He had been slipping – or jumping – into a dangerous love affair with a drug called mescaline. His schoolwork suffered and he dropped out of school altogether. Then through a 'straight' (in those days, it meant non-drug-using) girlfriend he had 'gotten saved'. He was now clean and sober, studying the Bible, re-enrolling in school, getting his life together. I saw something real in his life, something more robust and vigorous than I had experienced, and it left me a little envious.

Later that year, another friend invited me to a 'discipleship group' where some college students read the Bible, prayed and talked about their spiritual growth. I didn't exactly fit in this group: they were older and smarter and more serious than I was, and I was already planning my escape from a hyper-religious life. But again, I saw something real in their lives, something I didn't have. If I ever did become a more spiritual person, I wanted to be like them, I thought.

Along with my attraction, I must admit I felt a lot of revulsion. To a teenager in the early 1970s, church culture seemed like a throwback to the 1950s – or the 1750s, or 1850s, take your pick. To a guy interested in science, all the anti-evolution rhetoric seemed unnecessary, even a little silly. To a kid growing a scruffy beard and playing in a little rock and roll band, the crew-cut, white-shirt-and-tie-clad, pro-war, anti-hippie churchy role models seemed singularly creepy – just as I must have seemed to them. I felt stuck in a religious twilight-zone, not in, not out.

Right in the middle of all this ambivalence, some neighbourhood buddies, similarly conflicted, I think, invited me on a weekend retreat with the youth group from their Southern Baptist church. And that's where spirituality snuck up and crashed upon me, like an unexpected wave at the beach. The retreat leader sent us off on Saturday afternoon for an hour of silence, during which we were supposed to pray. I climbed a tree – being a back-to-nature guy – only to discover that my perch was along an ant-superhighway and that mosquitoes also liked the shade of that particular tree. But eventually, between swatting and scratching, I actually prayed. My prayer went something like this:

Dear God, before I die, I hope you will let me see the most beautiful sights, hear the most beautiful sounds, and feel the most beautiful feelings that life has to offer.

No, it wasn't an altruistic prayer asking God to end world hunger or war. No, it wasn't focused on repenting of my many sins, although like any hormonally-infused teenage boy, I had my share of things to feel guilty about. No, it wasn't a theological prayer affirming important tenets of faith. In fact, it was pretty adolescent and some might say trite. But it was *my* prayer – honest, and at least a little more lofty than my occasional pleas for a cute girl in Spanish class to get a crush on me, or for help on the algebra quiz I forgot to study for.

In spite of my sincerity, absolutely nothing happened. As the other fifty-seven or so minutes stretched on, I couldn't think of much else to say. I scratched mosquito bites, flicked ants off my legs, felt my butt go numb, and eventually climbed down the tree and wandered back to the retreat centre for supper. There were evening activities and then we were supposed to go to bed, I think. But somehow, a few friends and I snuck away to a hillside and found ourselves sitting under one of those sparkling autumn night skies. I walked several paces away from my friends and lay back in the grass, fingers interlocked behind my head, looking up, feeling strangely quiet and at peace. Something began to happen.

I had this feeling of being seen. Known. Named. Loved … by a Someone bigger than the sky that expanded above me. Young science geek that I was, I pictured myself lying on a little hill on a little continent on a little planet in a little solar system on the rim of a modest galaxy in a sea of billions of galaxies, and I felt that the great big Creator of the whole shebang was somehow noticing little tiny me. It was as if the whole sky were an eye, and all space were a heart, and I was being targeted as a focal point for attention and love. And the oddest thing happened as this realisation sank in. I began to laugh. I wasn't guffawing, but I was laughing: at first gently, but eventually almost uncontrollably. Profound laughter surged from within me.

It wasn't a reactive laughter, the kind that erupts when you hear a good joke or see somebody do something ridiculous. It was more like an overflowing laughter, as if all that space I had been feeling opening up inside me was gradually filling up with pure happiness and once it reached the rim, it spilled over in incandescent joy. *God loves me! Me! God! At this moment! I can feel it!*

11

The joy felt huge, so big that I got a little scared. My stomach started to hurt because I was laughing so hard. Not only had I never felt anything like this before; I had never heard of anything like this before. I started to feel as though I might burst apart because the joy felt bigger than I could contain. I felt that my universe was turning upside down, and I might fall off the planet and out into the depths of space. I prayed again: 'God, I don't think I can take much more of this. Maybe you'd better tone it down a little.' Gradually, the euphoria subsided and I quietly moved back towards my friends.

While I had been having my private spiritual experience, they were having a spiritual experience of their own, one of a more social nature. I remember hearing one of them say to the others, 'I love you guys. I really love you guys.' And then they all started telling each other how much they appreciated each other – saying the kinds of gushy, sincere, vulnerable things that teenagers normally say only when they're graduating, at a funeral, or getting drunk. I don't think I said anything, but I know I felt caught up with them in something spiritually tangible – theologians would call it the Holy Spirit – and I was bound together with my friends and with God. Soon most or all of us were all sniffling, moved to tears at the connection we were feeling – to each other and to God.

Then I remembered my prayer in the tree a couple of hours earlier. Wham! It hit me: *God had answered my prayer!*

In the previous few minutes, I had seen the most beautiful thing that eyes can see: the glory of God shining in the radiance of creation. I had heard the most beautiful thing that ears can hear: friends telling friends that they love one another. And I had felt the most beautiful thing that any heart can ever feel: the love of God and the love of others. And at that, my sniffling turned into quiet sobs, again coming from a deep part of me I had never even been aware of before.

If my private laughter was chapter one of my first spiritual experience, and if those shared tears were chapter two, chapter three came later the same evening when I had a vision. I wouldn't have known to call it that at the time, but looking back, I think that's what it was. I was praying again, and in my imagination, I could see a pair of sandalled feet. I knew the Bible story about a sinful woman weeping at Jesus' feet, and it was as if I were being brought into that story, not as an observer, but as a participant. I saw myself as a pool of water, of tears, spreading around Jesus' feet. I was filled with a profound desire to pour myself out for Jesus, in simple, pure, selfless love. Whether or not I was a true Christian before that night, I don't know and it doesn't really matter. But from that night on, I was a wholehearted lover of the Creator, a person thirsty for the Holy Spirit, and a devoted follower of Jesus. That was my triune baptism into spirituality.

I don't like to talk about these experiences much. Talking about them has a way of cheapening them. The memory of the experience itself gets replaced by the memory of telling the story about it. Eventually the experience itself all but disappears and pretty soon the story being told has little connection to anything that actually happened. Meanwhile, a suspicious psychologist could, I'm sure, offer plausible explanations for what happened to my friends and me that night. There's a time and a place for that kind of scrutiny and analysis, and I don't see neurological, psychological, sociological and spiritual categories as mutually exclusive.[3] But even so, sharing experiences like this can feel like casting one's heart before analytical critics, which is not a pleasant thing.

In spite of those misgivings, I've shared this dramatic experience for three reasons. First, I think it's important for you to know that I'm not writing about spirituality as a dispassionate observer. Since that starry night, I've been an insider to spirituality. And since that initial spiritual baptism, many other kinds of spiritual experiences have similarly snuck up and surprised me. Some of them have been equally dramatic, some more, most less, but still very meaningful. Sometimes they haven't come when I felt I needed them most, and others have felt like bounty poured upon bounty. They've never been an on-demand, push-button kind of thing for me. But usually, even when I'm in the middle of a tough and draining day or season, if I'm quiet for even a few seconds, I have been able to find that sacred space at the centre of my life where there is at least a faint, quiet glimmer of that same joy, love and unity that I experienced that night under the stars. My initiation into spirituality stuck and it has persisted through life's many dangers, toils and snares, as the old hymn says. So everything I write about spirituality today has been tested in the crucible of my own experience during the nearly forty years since that night.

Second, I want to distinguish the wine of spirituality from the wineskin of the religion in which I experienced it. That dramatic experience took place at a Southern Baptist retreat centre, around the fringes of charismatic renewal, in the context of the Jesus Movement, in the broader context of conservative Evangelicalism – the same basic matrix, incidentally, that gave birth to the Religious Right. At the Bible studies, conferences, youth events and religious festivals I began attending after that night, I would regularly hear sermons against evolution and for six-day-creationism – sermons that never sat right with me. When I listened to Christian radio – as I did religiously – I would be warned against every approach to the Bible except fundamentalist literalism, about which I always had my doubts.

When I went to youth rallies, I would be told repeatedly that anyone who had not said the required 'sinner's prayer' would miss out on 'the abundant life' before death, and would go straight to hell afterwards. Again, I always had misgivings about this dualism. When I went to church and Christian conferences, I was consistently taught why women shouldn't be leaders, why gay people should be stigmatised and why liberals were anti-God; although I probably nodded in agreement and maybe even voiced a flimsy *amen* from time to time, I had my doubts. And to top it all off, in popular books and through little tracts and scary propaganda movies, I would be reminded that something called the Rapture would occur any day – so we shouldn't concern ourselves with social issues but only focus on saving souls and helping them become born-again, Spirit-filled, elect, Evangelical Christians just like us.[4]

Now, almost four decades later, I cringe when I hear the teachings that were standard fare back then. I have discarded those theological wineskins ... but I treasure more than ever the wine of the Spirit that was somehow conveyed to me through them. That suit of theological clothing doesn't fit me any more, but the naked spirituality that sustains me today originally came to me dressed in it. I hope you can see that even if a particular style of religious clothing now feels stiff, tight and ill-fitting for you – Roman Catholic or mainline Protestant, Evangelical or Pentecostal, Sunni or Shiite, Reform or Orthodox – the possibility of naked spirituality remains a live option.

Third, I want to acknowledge that dramatic spiritual experiences happen, but they are, by definition, pretty rare – otherwise they wouldn't seem dramatic. Beyond that, although they solve some problems, they can create others. Some people, for example, seem to develop an addiction to dramatic spiritual experiences that disrupts their life as other addictions would. Most important, dramatic spiritual experiences simply aren't the point. Whatever the value of extraordinary dramatic spiritual *experiences*, to which some people seem more prone than others, I'm convinced that what matters most – and is available to everyone – is daily, ordinary spiritual *experience*. With or without dramatic experiences, we can all find, expand and hold a quiet, sacred space at the centre of our lives, a space where we experience vital connection to the living God. We can all learn to tap into the quiet current of sacredness and love that runs from the Creator through all creation. Dramatic experiences can awaken some of us to the reality of the spiritual life, but they are not sufficient to strengthen, sustain and deepen us as truly spiritual people.

But how do we become 'truly spiritual people'? How do we learn to strip away the superficialities so that, in Richard Rohr's terms, our naked souls can encounter the naked God? How do we nurture daily spiritual experience, with or without dramatic spiritual experiences? That's where spiritual practices come in, and that's what we will explore together in the pages ahead. We will root twelve essential spiritual practices in one simple word each. These twelve practices will not in any way be exhaustive, but they will be essential – essential for strengthening a vital, vigorous, naked spirituality.

Chapter 2

But I'm Spiritual

True religion helps us to grow, but pseudo-religion hinders growth, for it creates and maintains obstacles and barriers. Thus it is that much religion merely censors experience and does not liberate it, stifles human potential and does not allow it to blossom. Much religion is superficial and does not help the journey inwards which is so necessary to spiritual health. There has to be a movement towards the still centre, the depths of our being, where, according to the mystics, we find the presence of God.

Kenneth Leech[1]

I started as religious and then was plunged into spirituality that night under the stars. Others do the reverse, starting with spirituality and then exploring religion. But a lot of folks I meet feel a tension between spirituality and religion. 'I'm not religious myself,' they say, 'but ...' Why does the word *religious* almost demand to be followed up by a *but* for so many people?

To find out, when I hear 'but I'm spiritual', I often follow up with a question: 'I'm curious. What do you mean by *spiritual*?'

Four answers come up again and again, and each rings true

in my own experience. First, when people say 'I'm spiritual', they mean that secular science, politics and economics don't ... believe life has a sacred dimension ... formulas, rules and numbers. They believe human ... an't be fed by facts alone, ... us 'invisible hand of the market.'

Second ... mean that organised religion doesn't have all the answers for them either.[2] They're concerned that religious institutions are complicit in too many of the world's problems, and that they lead their adherents on too many adventures in missing the point.

Third, the word *spiritual* signals for them an inner sensitivity to aliveness, meaning and sacredness *in* the universe. They can't in good conscience assign God, heaven, meaning, values, souls, worship, afterlife and eternity to the sacred category and consign everything else – including bodies, sexuality, work, animals, plants, the earth, daily life and history – to the profane. Instead of separating the two, instead of denying one in favour of the other, and instead of reducing one to the other, they want the former to infuse the latter, and the latter to be enlivened by the former. They want to marry God and creation, heaven and earth, soul and body, eternity and history, afterlife and life ... not divorce them. They want to integrate both categories in a vital, intimate – can we say *naked?* – communion.[3]

Fourth, spiritual people seek practical ways to nourish that sense of integration and communion. It might be meditating, hiking on a wilderness trail, volunteering at a soup kitchen, doing yoga, going to art galleries, participating in festivals, or going on pilgrimages. It might be fasting, feasting or having deep talks with a few friends. Whatever the specifics, spiritual people have – or at least wish they had – some set of moves, rhythms, habits or practices, things that to some degree at least, keep them from sleep-walking or going on auto-pilot, so they live with a greater sensitivity to the sacred aliveness and meaning that surround them.

The truth is that these four characteristics of spirituality are also at the heart of true religion, as the etymology or origin of the word 'religion' makes clear. The root of the word is *lig*, which you see in the word *ligament*. It means to connect, to join together, to unite, to bring everything together in one body or one wholeness. And of course *re* means *again*. So you might say that good religion is about connecting us together again.[4] Most deeply it is about binding us together into one body with God, acknowledging that different religious denominations and families have differing ways of describing and relating to God.[5] It is also about bonding us and uniting us again with one another, and with all creation – the trees and the mountains and the animals, the stars and space and wind. In this light, true religion and naked spirituality are two names for the same thing: *seeking vital connection*. And seeking vital connection, it turns out, is another name for love.[6] So, we might say, both *spirituality* and *religion* are, at their best, two names for *love*.

In that light we can better understand the 'but' in *I'm spiritual but not religious*. What many experience in religious communities on a popular level seems closer to the opposite of love. Religion as they experience it promotes conflict and selfishness rather than generosity and otherliness. It teaches them to prioritise their own personal salvation and religiosity over the well-being of others. It teaches practices and beliefs that make some fear, dehumanise and judge others, straining or tearing the ligaments of creation instead of strengthening them. In this way, religions can actually become anti-religions, de-ligamenting us instead of re-ligamenting us. Maybe if we name this kind of false or unspiritual phenomenon *de-ligion* instead of *religion*, we can save the latter word for the traditions that enhance and support naked spirituality.

That's why in the end, I don't think we need to pit religion against spirituality, any more than we would pit clothing against nakedness. Nakedness is a good thing, and clothing is a good thing too. In the middle of a blizzard, a parka and boots come in handy, just as sturdy jeans and a long-sleeved flannel shirt do when you're walking through a forest full of nettles and mosquitoes. The lack of appropriate clothing in a hostile environment can kill you. So can the presence of inappropriate clothing. So the issue isn't clothing versus nakedness, but appropriate versus inappropriate ways to clothe nakedness. And we might say the problem isn't religion, but rather inappropriate religion – religion that doesn't serve, protect, enhance, or express the naked life within it.[7]

Jesus worked with these images of clothing and nakedness quite a bit, especially in Matthew's Gospel. Dressing up a wolf in a sheepskin doesn't change its ravenous nature any more than dressing up spiritually greedy or vicious people in religious garb does, he said (7:15). The naked beauty of 'the lilies of the field' surpasses the fine wardrobe of King Solomon (6:28–29). Hypocrites use both their fancy religious garb (23:5) and their flowery public prayers (6:5) to impress other people, but God isn't impressed. In contrast, he urged his followers to go into the closet – the place where you undress and dress in private, the place where you are naked – to pray 'in secret' (6:6). Isn't the body 'more than clothing?' he asked (6:25), and we might similarly imagine him asking, 'Isn't spirituality more than religiosity?'

In John's Gospel, Jesus explores the same theme with a variety of vivid images.[8] Imagine, for example, Jesus standing by a well in the blazing desert heat of a Middle-Eastern day, sharing a drink of cool water with an unnamed woman who has since been known as 'the woman at the well' (4:7–26). She was a lot like so many spiritual seekers today: confused and frustrated by the conflicting claims of what we're calling de-ligions. One of the hot-button de-ligious arguments in those days centred on which mountain was the most holy, which mountain worshippers were supposed to ascend for bona fide, certified worship. So she brings up this my-mountain-is-better than-your-mountain controversy, inviting this itinerant rabbi to render his opinion on which group chose the right piece of topography.

Predictably (if you're familiar with Jesus' approach to de-ligious controversy), Jesus doesn't answer her question. Instead he says, in essence, 'That's a surface question of de-ligion, but you're looking for something deeper and more satisfying: a cool drink of pure, life-giving, thirst-quenching spirituality. Dressed-up de-ligion divides people based on arguments about mountains, but it sends everybody away thirsty. Naked spirituality invites people to a deeper level and unites them there, and their spiritual thirst is fulfilled. God is Spirit and those who approach God must come to God in a spiritual and authentic way.'[9]

So Jesus turns her attention away from a solid, external, fixed *mountain*, and helps her imagine instead a flowing, internal, spiritual *fountain*, like the one that sources the well beside which they stand. He asks her to think deeper – about *living water* that flows up from within you, wherever you are, on this mountain, on that mountain, or anywhere else. There are any number of mountains of de-ligion – systems that fracture communities socially into in-groups and out-groups, us and them. But there's one fountain of Spirit, he suggests, accessible to everyone. Religious people argue endlessly about which mountain is higher and more scenic than the others. They stake their claim to this religious mountain or that one. They defend theirs and attack others. But naked spirituality is different. You don't argue about the fountain: you drink from it and experience its movement and flow within you. It's flowing under everyone's feet, as it were, and can well up in the soul. When you have the fountain flowing within you, you don't need to travel to some distant mountain to find what you're thirsty for.

Immediately before this encounter, Jesus had another conversation, this one by night rather than at midday, presumably indoors rather than outdoors, with a traditional religious man named Nicodemus instead of a marginally-religious anonymous woman. Like a lot of religious people, Nicodemus was preoccupied with teachings and miracles. Jesus told him that this approach would get him nowhere. He needed to become like a little child and start learning about naked spirituality from square one. 'You have to be born of Spirit,' he says.[10]

This time, instead of comparing Spirit to water in the aquifer beneath their feet, he points out the window to the wind blowing free in the trees above them.[11] 'Hear that?' he says. 'God is like that. Wind. Spirit. Mysterious. Powerful. Wild and untamed and uncontained. Always moving. You can't see wind or nail it down or catch it in a bottle. That's how Spirit is.' In both encounters, the pattern is amazingly similar: Jesus points away from de-ligion and toward Spirit. He leads people away from religious structures and controversies that divide people into in-groups and out-groups; instead he leads people to a different space entirely, where we can all experience the same Spirit.[12]

He does this sort of thing in John's Gospel again and again.[13]

In the episode that comes right before this encounter with Nicodemus, Jesus uses yet another dynamic image for Spirit.[14] He is at a wedding banquet where the wine has run out – a big embarrassment for the groom and a big disappointment for the guests. Jesus points to six ceremonial stone jars (the kind used in religious purification ceremonies, each holding twenty to thirty gallons) and directs them to be filled with water. When the banquet organiser tastes a cup drawn from the stone jars, he is amazed: it's better wine than any that had been served previously. Spirit-wine that fills empty religious containers ... and at a wedding banquet, a celebration of joy, love and union ... the symbolism is as delicious as the wine must have been!

Whatever imagery he uses – wine, wind, or wellsprings – it's clear that Jesus wants to focus on naked spirituality, not the religion that clothes it. In fact, when he shows up at the Temple, the headquarters of the regional religion, he stirs up so much trouble that Temple personnel begin plotting for him to be arrested and killed. The Temple, he says, has already become obsolete, and the Spirit will do just fine even if the Temple is destroyed (John 2:19–21; 4:21–24). It's the same for the movement that arises in his aftermath, as every page of the New Testament makes clear. It's all about Spirit. Sometimes New Testament writers depict us as entering into the Spirit, like a person plunged into a cleansing bath, like a ship launched into water, like a branch grafted into a vine, or like a person born into the wide world.[15] In other passages, the Spirit comes into us, like wine into a body, like sap into a branch, like breath into the lungs, like an inhabitant into a house.[16] Sometimes, marital imagery is used: we are united with the Spirit like a bride with a groom, and we become pregnant with Spirit-life that will be born through us into the world as good and beautiful works.[17]

A spiritual life is a Spirit life, a life in the Spirit, and Jesus' life and work come into proper focus when we realise his goal was not to start a new religion – and certainly not to create a new religion that would seek to compete with or persecute his own religion of Judaism! No: his goal was to fill with Spirit-wine the empty stone jars of religion – his own religion and any other one, I'd say. His goal wasn't to start a new religious argument about dogma-mountains; it was to fill hearts with Spirit-fountains. His goal wasn't to replace one group of powerful religious grown-ups (like Nicodemus) with another, but to help everyone become like little children through Spirit-birth.

When people say, 'I'm not religious but I'm spiritual', many of them, I think, see what Jesus saw: the Spirit's realm of activity can't be limited to the sphere of religion in general, much less to any particular religion. The Spirit of God is the fine wine of justice, joy and peace, the uncontained wind of creativity, comfort and liberation, the living water of holiness, beauty and love. Whenever people encounter justice, joy, peace, creativity, comfort, liberation, holiness, beauty, love, or any other good thing, they are in some way encountering the Spirit, or at least the signature or aftermath of the Spirit. The Spirit, then, is bigger than any particular religion or religion in general. Nobody has a Spirit-monopoly.

Get that straight and a thousand other things begin to fall into place. We can put ourselves into the sandals of that woman drawing water from that well, or Nicodemus hearing the wind in the trees, or the disciples tasting that wine drawn from those ceremonial stone jars. We might just dare to believe that we too can experience the water, the wind and the wine.

Chapter 3

Twelve Simple Words

Better a single word spoken from a heart of love than a thousand from a heart of indifference.

Evagrius Ponticus[1]

Spiritual experiences like the one that I had under the stars that night are wonderful – but not very dependable, which raises the question of how we can experience a life with God day-by-day and moment-by-moment, as a way-of-life. How can we build a naked life with God that is rich in spiritual *experience*, with or without dramatic *experiences*? On this question both our ancient religious traditions and our contemporary theories of education and human development agree: a way of life is formed by practices. By practices, we mean doable habits or rhythms that transform us, rewiring our brains, restoring our inner ecology, renovating our inner architecture, expanding our capacities. We mean actions within our power that help us become capable of things currently beyond our power.[2]

Our ancient traditions and contemporary theories also agree: there are personal and social dimensions to practices.[3]

On a personal level, practices have little or no impact on us unless we experiment with them and learn to work with them over time. But in order to experiment with and participate in them, we need a community or society which has embodied, refined, taught, preserved and enhanced them generation by generation. So in order to learn a set of practices personally and make fullest use of them, we must find a community that embodies them socially.[4]

So, for example, I'm incapable of speaking Chinese today. But if I find a social group of fluent speakers, and in their company I begin practising a single new word or phrase or series of phrases day by day, I will one day be reasonably fluent myself. I'm incapable of running a marathon today. But if I find a group of runners who can teach me a time-tested training regimen, I can start with a half-mile today. Then in six months, following their regimen, I will be able to run all twenty-six miles. I'm incapable of playing the violin today. But if I find a master violinist and join her circle of dedicated students, with some months or years of practice, I will someday be able to contribute to a band or orchestra and play an Irish jig or Mozart symphony.

Similarly, I may be incapable of accepting an insult without retaliation today. I may be incapable of remaining grateful in the midst of fatigue. I may be incapable of receiving attention for successful achievements without becoming conceited. I may be incapable of loving my enemies, or seeing things from their point of view, or overcoming discrimination, or resisting the urge to consume or pollute, or remaining patient under stress. I may be incapable of remembering that God loves me and knows my name, or that God graciously accepts me apart from my performance, or that God loves and knows 'the other' no less than me.

But what if there were some practices by which what is now spiritually impossible for me could actually become possible? What if there were practices that made space for the well of living water to flow, for the wind of the Spirit to blow, for the stone jars in my life to be filled with a nobler cause and a more meaningful, joyful purpose? What if there were communities focused on embodying those practices, and what if they were ready to welcome me to learn among them?[5] Would I want to learn those practices, and enter into those communities?

You might think, 'Yes, I would want to. But I've wanted to learn to speak Chinese, run a marathon, and play the violin too, and I've never been able to discipline myself to engage in the necessary practices. So if these practices are going to require an hour a day or something, it's not likely I'll follow through, as much as I should, as much as I might wish I would.'

The point is well taken. If the only people who can embark on a spiritual journey are those blessed with a lot of self-discipline and sufficient free time, many of us are in trouble. That's why we need simple, doable, durable practices that can be integrated into many things we are already doing ... taking a walk, commuting, cooking or eating, resting in bed, relaxing at home, taking a break at work, waiting for an appointment, enjoying a hobby.

In the coming chapters, I would like to introduce you to twelve spiritual practices that have passed the *simple, doable and durable* test for me. They are part of our ancient traditions and they can provide twenty-first-century people like you and me with a basic curriculum for our spiritual novitiate. You can think of them as twelve stretches for runners, twelve moves in martial arts, twelve basic positions in yoga, or twelve warm-up exercises a musician might employ. You can do them in groups, and I hope you will, but you can begin on your own, in private, today. Like learning your first few chords on a guitar, you'll find it amazingly easy to begin to play with these practices. But like expanding on those basic chords in order to become a guitar virtuoso, you'll also find these twelve practices endlessly engaging and challenging.

I stumbled into this simple-doable-durable approach to the spiritual life over many years, and to some degree, it arose out of frustration. For a while after my experience under the stars I enjoyed a kind of spiritual honeymoon. My problems seemed to be quickly resolved when I prayed; my questions were easily answered when someone showed me the right Bible verse. But that season of simplicity didn't last.

Eager to learn and grow spiritually, I started consuming books, sermons and tapes (remember 'cassettes'?) by the dozen, and many of them smuggled two dangerous words into my heart – *not enough*: 'You don't pray enough. You don't study the Bible enough. You don't share your faith enough. You don't attend church enough. You don't give enough money,' and so on. To the degree that I believed God was as demanding as these teachers, authors and preachers whose products I was eagerly consuming, I started to experience a kind of spiritual malpractice and malformation. When I thought I succeeded in doing enough, I would fall prey to spiritual pride. When I felt I wasn't doing enough, which happened more often, I would fall into vicious cycles of guilt and discouragement.

The tyranny of *not enough* ushered me firmly from that initial season of simplicity into a season of complexity. In order to be anybody in the religious communities to which I belonged, I needed to amass more and more Bible lore – so that if someone

28

mentioned Zephaniah, Meribah, Meggido, Huldah and Berea, I'd immediately know which were people and which were places, what era of biblical history they hailed from, and why they were important. But that was still not enough: I also needed to know the complexities of theology. I was raised in a school of theology known as Dispensationalism, which itself involves a good deal of complexity – detailed charts, timelines, arguments and counter-arguments. Then I was introduced to Calvinism with its even more intricate complexities, and then to Pentecostalism, and so on. On top of being conversant with the complexities of the theological systems I subscribed to, I needed to understand alternative systems enough to refute them (which often meant misunderstanding those systems enough to caricature them). On top of that, each theological system included dozens of sub-systems, each with its own fine nuances, intricacies, and bitter disputes: eschatology, apologetics, pneumatology, missiology, hermeneutics, and so on.

I applied myself diligently to each new challenge. And I became at least as complexity-competent as anybody I knew. But there were three problems with all this complexity. First, mastering more and more of it got really fatiguing. Since there was no end to the complexity, there was no end to the fatigue either. Second, I could see absolutely no correlation between the amount of theological complexity and the amount of spiritual vitality, Christ-likeness, or fruitfulness – in my life, or in the lives of others. In fact, for a lot of people I met, the more they knew, the meaner they got. All their knowledge turned into ammunition, which just made them more dangerous and less pleasant to be around. Complexity, I concluded, was overrated.

That introduced me to a third stage in my spiritual life:

perplexity. The perplexity only intensified when I became a pastor. Our little congregation had people from many different denominational backgrounds, each with their own brands of simplicity and complexity, each feeling frustrated that the others weren't 'normal'. Managing these competing assumptions and expectations was, on some days, downright maddening and miserable. The perplexity further intensified when we began welcoming a lot of people who were completely new to the faith. Did I want to baptise all these new spiritual seekers into a naïve simplicity that I knew wouldn't last? Or did I school them in the complexity that I felt was little more than a rat race? Or would I mire them in the painful perplexity that I was experiencing? Jesus' haunting words to the Pharisees often came to mind: 'You travel over land and sea to win a single convert, and when he becomes one, you make him twice as much a son of hell as you are' (Matt. 23:15, NIV). That wasn't exactly my idea of a great way to spend my life!

So with increasing desperation, I kept looking for ways to jettison excess baggage. I kept trying to get down to the naked essence, something beyond the first three stages that distilled the best and stripped away the rest. I needed a new approach to spirituality for my own spiritual survival, but no less for the well-being of the people I was called to serve. Eventually I felt I had broken through to a fourth stage which I later called harmony – because in it I could see the strengths as well as the limitations of earlier stages, and I could see that each stage had its own beauty. From that new vantage point, I felt I could see the first three stages with greater clarity – and empathy – than ever before.

Perhaps you already see what was so hard for me to realise back then: my frustrations were teaching me exactly what I needed to understand to better help myself and others on the spiritual journey. I was learning – the hard way, no doubt – that there are predictable stages or seasons in the spiritual life. A period of relative coherence and stability was followed by a period of restlessness and turbulence, after which a new period of coherence and stability would unfold, followed by yet another period of restlessness, and so on. I came across a number of thinkers and theorists who had reached similar conclusions and mapped out these periods in various ways.[6] By integrating their scholarly work with reflection on my own experience as a spiritual person and as a pastor, I sketched out a four-stage framework that has been extremely helpful to me and to many others for over two decades now: simplicity, complexity, perplexity and harmony.

Some years later when I was exposed to the concept of spiritual practices (it was a radically new way of seeing things for me back then), I tried to correlate specific practices with the four stages or seasons in the spiritual life. Just as a child needs to master addition before subtraction, multiplication before division and algebra before calculus, I felt there must be some natural sequence in which spiritual practices could best be acquired. I decided for both theological and pastoral reasons to focus on the primary practices that deepen our life with God. Eventually I settled on three practices for each stage, or twelve in total, and they will be our focus in the coming pages.[7]

As I experimented with these practices in my own life and tried to teach them to others, I started lodging each practice in one simple word. Why one word? The honest answer is that in my own season of Stage-Three perplexity, I couldn't manage much more than one word. I had become so tired of the words-piled-upon-words that characterised Stage Two that one simple word for each practice seemed to lighten the burden and bring clarity to the chaos. As I deepened in Stage Four, I sensed the need to slow down the pace of my inner life, to live in a more contemplative way. One word slowed me down in a way that many could not. The more I taught this framework of practices and stages to others, the more I realised that people in Stage One – who want above all else to get things exactly right – could get one word exactly right. And people in Stage Two – who are all about mastering complex challenges – could see the whole framework as just the kind of challenge they were waiting for. So this framework of stages and practices offered something appropriate to people at each stage, even as it invited them to move forward when they were ready. Here's the framework, with the twelve practices arranged in the four stages:[8]

Simplicity: The spring-like season of spiritual awakening

Here   the practice of invocation and presentation: awakening to the presence of God

Thanks!   the practice of gratitude and appreciation: awakening to the goodness of God

O!   the practice of worship and awe: awakening to the beauty and joy of God

Complexity: The summer-like season of spiritual strengthening

Sorry!   the practice of self-examination and confession: strengthening through failure

Help!   the practice of expansion and petition: strengthening through weakness

Please!   the practice of compassion and intercession: strengthening through empathy

Perplexity: The autumn-like season of spiritual surviving

When?   the practice of aspiration, exasperation and desperation: surviving through delay

No!   the practice of rage and refusal: surviving through disillusionment

Why?   the practice of lament and agony: surviving through abandonment

Harmony: The winter-like season of spiritual deepening

Behold   the practice of meditation and wonder: deepening by seeing

Yes   the practice of consecration and surrender: deepening by joining

[...]   the practice of contemplation and rest: deepening by being with

As you think of these four stages, you might imagine an ascending spiral that grows wider every year as you pass through spring/simplicity, summer/complexity, autumn/perplexity and winter/harmony afresh.[9]

Although we're working within the metaphor of predictable patterns of the seasons, we must acknowledge that unpredictable storms also arise in each season. And although our calendars give the illusion that one season ends on a certain day and another begins the next day, we've all experienced those surprisingly mild days in winter and surprisingly cool days in summer, not to mention the nearly constant surprises of spring and autumn. So there's unpredictability and surprise inherent in our simple framework of four seasons in the spiritual life.

Through these seasons we shape a spiritual life that is deep, honest and strong. The point isn't to stay in spring or summer forever, nor is the point to get to (or through) winter as soon as possible ... any more than the point of life is advancing from infancy to old age as soon as possible. No, the point is to live each stage well, to learn well what each day and season has to teach, to live life and enjoy life and bear the good fruits of a life with God through all of life's seasons.

By the time we've passed through these seasons a few times, these twelve practices become to the soul what the rhythms of breath, sleep and pulse are to the body: constant, natural, life-giving, unconscious, effortless. Our spiritual life becomes our way of remaining awake to God and aliveness, our way of being at home in the universe with (as St Francis said) brother sun and sister moon, brother fox and sister fire, connected and at peace with everything. Together, we and God are like an elderly couple, bound together through a lifetime of joy and heartache, holding hands with the one we love and with whom we have shared everything. (Or, like the fourteenth-century Persian mystic Hafiz said, we become like two giant fat people in a boat who keep bumping into each other and laughing.[10]) So little needs to be said as we sit together looking at the sea, watching the waves roll in. We start with one kind of simplicity and we'll someday arrive at a second simplicity that has much in common with the first but has been deepened, broadened and strengthened through all we've experienced and endured in between.

One

Simplicity:
The Season of
Spiritual Awakening

Simplicty

Many of us have memories of when our spiritual lives first came alive – the season of our 'first love'.[1] For example, in those initial months after my experience under the stars, I felt the Bible speak to me as never before. The simplest word or phrase would stir my soul. My weeks centred around Tuesday nights – the time of the 'Jesus people' prayer and teaching gathering I attended with some friends. I started wearing a big wooden cross around my neck and I carried a big, green Living Bible on top of my high school books – in hope that someone would ask me about either of them so I could 'bear witness' to my exuberant, contagious faith. I loved to insert 'Praise the Lord!' into my speech as often as possible – which elicited 'Amen!' from my Christian friends and surprise or annoyance from my other friends. Speaking of my Christian friends, we could often be found huddling in a stairwell or even the 'smoking court' (a fixture of US high schools back in those days) – not smoking, but praying for a miraculous intervention of some sort. And our prayers, it seemed to us, were answered way beyond the statistical norm. We seemed to 'live and move and have our being' in the holy glow of God's presence. It was spiritual springtime, and we assumed it would never end.

Spring is an amazing mixture of fragility and vitality. Each new sprout is delicate, but what can compare with the combined power of millions of leaves bursting out, drawing energy from the sun? The first season of the spiritual life similarly combines tenderness and toughness as tiny seeds sprout and display the magnificent power of life and growth.

Just as all higher mathematics depends on learning basic arithmetic, and just as all more sophisticated music depends on mastering the basics of tempo, melody and harmony, the spiritual life depends on learning well the essential lessons of this first season of simplicity. If these lessons aren't learned well, practitioners will struggle in later seasons. But if in due time this season doesn't give way to the next, the spiritual life can grow stagnant and even toxic.[2] Nearly all of us in this dynamic season of simplicity tend to share a number of characteristics.

We see the world in simple dualist terms: *we* are the good guys who follow the good authority figures and we have the right answers; *they* are the bad guys who consciously or unconsciously fight on the wrong side of the cosmic struggle between good and evil. We feel a deep sense of identity and belonging in our in-group. This in-group loyalty is constantly reinforced by our Stage-One leaders, who offer us clear, authoritative, black-and-white answers to every question of belief or behaviour, reminding us of the great danger of being misled by *them* into accepting wrong answers or following the wrong rules. As a result, our relationships in this stage tend to be dependent or even co-dependent; we need our in-group and its confident, charismatic leaders to know who we are and what we're about.

God, from this vantage point, is our ultimate Authority Figure, giving us simple truths to believe and simple rules to follow, leading us into battle against evil and blessing us by being ever on our side. This simple, dualist faith gives us great confidence.[3]

This confidence, of course, has a danger as the old Bob Dylan classic *With God On Our Side* made clear: 'You don't count the dead when God's on your side.' The same sense of identification with an in-group that generates a warm glow of belonging and motivates sacrificial action for *us* can sour into intolerance, hatred and even violence towards *them*. And the same easy, black-and-white answers that comfort and reassure us now may later seem arrogant, naïve, ignorant and harmful if we don't move beyond simplicity in the fullness of time.

So what are the important and essential lessons of simplicity, and how can we learn them well without getting stuck there long after 'the fullness of time' has expired? Those questions lead us to the first three practices of naked spirituality: awakening, gratitude and awe.

Chapter 4

Here: Starting Right Now

The Practice of Invocation and Presentation: Awakening to the Presence of God

Alternative words: Now. You. Who? We. Open. Home.

> You will find stability at the moment when you discover that God is everywhere, that you do not need to seek God elsewhere, that God is here, and if you do not find God here it is useless to go and search elsewhere because it is not God that is absent from us, it is we who are absent from God ... This is important because it is only at the moment you recognise this that you can truly find the fullness of the Kingdom of God in all its richness within you.
>
> Metropolitan Anthony Bloom[1]

It was a sunny October afternoon twenty years ago. I was far away from civilisation, deep in the mountains of Pennsylvania, fishing for native brook trout in a pristine valley, under a canopy of hemlocks and white pines that spiced the air with their sweet scent. I had taken a few days away at a retreat centre for personal rest and recharging, hoping to de-stress and let my soul revive a bit from the pressures of the ministry to which I was devoting my life. I was kneeling beside a freestone stream, releasing a trout, admiring its beauty – the magical wash of reds, greys, oranges and whites that shimmered at the intersection of clear mountain water and clear autumn light. Over the sounds of the brook, I thought I heard a voice calling in the distance. I stopped and listened, and then nothing.

Maybe it was a dog barking, I thought. A few more times I thought I heard something, but when I paused, I heard over the running water only the calls of crickets and crows. A half-hour later I had rounded a bend in the stream, and this time, I knew I heard a human voice, a long, faraway shout, two tones, the first higher, the second lower. 'Somebody must have lost a hunting dog,' I thought. I couldn't think of any reason for anyone else to be this far out in the forest calling for somebody.

It was maybe another half-hour later, a few more bends downstream, when I heard the voice again, and realised that the name being called was my own. My heart started pounding. Nobody names a dog Brian, and nobody would have gone to this much trouble to find me unless there was something seriously wrong. Was it one of my parents? My wife in an accident? One of my kids? I scrambled up the bank, imagining a thousand tragedies, and once I mounted the dirt road that led up and out of the valley, I started yelling at full volume, my voice breaking: 'Here!' I called. 'I'm *here*!' A few minutes later, my pulse racing and my chest heaving, I came across an employee from the retreat centre. A group of people had spread out across the area, by car, on foot, and using off-road vehicles, looking for me, he explained. 'Your wife called. It's an emergency. She's at the hospital with your younger son.'

41

That began a long adventure. In the coming days we learned that Trevor had a serious disease – either aplastic anaemia or leukaemia. As soon as the diagnosis came in – it was leukaemia – we began treatment, which, thank God, effectively cured him three years later. But still today, when I'm walking in the woods, my heart skips a beat if I hear – or think I hear – someone calling in the distance. And that simple word *here* has taken on new meaning for me, whether I'm calling out to someone else – *Is anyone here?* – or whether I'm answering a call, *I'm here!*

I had a five-hour drive from the mountains to the hospital. As you can imagine, I cried and prayed the whole way. As that disorienting day gave way to another and another, something emerged through the chaotic emotions and disrupted schedules. My wife Grace and I knew that we were not alone, that our son was not alone, that our family was not alone. We knew that God was *here*, with us, even in *this here*.

Here is the simple word by which we show up, respond to the one calling our name. *Here* is the way we name where we are – pleasant or unpleasant, desired or not – and declare ourselves present to God's presence. Before settling on *here* as the simple word in which to lodge our first spiritual practice, I considered several others. An obvious choice would have been *God* or *Lord* or *You*. Direct address of the soul to its Source must surely come early in any exploration of the spiritual life. But something held me back from making these obvious choices, and I wasn't sure what it was. Now I think I know: when we begin by naming God, too often we assume that we know more about the one we're addressing than we may actually know. The name carries too much unacknowledged conceptual freight for us.

Author and literary critic C. S. Lewis tried to capture this danger in a poem he wrote called 'Footnote to All Prayers'. When we pray, he said, we bow toward God and refer to God with familiar symbols – like father, judge, king and so on. In so doing, we may falsely assume that our idea of God is identical to God, that the real God 'out there' is no bigger than and no different from the idea we have 'in here' in our heads. Our cherished symbols, our familiar language, he warned, may carry the distortions of 'our own unquiet thoughts' or the confining shape of a 'folklore dream' – concepts of God that are partial at best, misleading at worst. We may forget that our best symbolic representations are in the end merely 'frail images' of God, images that 'cannot be the thing' that God is.[2] Whatever the reality actually is to which the word or name *God* points, we know that God's reality must always be far higher and greater and other than our concepts and images of God – even our best concepts and images. So if, like archers, we aim our arrow-prayers toward the bull's-eye of our conceptual target – at our limited ideas of God instead of beyond and above our ideas – our prayers will simply arc back down into the dirt. Our only hope is that God finds our arrows mid-flight and magnetically draws them to their intended destination. That hope in God's 'magnetic mercy' inspires Lewis's poem-prayer.

So I decided to work with the simple word *here* because it subverts the assumption that we have God named, figured out and properly 'targeted'. Instead, it places us out in the woods, so to speak, calling out so that we can be found by the one seeking us: *Here I am, in the presence of a mystery. Here I am, in the presence of a Presence who transcends, surpasses, overflows and exceeds every attempt at definition, description*

43

and even conception. Here you are, whoever you are, however similar or dissimilar you are to my preconceived notions of you. May the real I and the real you become present to one another ... here and now.

Whether I feel I'm seeking God – calling out, *Is anybody here?* – or whether I feel God is calling out to me and I respond, *Here I am!* – I think the simple word *here* can do something amazingly comprehensive. Through it, I show up. I come out of hiding. I let myself be found. The teacher is taking attendance, and I tell the teacher that I'm present and ready to learn. This acknowledgement of mutual *here-ness* becomes the prelude to mutual *nearness*. Through mutual presentation, the soul and God open the way for deep connection.

There is an old theological term for this first practice of awakening, of becoming present to the Presence: *invocation*. The word suggests a summoning, but of course, God isn't busy out in the back yard, needing to be called inside to meet us in the kitchen.[3] No, God has been with us all along, even though we may have been too busy or distracted, too groggy or sick, or simply too immature to notice. Through invocation, we are calling inward to our own souls, summoning ourselves to wake up so we can attend to the Presence in whose attention we are held and in whom we live, move and have our being.

Here can help awaken us to our own situation as well. Here I am at this point in history, within today's swirl of politics and economics, within epochal shifts in climate and plate tectonics, and within the ongoing drama of human civilisation and its discontents. Here I am, at this point in my own story – as a child, a teenager, an adult, a senior citizen. Here I am, on this hill, on this grass, looking up at this sky. Here I am, on this unique day in the history of the universe, with that bird singing over there, those planes flying overhead, these plants springing up around me, each thing with its own unique luminosity. Here I am, in this predicament, in this catastrophe, in this boring afternoon, in this hospital bed with all this beeping, buzzing, humming equipment. Here I am, with all my problems and faults, all my embarrassments and mistakes, all my whirring conscious thoughts and all my subconscious rumblings and doubts. Here I am, walking down this aisle, taking this exam, in between these contractions, about to deliver this lecture, in the middle of this divorce, writing this book. I don't have to be somewhere else: right here is OK. In fact, it's the only place I can be to begin to awaken spiritually. Here. Now. Just as I am.[4]

Being present here where we are can actually be tougher than it seems. I'm always tempted to be partially somewhere else, to pretend I'm not where I am, who I am, how I am. I'm always tempted to pray elsewhere than here, to shift my weight into a kind of religious fantasy-land, a doctrinal matrix, a state of emotional hype, some other kind of not-here in which to encounter God. But no. When we want our spirituality to be naked, simple, and authentic, we resist escapism, realising that a God who cannot be found here is not really God. So we say, 'Let's start … here. Now.'

That's not to say it's wrong to choose a special place as our *here*. Jesus frequently withdrew into the countryside, away from the crowds. The early Celts identified certain special 'thin spaces' where the membrane between the visible world and the unseen world felt especially permeable to them. Leaders as diverse as Moses, the Buddha, the desert fathers and Mohammed all recounted powerful spiritual experiences during times of withdrawal and solitude. To plug into the naked *here*, sometimes we need to unplug from the thousand distractions and demands that keep us not-here in fantasy or render us only half-here in anxiety. To awaken to non-virtual reality, we may need to unplug from the video game or website. To resituate ourselves in the down-to-earth presence of God, we may need to unplug from our heady -isms, whether economic, political, or even theological.[5] So withdrawal to a place less fraught with distraction and more hospitable to awakening makes sense. But the purpose of practising a retreat to a thin-place *there* is so that eventually we can practise awakening *here*, wherever that may be. When we practise awakening to the here-ness of God in solitude or out in nature, we gradually learn to stay awake to God's here-ness in the midst of the crowds, the noise and the rush and crush that threaten to derange us.

If I resist de-rangement in the hustle and hassle, I can be re-ranged and re-arranged in what Richard Rohr calls the *naked now*, another way of saying the *naked here*.[6] If I can unplug from fantasy and bring the real me to the table, the real me as I am at this moment, then I can make room for the real God as well. Not just the God other people told me about. Not just the God I was told I had to believe in. Not just the God who is the projection of my wishes, 'unquiet thoughts' or 'folk-lore dreams'. But the God who is here – as present as gravity, light, heat, friendship, hope, love – the real Presence who is really present.

Just yesterday, this practice sustained me. I was on the subway in Washington, DC. The seats were all taken, so I was standing, holding one of the support poles in the rumble and sway of commuting. I closed my eyes briefly and said, 'Here. I'm here, God. You're here. We are here together.' I simply tried to hold that awareness that here, now, in the commotion and clatter, I was with God. I held that here-ness as I exited the subway, ascended the escalator, weaved my way through crowds on side-walks and crosswalks, and entered a meeting with lots of impor-tant people. In those situations, I often become more aware of their presence than God's, so as I walked into the meeting, I whispered, 'Here, Lord. I'm here with you. You're here with me.' When I found my seat, in between hellos and handshakes, I tried to stay centred in the presence of God, simply breathing here, here, here; in each here, staying awake to God's presence above me, before me, behind me, beside me, beneath me and within me, as the old Celtic blessing puts it.

When I just used the term *God* to name the Presence, I wasn't actually using a name, strictly speaking. *God* and *Lord*, like Father or Mother or Doctor or Professor or Your Majesty, are titles, not names. Titles usually imply a relationship. Whenever I use a title to address God, I can awaken myself not only to God's presence, but also to my presence in a multi-faceted relationship with God.

This is a precious thing to savour. It's deep, and huge. When I realise I am here with God our Creator, God our Father, the Lord my Shepherd, I am awakening to the relationships in which I live – as creature in creation, as child in family, as member of God's flock. But dare we move beyond this language of relationship? Dare we go even farther – to address God not simply by title but even by name?

Dare we move from *here* to *who* and *you*? This is exactly the move a young zealot named Paul makes when he is knocked off his feet on the Damascus Road. Paul shows the typical strengths of a Stage-One pilgrim, deep in the season of simplicity. Fuelled by the anxieties and furies of de-ligion, he is out to imprison those who defy the religious system to which he is so desperately devoted. But along the way, he experiences a blinding light. Somehow, in that light he hears his own name, repeated twice. His response suggests that up until now, he has known exactly who God is and what life and religion are about, or at least, he has thought so. But now, as he experiences a kind of new birth and new beginning in an actual encounter with the living God, he must let what he knew with such certainty be deconstructed and fall behind him. He must reopen the question: *Who are you, Lord?* This question is essential in the shift from de-ligion to deep religion, from religiosity to spirituality. We must hold that question open to God: *who are you?* Without doing so, we will pray yet again to our frail images of God, our set of pre-conceived notions of God, our familiar boxed and framed conventions and our comfortable stereotyped assumptions about God. By holding *who?* before God, we open and present ourselves to the God beyond our notions, to the living *You* who is actually here.

This kind of awakening begins the transformation of a religious (or de-ligious or non-religious) life into a spiritual life, a life with God – not later and elsewhere, but here and now. How much higher and wider and deeper and richer our lives become when we awaken to the presence of the real, wild, mysterious, living God who is bigger than our tame concepts of God, when we sense an inward vocation from God and toward God, and we respond with presentation, saying, *Here I am, Lord. I present myself to you, presenting yourself to me.* We live with a perpetual *Here I am, and here you are,* in our hearts, inviting constant, vital connection, unbroken communion, lifelong friendship ... starting right here, starting right now.

Chapter 5

Here: Naming the Mystery

The Logos, the Word ... that informs the cosmos – all
things great and small – is still spoken in sparrow song,
wind sigh, and leaf fall. An electron is a single letter, an
atom a complex word, a molecule a sentence, and a mock-
ingbird an entire epistle in the great ongoing saga. The
ocean still whispers the song that originated with the big
bang. Listen to the longing in your heart for love and
justice, and you may hear the sacred word. To live in a
reverential manner is ... to create an autobiography in
which we tell the stories of the unique epiphanies that
have informed our lives.

Sam Keen[1]

The bush is burning, but it's not burning up. How could that be?

That's the paradox that Moses faces in Exodus 3 in one of
the Bible's paradigmatic encounters of a human being with
the mysterious Presence of God.[2]

Moses is tending sheep in the middle of nowhere one day
and sees a common bush filled with uncommon fire. He is
drawn to the flame, not necessarily out of reverence – he's at
something of a spiritual low point when the encounter happens
– but out of curiosity. It's fascinating that God would self-

manifest in a flame, since by its very nature fire (like the wind, water and wine we considered in Chapter 2) is mysterious, at once attractive and intriguing and in some ways scary and dangerous. It's equally fascinating that this extraordinary flame is fused with an ordinary bush. It's still more fascinating to think that the ordinary isn't destroyed by the extraordinary, or to put it differently, that this is a fire that doesn't consume; it burns but doesn't burn up – a curious paradox that draws Moses in.

Interestingly, the conversation begins not with Moses invoking God, but with God invoking Moses – by name. God doesn't say to Moses (as God does say to some other people in the Bible), 'Attention: Earthling!' or 'Now hear this, Human Being!' Instead, Moses simply hears his own name – twice, in fact, just as did Paul centuries later – 'Moses! Moses!' I wonder if Moses, out in the barren desert, felt as I did that day walking along the stream; I wonder if his heart pounded and his breath was taken away.

This story is deeply suggestive about our awakening to God. First, as we've seen, it suggests the uncontainable mystery and wonder of the Presence who calls to us.[3] Second, it suggests that as we approach God, we begin not as knowers but as the known. We are named before we name, called before we call, spoken to before we speak. What feels like an initiative on our part turns out to be the response to a prior initiative taken by the one who calls us. So we are not, through our invocation, waking up God and getting God's attention. We are being awakened, and God is attracting our attention, and we respond to the one who was already *here* but we didn't realise it.

Third, the story suggests that an encounter with God requires a response. Moses' responds by presenting himself to the mysterious presence who has called his name. *Here I am*, in this sense, would mean *reporting for duty*, and *in-vocation* would mean a call to enter a *vocation* or mission.

After cautioning Moses to keep his distance from the fire and to remove his sandals as a sign of being in a holy place, God then self-introduces in a fascinating way: 'I am the God of your father, the God of Abraham, the God of Isaac, and the God of Jacob.' God doesn't self-identify by giving God's personal name, but by naming persons Moses knows. God shows up, we might say, behind familiar faces – the faces of Moses' own ancestors.

So then, in this encounter, God first wants to be known through a dynamic image beyond words – a dancing flame that doesn't destroy what it fills. Then God wants to be known through a heritage, a tradition, a story, as if God is saying, 'You are now encountering the one that your ancestors have encountered over many generations.' Yes, God says, this is an unprecedented experience for you, but it is not unprecedented in history: it is your time now to enter into a conversation your ancestors participated in.[4] Might we hear the same message coming to us, here and now?

As the conversation unfolds, God gives Moses a mission and promises to be with him in its fulfilment. But Moses' response is surprising. He doesn't say, as we might expect, 'Yes, sir! Your wish is my command!' Instead, Moses – and this is really stunning, when you think about it – argues. During a paradigmatic experience of God, one is capable of quarrelling, questioning, debating and doubting.

This pattern, amazingly enough, holds true throughout the Bible. The experience of God is not normally so overwhelming that one is reduced to quivering mush: instead, it invites one to stand tall (though barefoot), to push back, to question, even to resist.[5] At one point in the give and take, after God says, 'Here's what I want you to do,' Moses replies, basically, 'No way. You have the wrong guy.' Then, as if negotiating a business deal, Moses says, 'OK. Suppose I do agree, and I go and tell people that God has sent me on a mission, but then people say, "Which god? What's the name of the deity who sent you?" What do I say then?'

Now Moses is asking for something beyond a title like 'Father', 'Mother', 'Sir', 'Your Honour' or 'the God of your ancestors'. Moses is asking, 'What is your name? Your personal name? If I am Moses, who are you?'

Moses' experience echoes two experiences of his distant ancestor Jacob (Gen. 28:10–22; 32:22–32). Jacob also had an encounter with God – in a dream of a ladder to the sky instead of a vision of a burning bush in the desert (Gen. 28). God self-introduced in the same way, 'I am the Lord, the God of Abraham your father and the God of Isaac', and similarly added a promise to be with Jacob (28:13). Many years later, Jacob had another encounter, again at night, this time with God strangely manifesting not from the top of a celestial ladder in the sky, and not from within a burning bush on the ground, but as a powerful assailant determined to overcome Jacob in a wrestling match (Gen 38). Jacob's impulse was the same as Moses': to get this being's name. Interestingly, the mysterious night-time wrestler did not capitulate, but instead turned the tables and demanded Jacob's name, and then, when Jacob acquiesced, changed Jacob's name to Israel.[6] Quite an interchange!

When we approach God through the awakening practice of *here*, we're entering into this primal drama of human beings encountering the one who knows them, who knows their names, and who can never be captured or pinned down in any single name. When we begin to pray, we too are Jacob wrestling, refusing to let go. We too are barefoot Moses, curious yet resistant and bargaining, grappling with mystery. And like Jacob and Moses, we will be changed through our encounter.

God's voice, still emanating from the burning bush, answers Moses, 'I AM WHO I AM' (Ex. 3:14); an enigmatic name theologians are still pondering millennia later. What does the phrase mean? Perhaps it means, 'I will be whoever I will be, Moses, so get used to the fact that you can't wrestle my identity down.' Perhaps it means, 'I am the essence of being itself.' Perhaps it means, 'None of your business! Who do you think you are to try to nail down my identity in a little word that your little brain can manipulate? I am who I am, and that's as much as you'll be able to grasp.' Some scholars see a kind of future tense to the statement, as if God is saying, 'I will be who I will be', or in other words, 'I am the one you will gradually get to know, always at hand but never in hand.' I imagine it means all of these, and more.

This same tension – that God wants to be in dialogue with us, but yet God's full identity must always remain mysterious to us, above us, beyond us, ahead of us – is captured in the opening lines of the prayer Jesus taught his disciples. 'Our Father in heaven' refers to God through a title, a title that implies relationship: God is our source and parent, God cares about us, we are part of God's family – and not just we as individuals, but all of us, because we are taught to pray 'Our Father', not 'My Father in heaven.'

But then Jesus teaches the disciples immediately to follow 'Our Father' with these words: 'hallowed be your name', or 'may your name be revered'. Quite certainly Jesus is here evoking the mysterious name 'I AM WHO I AM', the elusive name that names truly by not naming concretely. If the first line evokes the possibility of a personal relationship and intimacy ('the God of your ancestors, Abraham, Isaac and Jacob ... our Father in heaven') then the second line evokes mystery and transcendence – 'may your unspeakable name be held in reverence, the name I AM WHO I AM, I WILL BE WHO I WILL BE.'

This sacred name for God, which occurs 6,828 times in the Hebrew Scriptures, was considered so holy that it would rarely be spoken, a tradition I respect and try to follow myself (which explains why I am not offering an English transliteration of the Hebrew name). Many of Jesus' Jewish brothers and sisters through the centuries, to retain appropriate reverence for God's mysterious name, began to encode it in an alternative name. They created this code name – *Jehovah* – by mixing the four consonants of the holy name with the vowels of the word Adonai, which is a title of respect used for God and for powerful human beings too, like 'my lord' or 'sir' or 'your majesty'. In written English today, translators often render the name as *the LORD* (in capitals) or as *G-d*. At points in this book where I am especially eager to remind us of G-d's otherness, G-d's definite undefinability, I will employ this practice as well.

One way or another, we are wise to retain this dynamism so that reverential awe dances like a flame within us whenever we make the first move in the spiritual life, when we show up to G-d seeking mutual nearness in mutual here-ness, whether we say 'Lord', 'Our Father in heaven' or 'Mysterious Presence'. We must preserve this essential dynamic tension in addressing

God, who names us accurately and knows us utterly, while acknowledging that we can neither fully know nor adequately contain the Divine Mystery in any name. Throughout the Bible (and the Quran and many other sacred writings too, by the way) we feel this tension in the spiritual life, this tension between naming God and not reducing G-d to a name, this tension between addressing God through a name but never possessing G-d in a verbal or conceptual address, this electricity between what theologians call God's immanence or accessibility and G-d's transcendence or complete otherness.

When people experience breakdown in the spiritual life, it's often because they don't maintain this tension. If they resolve the tension on the side of transcendence or otherness, God becomes distant – at first a kind of remote deity, then a kind of abstract principle, then an impersonal cosmic force or energy, and eventually, God may disappear entirely, leaving us in a world of numbers and equations without meaning or purpose. Moses' bush no longer burns; Jacob's ladder leans against a wall, and his mysterious assailant is just another mugger. We call out, but nobody is home.

If people resolve the tension on the side of immanence or nearness, G-d becomes too much the chum or mascot or even guard dog, a genie who comes obediently when summoned by the magic words. When this happens, prayer is like rubbing a magic lamp or commanding guard dogs to attack an intruder. One's religion starts looking a lot like superstition or witchcraft. And magical religions in this mode too easily turn homicidal and genocidal because, quite conveniently, 'God' hates the same people its adherents hate and is happy to share their malice.

Naked spirituality differs from magical religion as love differs from lust. Where magical religion tries to harness cosmic powers so that 'my will may be done', naked spirituality seeks to unleash my powers so that 'God's will may be done'. Where magical religion tries to possess God for one's own benefit, naked spirituality seeks to be yielded to God for God's will, the common good.

So our first simple word is truly significant. The posture of invocation and presentation – holding our hearts open with *here*, brings us into an essential, dynamic and creative tension. This tension is essential for naked spirituality to break free from its husk like a seed in springtime. One name for this dynamic tension is *reverence*. Sometimes the Bible calls it *fear* as in 'the fear of the Lord', but it's clear that *fear*, when used this way, doesn't mean the kind of spiritual terrorism to which many people are subjected in fire-and-brimstone sermons and God-as-Terminator theology. (If *fear* in this context were intended to mean anxiety in the face of danger, why would God's first words to someone experiencing God almost always be, 'Don't be afraid!'? see, for example, Gen. 26:24 or Luke 1:30.) No, reverence or holy fear suggests this dynamic tension of being drawn to the beautiful and mysterious flame while always remembering that the flame is powerful and transcendent beyond imagination. Reverence means wanting to avoid dual dangers: thinking of the living God as a distant, impersonal, uncaring force or faceless principle on the one hand, or reducing G-d to one's personal deity on a leash or a genie in a bottle on the other hand.

So, how do we try to maintain this dynamic when we pray? One answer becomes clear when we survey the invocations in any random selection of Psalms:

O God (79:1), O LORD (79:5), O God our Saviour (79:9),
O Shepherd of Israel (80:1), O LORD God of hosts (80:4),

O LORD Almighty, my king and my God (84:3), O God
of Jacob (84:8), O LORD, the God of my salvation (88:1),
O Judge of the earth (94:2)

You'll notice the range of ways that God is addressed. First,
whenever you see LORD (in all capitals), it's a sign in English
that the Hebrew name for G-d drawn from I AM WHO I AM
is being used in the original text. You'll also notice that in
addition to this mysterious name with all that it evokes of
God's transcendence, the sacred poets invent scores of other
names, a kind of torrent of images and metaphors for God:
king, shepherd, rock, friend, father, co-worker, potter, shepherd, wind, breath, vine, farmer, and so on. Then, if that
weren't enough, poets employ dozens of adjectives to name
God, so God is the Holy One, the Faithful One, the Everlasting
One, the Almighty, the Eternal, and so on. Then there is a
whole category of names in Hebrew that combine the two –
joining the unutterable name for God with words or images
that describe what God is or does for God's people: the LORD
my healer, the LORD my provider, the LORD our Creator,
the LORD our Banner, the LORD our justice, and so on.

In Islam, similarly, there are ninety-nine names for God –
stopping short of a hundred as if to say, 'No name is sufficient, and all names together still fall short.' Here are a few
that I especially love:

The All-Compassionate
The All-Merciful
The Pure One
The Source of Peace
The Inspirer of Faith

57

The Guardian
The Creator
The Maker of Order
The Shaper of Beauty
The Forgiving
The Giver of All
The Sustainer
The Opener
The Knower of All

So, our diverse traditions agree that to approach God with the dynamic tension of reverence, we need a wide repertoire of names and images for God, so we can avoid getting stuck in a rut in referring to God. We need to move from image to image, name to name, and never settle exclusively on just one. So I may let an image like *God my Rock* bring to mind God's unchanging dependability, or God as a shelter from enemies. But then I must avoid the tendency to let God seem static and heavy rather than dynamic and free by adding another image – God as Spirit, blowing like wind over the waters of creation, for example. And then I can move to God as Parent, King, Shepherd or Potter, as the Shaper of Beauty, the Opener or the Source of Peace. By never letting my mind reduce God to one image or one name, I keep my mind opened up and awake rather than shut down and half-asleep, and in so doing, I maintain reverence.

My own practice of reverent awakening or invocation often unfolds like this:

O God, you are my light … You are my Shepherd … You are my Friend … You are my Creator … You are the Holy One … You are the Shaper of Beauty.

Sometimes I take this exercise a step further, drawing from St Francis' way of prayer.[7] I begin with *here* and move to *who*, *who* as a question that I then answer in a variety of ways. The prayer goes like this:

> Here I am, Lord. Here you are, Lord. Here we are together. (Pause)
>
> Who am I, Lord? Who are you, Lord? Who are we together? (Pause)

Simply opening the question is more important than closing in on any single answer. In fact, it's the multiplicity of answers that counts. On those restless nights when I am struggling with insomnia, I decide to stop spinning in my hamster wheels of worry and inquietude. I climb off the wheel and awaken myself to God's presence using the prayer above. I move from *here* to *who*, letting answer after answer come to mind. Sometimes, this exercise helps me fall asleep. Sometimes it doesn't. Either way, it's OK.

One night, my responses to this exercise came together in this simple song:

> O, Lord, who are you? O, Lord, who am I?
> Who are we together?
> We are glowing fire in a burning bush.
> We are master and apprentice.
> We are lover and beloved.
> Giving birth to a better world together.

We are artist and work in progress.
We are vine and fruitful branches.
We are partners in this mission.
We are builders of a brighter future.

We are wind in swaying treetops.
We are mother and her child.
We are friends in conversation.
We are dancers who move to joyful music.

We are wide blue sea and leaping dolphin.
We are warm spring sun and growing seeds.
We are poet and living poetry.
We are singers who fill the earth with harmony.

In a moment, I hope you'll put this book down and take a few deep breaths. Allow yourself to slow down and rest for a minute. As you feel your weight settle on a chair or on the ground, let the weight of your soul rest back on the presence and love of God. Just be here. You might want to hear, in your imagination, the living God calling your name, repeated twice as with Moses and Paul (and others in the Bible too), inviting you to reply, *Here I am*. It might help you to repeat those words for a while, in rhythm with each breath. Simply present yourself to the Rock, the River, the Light, the Wind, the Shepherd, the Greatest, the Shaper of Beauty, the Merciful One, the Unnameable One, the Presence. *Here I am. Here you are. Here we are together.* Try this now.

You may then want to let your *here* progress to *who*: *Who are you? Who am I? Who are we together?* Try this now. Try letting the question give you permission to let your understanding and experience of G-d expand, transcend and surpass your current understandings and boundaries.

Hold the space with *here* and *who*. And then, if it feels right, try working with the word *home*. Affirm that to be here with God is to be at home, wherever you are. That home-base or home-space is simultaneously your soul (your space, where God is welcome) and heaven (God's space, where you are welcome).[8] The word *open* may also help you open yourself to God, and realise that God's embrace, God's front door, God's presence is also open to you, welcoming you. It may even help you to clench your fists, symbolising how we are often tight and closed off to God's presence, bringing to mind the things that have had you uptight lately. Then you can gradually open them as you open your heart to God, and perhaps then, *You* will be the most helpful simple word.

From that quiet, simple beginning, see what happens. See what unfolds. This is the beginning of naked spirituality.

Please don't just turn the page. Please don't simply keep reading. First, practice *here*...

Chapter 6

Thanks! The Happiness of Appreciation

The Practice of Gratefulness and Appreciation: Awakening to the Goodness of God

Alternative words: Again. This. *Dayenu.*

> If the only prayer you said in your whole life was 'thank you,' that would be sufficient.
>
> Meister Eckhart[1]

I'm in Guatemala. Some friends and I are driving through the countryside in an old car, no air-conditioning, the windows wide open until we see an approaching vehicle. Then we quickly roll up the windows so we won't be covered by the cloud of red dust that follows ... but within seconds, beads of sweat are forming on our foreheads and upper lips, so we crank the windows down again. Up and down our windows go as rusty buses, ramshackle pickups and other old weather-beaten cars approach and pass, mile after mile. We finally come to a little town. We stop, turn off the engine, step out, stretch, and as the red dust settles and the noise of the road fades, we hear a new sound off to the right, down through some scraggly trees, past a few bony, wide-horned brown cows standing in the shadows chewing their cud, beyond a fence with just a strand or two of barbed wire.

Beyond the cows and just outside a few strands of barbed wire, there's a stream and a little swimming hole sparkling in the full sunlight. In its brown waters a dozen children are splashing and wrestling. Their laughter rises like music, a cloud of joy as real as the cloud of red dust stirred by another car passing on the road behind us. I think, 'I've seldom heard this much pure happiness in my life.' We watch for a few minutes, smiles irrepressibly arising on our faces, and then decide to take a break and explore the town before continuing our journey. As I turn off to be on my own for a few minutes, I see the homes these children come from. They're small in size and modest in construction but often painted the most dazzling colours, this one coral-pink, the next aquamarine, the next tangerine-orange, the one over there, a light purple peeling off in places, showing a royal blue underneath.

There are some dads sitting in the shadows of a few trees, cigarettes dangling under the bills of well-worn baseball caps, sharing stories, playing cards, nodding and smiling as we walk by. There are some mums squatting on front porches, peeling potatoes, washing dishes in plastic basins, nursing babies, shooing flies. I smell coffee roasting, mixed with the scent of a farm not far away; I hear a muted accordion and a flatulent trumpet from a broken radio speaker. I hear the sound of someone sawing a plank, a rooster crowing in the afternoon heat, a dog bark twice off in the distance, and everywhere, the buzz of insects mixed with the music of children's laughter jingling in the background.

Maybe someday there will be televisions in every house, I

imagine. Maybe someday there will be video games and DVD players. Maybe the hum of air conditioners and the roar of many cars. But I don't think there will ever be more happiness in the air than there is today.

What is this extraordinary happiness? Where does it come from? Back home, kids with a thousand times more wealth and security are bored and whining in their carpeted living rooms, not laughing in brown creek-water; back home, parents are stuck in traffic and worrying about a thousand things, not enjoying an ordinary day.

Walking through that town in Guatemala, I remind myself of something we all know, but we don't take seriously enough: *it is not how much you have that brings happiness; it's how much you appreciate however much or little you have.*[2] Again, it's not the amount of stuff you have that counts, it's the amount of appreciation you have that matters, and appreciation means 'gratefully holding' rather than simply 'having without gratitude'.

Perhaps we need to update those famous lines from the American Declaration of Independence: that along with being endowed by our Creator with certain inalienable rights that include 'life, liberty and the pursuit of happiness', we are encouraged by our Creator to slow down and appreciate the gift of life, to employ our liberty in service for others, and to gratefully cherish the happiness we already have. Gratitude may be the greatest secret to happiness there is. But if that's the case, wealth comes with a hidden danger, a threat to happiness. The more we have, the more we need to practise gratitude; otherwise, we will begin taking more and more of what we have for granted. If we habitually take more and more for granted, our ingratitude will eventually lead to ...

unhappiness. And of course, if we have little, we will also need to practise gratitude, so our little that is greatly appreciated can count for more happiness than much that is little appreciated. So, well-off or poor, we all stand in utter need of great gratitude.

You have already anticipated, I imagine, why gratitude is so essential to a naked spirituality. First, because spirituality in today's world is constantly under assault by consumerism, which claims that the source of joy is not in God, or within, but in a new pair of shoes, a trip to southern France, or a new flat-screen TV. In relation to consumerism, gratitude could be called downright subversive. As I've detailed elsewhere, a lot of people spend a lot of money every day trying to keep you from being grateful.[3] They want you to think a lot more about what other people have than what you have, so you'll want more. They want you to think a lot more about what you don't have than what you do have, so you'll want more. And if you want more, you'll buy something from them, so they'll have more. But will they appreciate the money they gain from stimulating your greed? Probably not, because they too have been sucked into the whole 'never enough' vortex of consumerism, so they're seldom grateful and therefore never satisfied – which keeps them needling you to give them more of your money.

Consumerism thus robs the soul of happiness while it sells the soul more stuff. But this petty larceny on the individual level leads to far greater crimes. Just think of where this sick, never-enough system drives us: to mountains stripped for gold or coal, to oceans plundered of fish and seas toxified with oil, to hillsides denuded of trees and wildlife, to fields scraped by bulldozers and paved with tarmac so we can have yet another shopping centre (or storage facility) where we can buy (or store) more things we don't need and won't take time to appreciate. Habitats are thus stolen from other creatures, which means those creatures die and are stolen from other creatures that depend on them. Ecosystems that have developed over millions of years are tipped into disequilibrium and collapse. The cascade of extinction and imbalance rolls on like an avalanche or gushes out like an oil spill, stealing not just from the humans of today, but from the humans of forever. Economists tabulate the gross domestic product, but whose spreadsheet measures the gross domestic *destruct*? – the losses extracted in advance from our great-grandchildren when wild elephants, giraffes, thrushes, tortoises, sea turtles, chimpanzees, horseshoe crabs and swordfish have gone the way of the dodo?

We could give another name to the insanity of ingratitude: addiction. Just as it takes more and more heroin or cocaine to deliver the same high, ingratitude continually turns yesterday's luxuries into today's necessities. More and more stuff is required to give the same fleeting feeling of satisfaction. And just as addiction ultimately leads through insanity to misery and even death as the addict 'hits bottom', an economy driven by ingratitude – whether global, national, family or personal – races through overextension towards collapse. That's why gratitude is important, not just as a personal practice, but also as a group practice: it is a kind of immunisation against both personal and corporate addiction.

Gratitude is the spiritual practice that raises its fist in the face of this insanity; but that raised fist is actually a raised hand – reaching up in gratitude to God. The naked spirituality that fosters this kind of gratitude may, in the end, be the only thing that can save the planet. Consider that for a minute before moving on, OK?

If *here* suggests waking up and presenting ourselves to the presence of God, *thanks* means waking up to the presents of God ... waking up to the abundant gifts of life with which we have already been blessed. Joni Mitchell had it right – or almost right – in her song *Big Yellow Taxi*. You don't know what you've got 'til it's gone ... unless you practise gratitude.

When I was still a teenager, my friend Mary – one of the people who shared that dramatic experience on the hill that night under the stars – asked me, 'How much money would you give to keep your eyesight if you knew you were going blind?' A lot, I answered. Everything. Then she asked, 'What if it was your ability to walk – if you had a disease that would leave you wheelchair-bound unless you could pay for a cure. How much would you spend?' Everything, I said. I'd liquidate everything I own and go as far into debt as I could to save my mobility. 'How about your hearing?' The same, I answered. 'How about your sanity – your mental health, your intelligence?' Finally I asked, 'What's your point?'

'I'm just trying to save you from BYTS – the Big Yellow Taxi Syndrome,' she said, evoking the newly released Joni Mitchell song. 'If you were to lose any one of these abilities, you would pay millions of dollars to recover it, so each one is worth millions of dollars to you. You would rather have the ability to see or hear or move or think than tens of millions of dollars in the bank. Well ...' she smiled and gave me a little shove, ' ... you have them! Which means you're better off than a multi-million-aire! You have to know what you've got before it's gone.'

That's not a bad place to start with gratitude: with our own bodies. When I want to practise thanks, I can start with my toes – which, by the way, are under-rated until you break one as I did recently, and then you realise, limping, how much you depend on all ten every day. So, I can be grateful for working toes, then for working feet, then for mobile ankles, then for strong calves, then well-lubricated knees, and so on. Each part of my body that functions – that doesn't wrack me with pain, that makes possible other benefits and pleasures – can be counted, enjoyed with gratitude, not taken for granted.

Then, I can continue my practice of gratitude with physical possessions. I can start outdoors – with the landscaping I enjoy, the pleasure of having a garden, the trees on my property that bring me such joy, then the car in my driveway with all its features – good mileage, a good sound system, air conditioning, and so on. Then I can work my way room by room through my house, from basement to attic. Recalling my friend Mary's mental exercise, I can imagine my home being levelled by a tornado or flood, and see myself sifting through the wreckage, to find one shirt, salvage one photo, rescue one piece of furniture. How glad I would be to have that one thing! In my gratitude exercise, I realise that I do have all these things, and I can turn to God to share my joy.

I can then extend my practice of gratitude to my family, each member, one by one. As I shared previously, one of my adult children survived cancer as a boy, and so my wife and I experienced, day after day, the realisation that the child we had that day might be gone from us a year later. Although cancer took a lot from us, by stimulating gratitude and treating the Big Yellow Taxi Syndrome, it gave us far more than it took.

From my body to my possessions to my family, I can continue my practice of gratitude by moving out to other people – friends, pastors, colleagues. Then I can take it a step further – institutions like the courts, the police and other security forces, government and its many important duties, sports organisations, the music industry, entertainment. Every week or so, I'll hear a song by one of my favourite musicians – yes, Joni Mitchell and Bob Dylan, Bruce Cockburn, David Wilcox, Keith Jarrett – or I'll see a comedy routine by Steve Martin or Stephen Colbert or Jon Stewart, or I'll watch a great film or enjoy a good sporting event, and I'll breathe out a simple thanks: *Thanks, God, for the chance to be alive at the same time as these amazing people, to enjoy their talents, to watch their development over time. Thanks.*

My practice of gratitude can continue expanding outward … to those elephants and giraffes, those thrushes and horseshoe crabs who are my neighbours on this planet. Mountains, rivers, oceans, continents … I can ponder each one while holding *thanks* open to God like a hand.

The other night, I was experiencing a bout of insomnia, so this is just what I did. I brought the blessings of my life to mind, one by one. I didn't name them; I just pictured them while holding thanks open before God. I pictured what I had eaten for dinner a few hours earlier. Then I pictured the farmers who made it. Then I thought of all farmers everywhere, my mind quickly imagining scenes of rice paddies and wheat fields and vineyards and ranches and aquaculture ponds, from America to China to Argentina to Russia to Uganda to Canada. Then I pictured the blessings of soil and sun and rain, which got me thinking about the water cycle and sunlight and the solar system and the galaxy.

And soon, my mind was dazzled with a sense of the one big thing we call the universe, and – this might sound silly, but it might not – I felt a profound gratitude not just for the gifts that pertain to me and my life here and now, but for the gift of ... everything, everywhere, always. Instead of seeing the universe and its many gifts revolving around me as, sad to say, I normally do, for a few minutes, I saw myself as one gift within the larger gift that we call creation. And I felt thankful, not just that certain gifts are part of my life, but more: I felt thankful that my life can be part of this bigger gift, this sacred Given-ness. I'm fifty-four years old, and I don't think I ever felt that kind of great big gratitude until the other night. There was a kind of ecstasy to it, a deep delight and weighty joy that stayed with me as I drifted off to sleep and remains with me now.

Chapter 7

Thanks! *Dayenu* – Enough, and More, and More

Never let yourself think that because God has given you many things to do for Him – pressing routine jobs, a life full up with duties and demands of a very practical sort – that all these need separate you from communion with Him. God is always coming to you in the Sacrament of the Present Moment. Meet and receive Him there with gratitude in that sacrament; however unexpected its outward form may be receive Him in every sight and sound, joy, pain, opportunity and sacrifice.

Evelyn Underhill[1]

Every time you eat, drink, or draw a breath, you are demonstrating that you are not a self-contained unit. Your skin might give you a sense of boundaries, but in reality, you are interconnected not only with others, but with all creation. You are an organism in an environment, vitally connected and utterly dependent on resources outside yourself – elements and minerals; chemical, biological, geological and even astrophysical processes; friends, family, mentors, public servants; ecological, social, political and economic systems. Your story flows from and into a million other stories; it's hard to know where your story ends and others begin. At a funeral, when the officiant says, 'From dust you came, and to dust you shall return,' he or she could just as easily have said, 'From stardust you came, and to stardust you shall return,' because even earth's dust has a story beyond itself. Ingratitude makes us foolishly forget the fragility of our skin and proudly deny our interdependency and interconnectedness. If true spirituality and authentic religion are about vital interconnectedness, you can see how essential the practice of gratitude must be.

Jesus addressed gratitude again and again in his teachings, directly and indirectly. In the prayer he taught his disciples, for example, he offered these simple but revolutionary words that acknowledge our dependence: *give us this day our daily bread*. The phrase evokes the journey of Jesus' ancestors through the wilderness under Moses' leadership in about 1400 BC. It reminds people of those days when they had to travel light because they were always on the move, when each day they had to collect manna, bread for that day. Nothing could be stored for the next day on their journey, so each day was lived in utter dependence on God's provision, and nothing could be taken for granted.

Their journey was a journey of liberation: they were being liberated from slavery in Egypt, where they had been dehumanised and exploited so that their elite Egyptian slave-drivers could build their own never-enough system. It was also a journey of discipline. They were learning values on the journey that would form their national character when they finally settled down – so they wouldn't become either slaves or slave-drivers in the future.[2] When we awaken to the addictive slavery of our contemporary never-enough system, we too want to go on a journey of liberation, and we too want to develop a humility of character enriched by daily dependence and daily gratitude, true thankfulness for our daily bread.

We are well insulated from this daily dependence and the gratitude it engenders. Bank accounts, insurance policies, even daily conveniences like refrigerators and air conditioners … they all build in us a sense of independence and invulnerability. But think a little deeper, and you see how thin the illusion of security can be. What if the sun stopped shining tomorrow? How long would any of us last – no matter how much money we had in the bank? What if the ocean currents shifted and the weather patterns changed? What if terrorists stopped the electricity from flowing or brought down the internet for a few weeks or months? What if an epidemic broke out that stopped first air travel, then car and truck travel? How vulnerable would we feel then? So Jesus' prayer teaches us to travel light: to realise that, as his follower Paul would later say, if we have food and clothing, we have enough (1 Tim. 6:8), which means we have plenty to celebrate.

Jesus reinforces the same theme elsewhere in his Sermon on the Mount (Matt. 6:25–33). He reminds us that we can't keep our hair from turning grey (or falling out, at which I'm an expert). Nor can we add a day to our lives or an inch to our height – no matter how much we exercise our anxiety. Like the sparrows flying overhead or the day lilies blooming beside the roadway, we live within creaturely limits, and we depend for our survival on resources outside ourselves. This awareness of our creaturely limitations, dependence and vulnerability doesn't make us less happy, Jesus suggests: it actually increases our happiness. It liberates us from the addictive drives of the never-enough system: more food, more drink, more clothes – always more, more, more. It liberates us to see ourselves as

God's beloved creatures within God's creation instead of as self-made consumers in a self-made economic system.

In those simple words, *give us this day our daily bread*, Jesus invites us to radical non-conformity, which means radical liberation from the never-enough system. If we seek to fulfil God's dream for creation rather than our own little ego-centric ambitions to have more, more, more, he says, 'all these things' that we need will come to us.[3]

Now that's not a promise of an easy life, because in many other places, Jesus makes it clear that a life lived to fulfil God's dream for creation will involve suffering. But even here, Jesus implies that there is reason for gratitude. You see it in the Beatitudes, Jesus' eight-fold way of happiness (Matt. 5:3–12). There is a blessing in poverty, he says: to the degree you miss out on the never-enough system, you partake of God's dream. There is a blessing in the pain of loss, he says: in your grief, you experience God's comfort. There is blessing in being unsatisfied about the injustice in our world, he says: as God's justice comes more and more, you will feel more and more fulfilled. There is even blessing in being persecuted for doing what is just and good, he says: you enter into the heroic experience of God's prophets, and you show yourself to be on God's side.

With these counter-intuitive sayings and others like them, Jesus enrols us in advanced classes in the school of gratitude. He shows us the disadvantages of advantages, and the advantages of disadvantages. He will make this paradox most dramatic through his own death; his suffering and crucifixion will eventually bring hope and freedom to all humanity, hope and freedom that could come no other way. Here is the deepest lesson of gratitude, then: to be grateful not just in the good times, but also in the bad times. To be grateful not just in plenty, but also in need. To maintain thankfulness not just in laughter, but also through tears and sorrow. One of Jesus' followers will say that we should even rejoice in trials, because through trials come patience, character, wisdom. And another will say, 'I have learned in all things to be content', and so he can add, 'In everything, give thanks.'[4]

The words 'in everything' shouldn't be confused with 'for everything', of course. But neither should they be thinned to mean 'in easy circumstances'. Even in pain, we can find a place of gratitude, a place where alongside the agony of loss we still count and appreciate what remains.

Perhaps it becomes clear, in this light, how the attitude of gratitude is more valuable than any insurance policy. You may lose your job, but you can still be grateful for what you have left. You may lose popularity, but you can still be grateful for what you have left. You may lose a loved one, or facet after facet of your physical health, but you can still be grateful for what you have left. And what if you lose more, and more, and more, if bad goes to worse? Perhaps at some point, all of us are reduced to despair, but my hunch is – and I hope I never need to prove this in my own life, but I may, any of us may – having lost everything, one may still be able to hold on to one's attitude, one's practised habit of gratitude, of turning to God in Job-like agony and saying, *For this breath, thanks. For this tear, thanks. For this memory of something I used to enjoy but now have lost, thanks. For this ability not simply to rage over what has been taken, but to celebrate what was once given, thanks.*

If we seek for other words to stand alongside the simple word *thanks* in expressing gratitude, I think one would be *again*, because one of the greatest obstacles to gratitude is the sheer bounty of God's generosity. Day after day we are given sunlight, water, air, breath, food, drink, family, friends, work, rest, sight, hearing and a million other blessings, again and again, and our great temptation is to take them for granted. So when I notice that I've been taking these gifts for granted – a sure sign of which is that I'm moaning and groaning and complaining a lot – I rededicate myself to the practice of gratitude: *Again, God, again you have blessed me. Again, I savour this gift. Again I appreciate. Again I say thanks. Again. Again.*

Another word might be *this*. This day. This kiss. This view. This meal, this taste, this breath, this moment, this song … instead of letting these treasures pass by as if they were nothing or as if we were unconscious of their beauty and wonder, we pause and savour them, and we lift our joy and appreciation up to God in gratitude. Because if God created these wonders, and if God created us with the capacity to enjoy them, what could be better than to enjoy them *with God*? Isn't that what gratitude is, in its purest sense, joining God in the enjoyment of the goodness of creation – the goodness that was celebrated in the first sentences of the book of Genesis, and the goodness that surrounds us now, in *this*, and *this*, and *this*, *again* and *again*?

For one more alternative word we can borrow from the Hebrew: *dayenu*. The word is from a Jewish song that has been a key part of the Passover celebration for over a thousand years. It means, 'It would have been enough', and it functions within the retelling of the story of God's goodness over the generations:

If God had brought us out of Egypt, *dayenu* – it would have been enough.

If God had split the sea for us, *dayenu* – it would have been enough.

If God had led us through on dry land, *dayenu* – it would have been enough.

If God had provided for our needs in the wilderness for 40 years, *dayenu* – it would have been enough.

If God had fed us manna, *dayenu* – it would have been enough.

If God had given us Shabbat, *dayenu* – it would have been enough.

If God had led us to Mount Sinai, *dayenu* – it would have been enough.

If God had given us the Torah, *dayenu* – it would have been enough.

Singing this song fills one with a sense of surplus, of being super-abundantly blessed, of being saturated with good things, of one's cup being full and running over. And it fills one with a corresponding appreciation of God's unlimited generosity: *Dayenu – but there's more! Dayenu – but there's more! And more, and more! Thanks be to God!*

I've been thinking these thoughts as I wander through this town in Guatemala. I get back to our dusty car and I lean against the trunk, waiting for my companions. I realise the little swimming hole is now empty. A few white ducks sit placidly on the rocks where the children were laughing an hour ago. The kids have gone home to dinner. Smoke is rising from dozens of cooking fires around town, and I smell chicken and onions cooking. A dog barks, a rooster crows, I take a deep breath, and I am smiling without even meaning to. I feel full, and buoyant, and alive. Something in me wants to sing. I'm too inhibited to dance here alongside the road in the golden late-day sun, but I nod my head and sway a little to the song I hear from a nearby radio. Life with God is good. This day, this moment is good. I feel the vital connection. *Thank you, Lord,* I whisper. *Thank you, Lord. Again and again, for this and this and this. Dayenu. Dayenu. Thanks. Thanks.*

Chapter 8

O! Practising Jubilation

The Practice of Worship and Awe: Awakening to the Beauty and Joy of God

Alternative words: Hallelujah! Glory! Amen! How...

> Oh, these vast, calm measureless mountain days in whose
> light every thing seems equally divine, opening a thou-
> sand windows to show us God . . . These blessed moun-
> tains are so compactly filled with God's beauty [that] the
> whole body seems to feel beauty when exposed to it as it
> feels the campfire or sunshine . . . No wonder the hills
> and groves were God's first temples, and the more they
> are cut down and hewn into cathedrals and churches, the
> farther off and dimmer seems the Lord himself.
>
> Adapted from John Muir[1]

I'm on a flight home from Africa. My carry-on bags are packed
tight with wrinkled, dusty clothing plus some gifts from my friends
there, and my heart feels even more densely packed with memories to add to those of previous journeys. Among the strongest,
sweetest and most mysterious memories for me on these trips
home – the experience of joining African friends in worship.

Imagine a dirt floor and no walls, but wooden posts supporting rough-hewn rafters that in turn support a vast tin roof that shades about a thousand cheap plastic lawn chairs – mostly white, some green – arranged in rows. In front, there's a rough wooden stage covered with random pieces of carpet and linoleum tacked or duct-taped together. A ramshackle sound system hums a little, background to the sounds of sparrows chirping and magpies scrapping in the sun outside. The place is empty now, but for the last few hours, it has been rocking with joy. Old ladies and little kids clapped their hands and smiles flashed like cameras at a celebrity event. The impossibly bright and varied colours of women's dresses swayed and swirled like so many flags, and dust rose from dancing feet in the rising heat. And the singing – harmony, echo, rhythm, call and response, punctuated by shouts and ululations. If you've ever worked up a sweat celebrating the goodness of God and life and love as they do in an African Pentecostal church, you know what I'm talking about, and if you haven't, I hope you someday will.[2]

I preached today, so for over half an hour I had a bird's eye view of the congregation. An older man in the front row had one leg, probably a victim of a land mine during the last civil war. Another man had a patch over one eye and scars malforming his mouth, probably machete wounds from the same ugly period of violence. Many of the women were nursing babies, and for many of those mothers, I'm sure sixteen years hadn't yet passed since they themselves were babies. The worshippers' clothing was clean and bright – which always amazes me in a dusty place like this, especially because I know that nearly all these folks live in shacks or houses with dirt floors. But I also noticed that many outfits looked a little loose because these are thin people, living on a dollar or two a day, often subsisting on a single meal a day and often depositing into their metabolic banks insufficient calories to compensate for withdrawals made by HIV and related diseases.

I have worshiped in the world's great cathedrals, and I love the grandeur, glory, reverence, dignity and history that wash over me there. But these tin roofs, these dirt floors, these smells of sweat and cooking fires, these animating rhythms and swaying bodies and resonant voices ... these mark for me worship at its most sublime. It's this simple, passionate, primal Pentecostal worship that speaks most deeply to my soul, whether it's in Africa or Latin America or Asia or among the rural or urban poor in my own country. Why is it this way? Why are the most blessed often the most restrained in their worship, and why are those who have the least in terms of health, wealth and safety the most ready to 'make a joyful noise and sing for joy to the Lord'?

Is it because they relate to God primarily from their heart rather than their head? Is it because necessity has forced the poor to discover the practice of intentional celebration, the cultivation of disciplined delight? Could it be that our accumulation of possessions and protections coat our souls like rubber gloves so that we touch, but do not feel? Could the growl of our roaring machinery and the glare of our bright screens and flashing signs relocate us among those with ears that do not hear, those with eyes that do not see? In this way, is the call to worship a summons to the half-dead, half-asleep and half-numb to strip down, step out and draw near to the one thing money not only cannot buy but may actually rob us of? Could it be that the conceptualised and formalised worship of the 'developed world' is actually designed to inhibit and control rather than foment joy?

Author and activist Barbara Ehrenreich suggests this very thing. Empires and dictatorships maintain social control, she says, by converting (or subverting) the energy of jubilant dancing into regimented marching.[3] Pews in churches, she explains, are a rather late architectural innovation, added in the Middle Ages to inhibit the dancing that apparently broke out from time to time (think medieval European Pentecostals). Straight lines, orderly rows, military conformity ... these suit the civilised state better than spontaneous outbreaks of collective joy. But, she says, rigid conformity and emotional inhibition stultify the human spirit, and so occasionally, people defy the authorities and dare to dance. They create what author Kester Brewin describes as Temporary Autonomous Zones (TAZs), places where the normal patterns of hegemony and homogeneity are broken.[4] True, TAZs like Woodstock, Burning Man, Carnival, Mardi Gras and many rock concerts and music festivals can be occasions for drunkenness and debauchery. But they can also be expressions, Ehrenreich says, of the human need for jubilation, of the human right to freedom, and even of the sacred quest for vital connection.

Perhaps the original experience of a TAZ was a holiday in its original sense: a holy day, when we transcend the normal patterns of hegemony and homogeneity, labour and domination, and we get a tiny taste of the way life is supposed to be. We engage in holy play, godly partying, sacred merriment. These 'holy TAZs' are, I believe, spiritual festivals of worship, where we make an empowering and vital connection to 'the joy of the Lord'.[5]

That, I think, is what I savour about my experiences of worship among 'pure' or 'primal' (as opposed to hyped-up and manipulated) Pentecostals, whether in other countries or my own. If our first simple word awakens us to the presence of God and the second to the presents or gifts of God, our third simple word awakens us to the heart of God which is – consider this – characterised by an essential, unconquerable, boundless, radiant, wonderful, infinite, exuberant, generous, glorious joy. I know that comes as a shock to many of us.

Many of us associate God with cranky nuns with hands on hips or stern preachers with pursed lips, nearly bursting with fury because we were *chewing gum in church*. We see God as a stern and controlling parent who was watching with simmering rage from the window when we were experiencing the thrill of our first kiss in a car in the driveway ... or as a terrifying judge who has been counting our life's infractions and will inevitably charge us, mercilessly judge us, and eternally punish us for our guilt.

But the scandalous truth – known by mystics throughout history and affirmed in the pages of our sacred texts is that when we connect with God, it is as if we are plugging our souls into a pure current of high-voltage joy. The joy that surprised me under the stars in my teens was exactly what the ancient Psalmist knew (16:11): that God is a joyful being and to enter or awaken to God's presence is to enjoy a bracing jolt of invigorating delight followed by increasing levels of unending pleasure. Yes, there is indeed a place for quiet reverence, the dignity of robes and the noble tranquillity of marble columns and pipe organs. But my suspicion is that among the barefoot poor, we learn something that the well-heeled seldom discover: God is joyful, and God's joy is contagious. When we tap into the joy of the Lord, when we step into the pure joy that burns like a billion galaxies in the heart of God, we'll soon find ourselves shouting, dancing, singing, leaping, clapping, swaying, laughing, and otherwise jubilating and celebrating.

Doesn't it make sense, then, for Trinitarian Christians like me to define worship as joining in the eternal, joyful celebration that erupts continuously among Father, Son and Holy Spirit? Is it any wonder that Jesus, describing the kingdom of God, conceived of it as party, feast, banquet, festival? Could it be that the kingdom of God is the ultimate TAZ, the ultimate liberation from the normal oppressive patterns of hegemony and homogeneity?

If we entered the sacred connection with the words *here* and *thanks*, what one word can capture the joy of worship and holiday?[6] It would have to be a word of wonder, thrill, ecstasy and – paradoxically – speechlessness. It would have to be a speech act that acknowledges the limits of speech.

A prime candidate would be that simple word *hallelujah*. The word is beautiful, almost musical. Though drawn from the Hebrew, it is recognised in nearly every language today. In Hebrew it means 'Praise G-d, all you people!' It expresses a vast range of worshipful emotion, from exuberant joyful celebration to tender, grateful adoration. The word *glory* would also be a prime candidate, simultaneously evoking visual brightness, weighty substance, social splendour and more. Maybe the word *amen* would also serve, since it is a way of responding to a moment of revelation or insight by saying, *Yes, that's right! Or Right on! Or I agree! Or I second the emotion!*

But there's another word, even more primal and simple, in which we could lodge the sacred connection of worship. We've seen the word already, but passed over it without comment when we looked earlier at the many names given to God in the Psalms: the simple, primal interjection or exclamation *O!* This shortest of all words turns out to be one of the most amazing, because it can express the widest range of emotion. The exclamation *Ouch!* expresses the feeling of pain. *Wow!* expresses delight or pleasure or surprise. *Ugh!* expresses distaste. And what does *O!* express?

O! erupts from within us almost involuntarily and uncontrollably, expressing our reaction to almost any deep or powerful emotion. It may be awe in the presence of beauty – 'O! What a glorious sunrise!' It may be gratitude in the presence of generosity – 'O! What a kind gift!' It may be relief in the presence of comfort – 'O! I'm so glad you're here!' It may be surprise – 'O! I didn't realise you were standing there all along.' It may even be agony that reaches out for empathy – 'O! My head is pounding!' or 'O! My heart is breaking!'

For our purposes, this little interjection of one letter, so tiny yet so challenging to define, can hold the joyful, amazing, loving wonder of awe, worship and jubilation, to express what surpasses normal speech.

> O come, let us sing for joy to the LORD!
> O come, let us worship and bow down.
> Let us kneel before the LORD, our Maker. (Ps. 95:1, 6)

> O magnify the LORD with me
> and let us exalt his name together! (Ps 34:3)

The form of the letter itself – a circle encompassing empty space – seems to beg us to fill it with all the emotion and thought we can muster. And this, I believe, explains why the word *O!* arises so frequently in worship: worship is an act of the whole being, uniting intellect with emotion, integrating reason with feeling, combining thought with affection, summoning both our brain's hemispheres and all our brain's layers and capacities in a joint eruption of joyful love and loving joy.

According to our best scientific estimate, matter and energy, space and time big-banged into existence about 13.7 billion years ago. About 8.4 billion years ago, our planet formed. Then about 3.8 billion years ago, the first living cells formed in Earth's warm seas. By about 0.6 billion years ago, the first somatic brains began functioning, reptile brains developed about 0.3 billion years ago, and mammalian brains about 0.2 billion years ago. And primitive hominid brains? They appear about 0.0025 billion years ago, and modern humans appear only 0.0002 billion years ago. And as for signs of religious sensibilities – cave paintings and ritual burials – they don't appear until 0.00003 billion years ago, the blink of an eye in deep time.

So when we come to the spiritual practice of awe, whether expressed in a Pentecostal dance in Africa or a soaring cathedral in Europe, we're talking about a very young art, and we human beings are, on earth, at least, its early pioneers. We are just beginning to unite brain and body, voice and movement, architecture and liturgy, word and music in this joyful discipline of drawing near to the joy of the Lord.

These young human brains of ours, it turns out, flowered into two hemispheres, each with its own strengths when it comes to worship. The desire to create analytical systems of belief clearly is a cortical function – probably originating in the left hemisphere – through which we apply our rational intelligence to questions of origin, destiny, personal and social morality, and divinity. The impulse to create works of art to celebrate and glorify God – temples, cantatas, poetry, icons, gardens – no doubt arises largely within the right side of the human brain. And the capacity for love in its most profound dimensions – *caritas*, altruism, generosity and humanitarianism towards our fellow creatures, and worship and love of God – would seem to arise within the highest capacities of both hemispheres working together.

The left-side analytical brain looks at a sunset and thinks about the spectra of light, ponders refraction and conceptualises the rotation of the earth in relation to the sun. Or it looks at a forest and names the trees, situates it in the conceptual scheme of forest succession and estimates the profit from harvesting its lumber or converting it into a theme park. Or it looks at a feeble old woman on a hospital bed and estimates her age, looks for symptoms of disease, notices a thousand details that might help in making an accurate diagnosis and predicts chances of survival. This left brain is abuzz with words, observations, calculations, theories, judgements, analyses.

But something happens when we expand from the left to the right brain. The hum and buzz of the cortical data-stream stops dominating. We rise from the busy dissection of analysis to the calm union of appreciation. We move from aggressive reasoning to receptive understanding. From knowing about to knowing-in-relationship. From facts to meaning. From taking things apart to seeing things whole. From knowledge to love, from prose to poetry, and from invocation and thanksgiving to the awe of worship.[7]

Whole-brained worship, in this way, must include the humble acknowledgement that 'more is going on than I realise'. The busy left brain feels the digital thrill of being able to name, define, compare, contrast, analyse, dissect, categorise, and so on. But eventually, it reaches its limits and invites the right brain into partnership. The right brain replies, as it were, 'Yes, yes, very good analysis, and all that is true and of some real value. But no matter how much you chatter on about many things, you'll never comprehend the whole. You'll never get the big picture. So step back now, and let's together acknowledge the beyond-ness, the more-ness, the more-than-we-can-graspness of what lies before us.' When this sense of awe and wonder is directed not just at a sunset, a forest, a mountain, or a night sky, but through and with and beyond them to the source of all good things, wide-eyed wonder becomes joyful worship. Worship, then, we might say, is the highest exercise of all the parts of our multiform brain. No wonder the Psalmist says, 'Bless the Lord, O my soul, and all that is within me bless God's holy name!'

But there's a problem. If we're not careful, our left and lower brains will reassert themselves and reduce our understanding of God down from the level of whole-hearted, whole-brained, all-that-is-within-me worship. Soon we start worshipping the thin cortical God we conceptualise in our left hemisphere. Or we start idolising the warm, sentimental God who suits our mammalian brains, who embodies the familiar, cosy sentiments of our little troop or tribe. Or worse yet, we descend into our reptilian brains and kneel before a reptilian God who is driven to fight, vanquish, dominate, assimilate or destroy the people we dislike having in our marked territory.

That's why, when we engage with the subject of worship, we must ask what kind or image of God we are worshipping, which is related to the question of which brain (or part of the brain) we are employing in worship. Andrew Newberg and Mark Robert Waldman explore this question at length in their book *How God Changes Your Brain*, and Michael Gerson summarises their findings like this:[8]

Contemplating a loving God strengthens portions of our brain – particularly the frontal lobes and the anterior cingulate – where empathy and reason reside. Contemplating a wrathful God empowers the limbic system, which is 'filled with aggression and fear.' It is a sobering concept: The God we choose to love changes us into his image, whether he exists or not.

For Newberg, this is not a simple critique of religious funda-mentalism – a phenomenon varied in its beliefs and motiva-tions. It is a criticism of any institution that allies ideology or faith with anger and selfishness. 'The enemy is not religion,' writes Newberg, 'the enemy is anger, hostility, intolerance, sepa-ratism, extreme idealism, and prejudicial fear – be it secular, religious, or political.'

Worship is the practice of uniting all that is within us to cele-brate the joyful goodness of God – and for us that must not be a reptilian and mammalian God of 'anger, hostility, intolerance, separatism, extreme idealism, and prejudicial fear', but rather the God described poetically by the Apostle John like this:

> This is the message we have heard from him and declare to you: God is light; in God there is no darkness at all … Dear friends, let us love one another, for love comes from God. Everyone who loves has been born of God and knows God … because God is love.
> God is love. Whoever lives in love lives in God, and God in them … We love because [God] first loved us … Those who love God must also love one another. (1 John 1:5; 4:7–21, NIV)

To worship is to exercise the highest capacities we have. It exer-cises the parts of our brains that transcend the reptilian, the mammalian and even the merely human: it invites us to contem-plate the glorious, transcendent living God of love and in so doing, to experience transformation into that image ourselves. This, it turns out, is a good and supremely joyful thing.

Chapter 9

O! Not Just a Word – a Way of Life

> Holy One of Blessing
> Your presence
> Fills creation.
> You have kept us alive,
> You have sustained us,
> You have brought us
> To this moment.
> *Shehecheyanu*, Traditional Hebrew Prayer[1]

When human beings enter into the joyful celebration of the glory of God and the goodness of God's gift of life, normal prose breaks into poetry, normal voices break into song, normal postures break into dancing, and people don't simply become more religious – they become more alive.

You can feel this dynamic in the ancient Hebrew Psalms:

> The LORD is my strength and my shield;
> my heart trusts in him, and I am helped.
> My heart leaps for joy
> and I will give thanks to him in song. (Ps. 28:7, NIV)

Praise the LORD!

Praise God in God's sanctuary ... in God's mighty firmament!

Praise God for God's mighty deeds ... according to God's surpassing greatness!

Praise God with trumpet sound ... with lute and harp ... with tambourine and dance ... with strings and pipe ... with clanging cymbals ... with loud clashing cymbals!

Let everything that breathes praise the LORD!

Praise the LORD! (Ps. 150)

It's ironic, I think, that at the moment we get a glimpse into the goodness, greatness, beauty and glory of God, we simultaneously seek words to celebrate what we have seen – and we know that no words can do it justice. So we grasp for strong, sturdy words like goodness, greatness, beauty, glory ... and we reach still higher for our loftiest words like wonder, sovereignty, power, holiness. And still we feel they fall short. So we then seek to describe by negation, using prefixes and suffixes like *in-, un-,* and *-less* ... infinite, limitless, boundless, endless, unfailing, unblemished, and so on. And still we are unsatisfied. So we reach for metaphors and similes, the tools of the poetic trade, and we summon our imagination to action. And when they fail us, we reach for riddle and paradox, as in this adaptation of some worshipful words of St Bonaventure, an early disciple of St Francis, whose words I adapted for a song:

You are within all things, but not enclosed. You are outside all things, but not excluded. You are above all things, but not aloof. You are below all things, but not debased. Your centre is everywhere. You have no circumference. Your fullness is everywhere.[2]

Even now, however inspired we feel, however our tongue becomes 'the pen of a ready scribe' (Ps. 45:1), still we aren't satisfied. So we bring in the sound effects of nature – crashing waves, thunder, wind in trees, waterfalls – but still we're falling short. So we add every sound we can create in human music – from tubas to piccolos, from drum kits to screaming lead guitars, from congas to steel drums to dulcimers to banjos to violins. And then we add gesture, dance, leaping, maybe even some 'holy rolling'. And that's not enough, so we reach into architecture. And storytelling. And drama. And painting. And sculpture. Still unsatisfied, we add ritual and vestment, incense and stained glass. We even invent new instruments, new media, on screens and through speakers seeking to express our tiny glimpse of the glorious wonder that radiates from God. And never for a moment, after all we've said, sang, danced and done, do we feel that we have overstated or even done justice to the glimpse of beauty, holiness, glory, love, power, kindness, purity, complexity, simplicity, depth, height and infinitude with which we have been graced.

A moment like this comes in what many consider Paul's magnum opus, his letter to the Romans. The letter is interpreted in widely varying ways, the commonest conventional approach perhaps being to read it as a treatise on the theological theme known as 'justification by faith'. I greatly appreciate this doctrine, but I have become convinced that this isn't actually the theme of the letter.[3] I now understand the theme to be this: *all human beings, regardless of their status as*

Religious Insiders or Outsiders, are invited into the new commu-
nity of God.

This thesis raised a big problem in Paul's day, though. The dividing wall between Insiders and Outsiders was high and thick, topped with razor wire and guarded by aggressive clerical rottweilers. In order to assert that the wall must come down, that all people must be welcomed as equals through the good news of Jesus, Paul has some ''splainin' to do'. And that's what he does for the first eleven chapters. I don't, however, read those eleven chapters as one long linear argument. I read them as a succession of short arguments, analogies, metaphors and logical experiments, like switchbacks by which a trekker zig-zags up a mountain. Paul tries one tack, then another. One analogy works for a while, but then breaks down, so he switches to another metaphor only to have that one hit a brick wall as well. After eleven chapters of this, it's as if he is taken by surprise by the end of a sentence that begins like this: 'For God has imprisoned all in disobedience...'

When he concludes, '... so that God may be merciful to all', something in Paul seems to snap. His own Spirit-led conclusion seems to have got out ahead of him, leaping out and surprising him with its grandeur at the climactic moment. The good news, it turns out, is even better than he imagined. His line of reasoning has seemed to take on a life of its own, rising like a tsunami and carrying him to a higher and bigger appreciation of the gospel than he has ever had before. (As a writer and preacher, I have experienced this myself. It's an amazing thing.) So his normal syntax breaks like a thin fishing line: worship explodes like a sailfish heaving itself up from the sea in a wild leap of defiance and joy. And there it is – our little word O!

O the depth of the riches and wisdom and knowledge
   of God!
How unsearchable are his judgments and how
   inscrutable his ways!
'For who has known the mind of the Lord?
Or who has been his counselor?'
'Or who has given a gift to him,
to receive a gift in return?'
For from him and through him and to him are all
   things.
To him be the glory forever. Amen. (Rom. 11:33–36)

Explanation gives way to exclamation, reasoned answer to rhetorical question. As the wave of wonder crashes on the shore, Paul gets control of himself again. He tries to shake himself back into normal prose, and pulls himself together to offer this conclusion in the next verse: 'OK. Now that we've got a breath-taking glimpse of the amazing, explosive, over-whelming mercy of God, I want you to join me in worship … not by offering a sheep or bull as a sacrifice as in the old temple system, and not even by going to church and singing, clapping, kneeling or dancing for hours on end. I want you to worship God by offering your whole lives, all you have and are, as an offering of worship to God.'

For Paul, then, the *O!* of worship translates naturally and immediately into a way of life, life lived not for self-interest (which Paul often calls 'the flesh', 'the old self' or 'the old humanity') but for the common good, or in Paul's words, 'faith working through love' (Gal. 5:6) and 'serving one another in love' (Gal. 5:13). This is remarkable, really: we might be less surprised if Paul had said, 'In view of God's mercies, I demand

that you spend at least one hour per day in church services, O
or one hour on your knees, reciting prayers to God.' But no,
the tsunami of God's grace inspires us to express our worship
not simply in religious activities, but in real life, through love
for one another. The prayer of worship that leaps up in a
simple *O!* must be translated into the gracious eloquence of
a good, kind and just life, in the grammar and syntax of everyday
relationships.

How can we infuse our daily lives with the poetry, song and
dance of worship and praise? I've tried to maintain several
disciplines of worship in my life through the years, each
involving a way to render my whole life a living sacrifice:

1. Give God the first greeting every morning

As I emerge from sleep into awareness, even before my eyes
are open, I try to turn my attention to God, moving from *here*
to *thanks* to worship: 'O Lord! Good morning! Here I am,
with you for a new day, and here you are, with me as always.
Thank you, Living God, for this fresh instalment in the gracious
gift of life! O Lord! I worship you for who you are, gracious
and compassionate, just and good, holy and forgiving, almighty
and gentle.'

2. Give God the first thanks at every meal

I believe the old practice of pausing to thank God before meals
is a wise and good one. It reminds me of my creature-liness:
like the birds of the air and the flowers of the field, I am
dependent on God for my daily sustenance. The simple act of
table grace can certainly be practised on mindless autopilot,
but when it is done mindfully and with awareness, it can connect
me at least three times a day with the Creator who supplies

soil and sunlight and rain to maintain the miraculous web of life, of which I am part. And true gratitude to God will also produce gratitude to my fellow creatures – wheat stalk, apple tree and corn plant; chicken, salmon and cattle; farmer, agricultural researcher, truck driver, grocer and cashier too. Closing your eyes is fine, but I often think it's even better to pray with open eyes, noticing the rich brown texture of wholewheat bread, the robust green of lettuce, the bold red of a tomato, the clearness of water.

3. Give God the first response to every pleasure

You've probably had the same experience I have: of being somewhere alone and witnessing some beautiful thing – a sunrise, an act of kindness, a rainbow, the Milky Way – and wishing a friend or family member were there to share it with you. We often forget that although another human being may not be present, our Creator is, and we can learn to share our joy with God. In so doing, we may come to feel that the opposite is in fact happening as well, that in this moment, God is sharing God's joy with us. The living God is the Creator of spinning galaxies and fluttering butterflies and towering mountain ranges and leaping whales and whirling subatomic particles. God is the giver of both good foods and the taste buds to enjoy them. God is the maker of the coral reefs of Costa Rica and Australia and the forests of Siberia and Tasmania and everywhere in between … and right now, at this moment, God sees and enjoys every glimmer of sunlight passing through the water on all the magical colours of every purple parrotfish and emerald angelfish and crimson wrasse and jade goby and red blenny and orange clownfish and blue damselfish and yellow tang. Imagine, then the joy of God, as God sees how wonderful these things are, and God savours their goodness, and God takes pleasure in them as artists take holy pride in their creations.[4] In worship, we take notice too – appreciating the art, and the Artist. In this way we share in God's joy and add to it through our spontaneous *O!* of worship.

With practice, it becomes natural and instinctive to turn to God as our first response to all experiences of pleasure or beauty – the robin whistling outside the window this morning, the way sunlight comes through the blinds, the simple green of grass and its smell when freshly cut. Each one becomes like a church-bell beckoning us to pray: *O! Glory to God!* But at various seasons of my life, when because of depression, pressure or pain these spontaneous expressions of praise are not forthcoming, I have been helped greatly through fixed-hour prayer, using various traditions to turn my attention several times each day to the goodness, wonder and beauty of God. And when I am dull or down, not appreciating the goodness of the moment, I can at least employ my memory for past pleasures, even the pleasures whose loss might be causing sadness in the present.[5]

4. Give God the first consideration in your weekly schedule

It has been my practice not only to begin each day with private worship, but also to plan each week around a special time of gathered worship where gifted people, drawing from rich liturgical traditions, guide a community of worshippers to ponder and celebrate the goodness of God in song, prayer, sermon, silence and more. For me, first and foremost, this is what gathered worship is about. It's not about satisfying the demands of scrupulous religious consumers, but about helping people continue to taste and see the goodness of the Lord, letting their private *O!* of daily personal worship harmonise with that of others to produce a glorious symphony of gathered worship. True, in other churches, what happens on Sundays is lacklustre and sometimes downright depressing, and in other churches, what happens is noisy and showy and maybe a little tacky. But my guess is that just about anywhere, if we have the right eyes to see, there is great value in gathering for worship – whether it's on Sunday, Saturday, or whenever, whether it's in a glorious cathedral or temple, a spacious megachurch facility, or a small local chapel, synagogue, or mosque, whether it's in a humble storefront, in a coffee shop or pub, or around a kitchen table.

5. Make God the first supervisor or customer for all work

'Just as you did it for one of the least of these you did it to me,' Jesus said, and that attitude can infuse all our work with new meaning. The apostle Paul was getting at the same thing when he said, 'Whatever your task, put yourselves into it as done for the Lord … you serve the Lord Christ' (Col. 3:22–24). So the chef whose life has been offered to God as a living sacrifice of worship seeks to prepare each meal as if God were her customer, and the teacher as if her students were God. Similarly, the gardener, the computer programmer, the project manager, the administrative assistant, the politician, the sales person and the banker seek to serve, honour, and worship God as they water, program, manage, assist, govern, sell and invest. They make their work sacred in this way, and my guess is, both their supervisors and their customers and clients will feel a difference.

6. Give God the first part of every pay cheque

I think it is best to see giving not simply as an act of duty to my faith community – although that's a legitimate dimension of giving – but even more as an act of worshipping God. When we are counting our blessings, having freely received enough and more than enough, we find it natural to freely give; when we're running in the never-enough addictive rat-wheel, the generous impulse rarely if ever arises.

7. Give God the joy of your creativity

Since God is at heart a joyful creator, and since you are made in the image of God, you no doubt have found (or will find) some ways you enjoy being creative. Maybe you write poetry or play the guitar or garden or cook. Maybe you design furniture or work with landscapes or sculpt or paint or take photographs or sketch portraits or do collage. Maybe you dance or climb mountains or build birdhouses or arrange flowers. Probably, in whatever you do, you apologise: It's not very good … I'm just an amateur … I never took any lessons … I really do it just for myself. My guess is that you do this for the same reason do: I really love my creative pursuits, and they are unspeakably precious to me, and the thought of them being evaluated or criticised or even mocked by others is so distressing that I decide to pre-empt the criticism of others with my own disparagement.

Let me make this suggestion, to you and to myself. Let's apologise less and create more. Let's think of creating for the approval of others less, and for the pleasure of God more. Think of the little girl who draws a picture for her mother. She uses crayons to compose crude stick figures – a blue person, a red car, a green and brown tree, a purple house, a yellow sun with squiggly lines radiating out from it. And what does her mother do? Critique it? No, she uses magnets to display it on the refrigerator, where it may stay until the girl graduates from high school. What if God is more like that mother than the critics we fear? What could give our Creator more pleasure than our creative offerings? I remember as a father, feeling pure delight as my children ran free at a playground with their friends, completely unaware of me because they were so taken up with the joy of play and playmates. But when they saw me sitting quietly on the bench, ran over and threw their arms around me, my delight was enriched all the more. And when they would climb the slide or the jungle gym and shout, 'Dad, watch this!' … I remember thinking that I would like very much to live this way with God: showing off, but not in an egotistical way – rather, humbly, generously and with childlike abandon seeking to bring pleasure to the One who gave me life. This, to me, is worship – not just words, but a creative way of life.

How fascinating that worshipping the Creator thus exercises the imagination and so drives us to creativity. Soon, in response to God's creativity and goodness, we fashion good works of art of our own, from Handel's *Messiah* to Bob Dylan's *Every Grain of Sand*; from grand cathedrals that all can see to a poem written in a private journal for no eyes other than God's. The *O!* of worship leads us to reach for a pen or paint brush or garden tool or guitar, an instinctive creative urge that reminds us that we are created in God's imaginative image. When we get a glimpse of God's creative glory, we ourselves become more creative and glorious ourselves.

The first sentence of the previous paragraph suggests that if we seek one more word to partner with *O!* or *hallelujah!* in the expression of worship, *how* is an excellent option. *How* functions in a fascinating way in the grammar of praise. Many of us experience it in the old hymn *How Great Thou Art!* It spans question and exclamation, and expands our imagination – *How wonderful? How wonderful! How kind? How kind! How glorious? How glorious!*

To be surrounded by so much goodness, beauty and wonder, and not to celebrate … to be given so much, but to fail to appreciate the source – wouldn't that spoil us? This realisation helps explain why the Bible (and other spiritual literature) overflows with exhortations to worship: it is not that God is insecure and narcissistic, requiring frequent affirmations to be saved from depression or a fit of rage. Nor is it that God is dominating and sociopathic, capable of happiness only when others are grovelling in deference. No: God wants us to be saved from being spoiled, self-centred, inflated and distorted with a sense of entitlement. It is for our good, not God's, that worship is so important. Psalm 149 creates just this kind of scenario. It calls people to create a TAZ, to erupt in jubilation, to sing, dance, bang tambourines and pluck stringed instruments in praise of God. And then it affirms that God takes pleasure in us as we take pleasure in God. God joins us in joy and we join in God's joy. In jubilation we strengthen the vital connection.

Yes, there are problems to be faced. Yes, in the pages ahead, as in the days ahead, there are prayers of complexity and struggle, prayers of perplexity and lament, prayers of confession and desperation and agony and terror. Yes there is a time to cry and groan in rage as well as a time to laugh and dance in joy. To these dimensions of the spiritual life we will turn presently. But before we go there, don't you agree we are wise to establish this baseline of spirituality as simple, pure, deep happiness in a life with God – of spirituality as a joyful awakening to the God who is here, near, with us, the One in whose presence we live and in whose attention and care we are held? Of spirituality as an overflowing thanks as we awaken to what can so easily and tragically be taken for granted? Of spirituality as a pregnant *O!* that arises when we see the wonders of creation and trace in them the signature of the Artist from whom all good things flow? Of spirituality as the essential *joie de vivre*, shared with the One in whom both joy and life originate, the One in whom all good things freely play, and the One from whom and to whom all good things flow like sparks rising or rivers running?

So in a moment, put this book aside. Let your mind ponder good and great and wonderful things, things you love. As each comes before you, simply hold it in a spirit of wonder, in the simple word *O!* And then take that wonder and love for the thing, and expand it out to the Source, the giver, the designer of all goodness, all greatness. Let your mind with all its capacities and your heart and imagination with all their powers see how good and great G-d must be, and in that awareness, let your *O!* resound to God – silently, within you, or aloud as a groan or shout or song.

And if the urge strikes you, put on some music and dance!

Two

Complexity:
The Season of
Spiritual Strengthening

Complexity

'There's a way to do this.' That's what I remember saying to myself again and again as I entered the season of complexity. How was I to find God's will for my life? Change bad habits? Avoid or repair conflict? Become more well-liked or effective? Find a mate or build a healthy family? Somewhere, someone knew how, and if I could find them, I'd learn their checklist, no matter how complex, and I'd master their techniques, no matter how difficult. I became an avid devotee of conferences and workshops at this stage – as I still am today. I scribbled copious notes on sermons and eagerly listened to religious broadcasts, wanting to glean every practical tip and memorise any step-by-step plan that might help me in my spiritual journey. Even today, decades later, I'm building on strengths I developed during my first journey through Stage Two.

When we're in Stage Two, we don't leave Stage One behind. We build upon it in three new movements of the soul. Without these three new skills or strengths, we remain dependent and immature, but with them, we learn increasing independence. Whether it's praying, reading and interpreting the Bible, sharing our faith with others, fulfilling a ministry in the church, or simply handling the inevitable complexities of life, in Stage Two our goal is to be able to say, 'I can do it myself. I can handle it. I know how.'

Our focus now shifts from right-versus-wrong to effective-versus-ineffective. To the degree we feel we have orthodoxy (right belief) nailed down, we now turn to orthopraxy (right behaviour). To our core of dualism we now add a new layer – pragmatism.[1] If the greatest sin of Simplicity was being wrong, now in Complexity the greatest sin is being apathetic or ineffective. If we previously were attracted to leaders who told us how to be and do *right*, now we are drawn to leaders who show us how to be and do *well*. If Stage One leaders taught us the rules of the game, Stage Two leaders now coach us in how to win it. (Right now, Stage-Two readers are saying, 'Yes. That's exactly why I bought this book!') We're no longer satisfied to be part of the right in-group; we now seek identity as part of a winning team. Within that team, we want to play our part well.

And that is our great strength as Stage Two people: we share the can-do, 'yes, we can!' spirit. Of course, as with every stage, we can get comfortable here and refuse to move on when this season has run its course. When reality refuses to comply with our complex schemes, strategies and techniques, we can blame reality and go into denial rather than question some of our assumptions. Stage Two is, after all, a really enjoyable time in life, and saying goodbye to it is so painful that many people never do.

But for those of us just entering Stage Two, there's no need to think about letting it go. Right now, there are skills to master, goals to achieve, challenges to conquer. At the age of eighteen, those challenges might include choosing a subject to study at university or navigating the complexities of romance. At twenty, they may involve a relationship that needs to be nurtured, a career, or finding a cause to work for. At thirty and forty, they might entail raising children, handling new opportunities at work, or caring for an unhappy spouse or difficult marriage. At fifty and sixty, life's challenges might include ageing parents or fading dreams, health setbacks or new freedoms. At seventy, eighty and ninety, they might involve surviving surgery or coping with grief or planning for the next holiday with the grand-children ... or preparing for death. Whatever the challenges, Stage Two is about learning three essential practices that help us survive and thrive, not cave in or give up.

What are those practices? First is the ability to self-examine, admit mistakes and process failure. Second is the habit of acknowledging our personal weaknesses and limitations, and seeking wisdom, strength and skill beyond our own. And third is the ability to empathise with others in their pain.

If Simplicity resembles springtime with its fragility and vitality, Complexity resembles summer – a time of hard work and getting things done during long sunny days.

Chapter 10

Sorry! Holier Than Myself?

The Practice of Self-examination and Confession: Strengthening Through Failure

Alternative words: Regret. Mercy.

> If there is such a thing as human perfection, it seems to emerge precisely from how we handle the imperfection that is everywhere, especially our own.
>
> Fr. Richard Rohr[1]

I have a friend we'll call Carlos, who for many years was, like me, a pastor. He is one of the strong, kind and holy people I've been privileged to know in my life. We see each other too seldom, but however long the absence, we pick up again where we left off. Over the years, Carlos has been a touchstone of spiritual authenticity for me. We have been confidants and friends to one another in some of our personal struggles. We have also had some monumental laughs together and played a couple of gut-busting practical jokes on each other.

Once I invited Carlos to speak at a weekend retreat for the leaders of the church I served. I won't go into the practical jokes that we played on each other that weekend, even though they were pretty funny and involved rubber snakes and showers. During a serious moment on the retreat, he said something to our little group that has stayed with me ever since. 'A secret to the spiritual life,' he said, 'is desiring to actually be more spiritual than you appear to be.' Then he added, 'The secret to hypocrisy is desiring to appear more spiritual than you actually are.'

People like Carlos and me, who for most of our lives have been paid to be spiritual leaders, live constantly in the orange alert of spiritual danger: it is perpetually tempting for us to desire to appear more spiritual than we are. But I think any person who is part of a faith community of some sort also faces this danger. Forget keeping up with the Joneses: I'm projecting a false Jones image that I want others to think is real, and I'm struggling to keep up with that. Forget *holier than thou*; I'm seeking to appear holier than *moi*. That kind of pretence piles layers of cosmetics and clothing on naked spirituality, which makes our next practice all the more important.

The fact is, we are all hypocrites to some degree. None of us wants to be known for our worst moments. Sometimes, like too many religious leaders of recent years (who, as religious broadcasters, were rewarded for projecting an image), we preach most loudly and passionately against the sins to which we are most subject – hiding our secrets out in the open, so to speak, fighting our personal demons 'in here' under the guise of fighting culture wars 'out there'. Sometimes, we find the best way to keep guilt at bay over our own inconsistencies is to pour guilt on others. As we do so, our souls go dark and dangerous, as do the religious communities we lead.

That's why another friend of mine, Gareth, says we all need to come out.[2] Reflecting on our agonised and often dysfunctional religious controversies about homosexuality in recent years, he says that the gay community is doing an invaluable service for everyone, gay or straight: by admitting they're homosexual, gay people are leading the way for the rest of us to admit simply that we're *sexual*. When we pretend we aren't, when we hide our sexuality in shame and secrecy, we create a dark, damp culture where shame and self-hatred grow like mould, a disconnected culture of tragic pretence and inauthenticity. Another friend, Mark, says that we should put a sign just inside the front door of all our churches: 'Let's pretend!' This way, we'll at least be honest about our dishonesty!

We've been considering the spiritual life in the season of simplicity. Life is indeed simple in many ways, but it is also more than simple. There are shades of grey between our black and white extremes, layers and folds of complexity under every simple surface. And nowhere must we face that complexity more directly than when we deal with our own behaviour. You're singing in a choir – maybe it's Handel's *Messiah*. Your eye catches the eye of another singer, and soon your imagination is writing a mental screenplay for a torrid affair ... even as your vocal cords and lips form the words 'Hallelujah! Hallelujah! For the Lord God Omnipotent reigneth.' You're working in a slum in Africa, helping orphans whose parents have died of HIV/AIDS, there at your own expense, there on your own vacation time ... and you're thinking about how you can post a blog about your experience to puff your image in front of your friends back home. You're writing a book on building a life with God, and at the same time you're wondering how it will sell and what status it will gain you in the eyes of your loyal readers and hostile critics.

Carlos is right: we all can be seduced by the appeal of appearing more spiritual than we actually are. Mark is right: we're all pretenders, all religious broadcasters, all of us false prophets projecting an image by which we hope to rake in profits – financial, social, relational, spiritual. Gareth is right: we all need to come out of the closet. We don't have to hide the real us – the sexual us, the insecure us, the doubtful us, the angry us, the complex, different, tempted, actual human us.

Novelist and essayist C. S. Lewis used to ask, 'What is the most significant conversation you have every day?' People would respond piously, 'Your conversation with God, of course.' 'No,' Lewis would reply. 'It's the conversation you have with yourself before you speak to God, because in that conversation with yourself, you decide whether you are going to be honest and authentic with God, or whether you are going to meet God with a false face, a mask, an act, a pretence.'

The practice of self-examination and confession acknowledges the tragic gap between our appearance and our actuality. Through confession, we say, 'God, I will not hide anything from you. You know already. Pretending in your presence is pure and pathetic insanity. I want to be who I am in your presence.'

When I utter the simple words, *I'm sorry*, I'm saying, 'I acknowledge what you already know.'[3] When I confess to God my secrets, the truths about which I fear rejection, I am rejecting de-ligion – which always involves a disconnection between who I really am and who I project myself to be. When I hold up to God the regrets and remorse I would otherwise try to hide in order to project a happy, likeable and 'spiritual' image, my

'I am who I am' can resonate with God's 'I am who I am'. When I try to appear no holier, stronger or better than I actually am, I keep the vital connection intact, unsevered.

Two powerful moments in the Hebrew Scriptures have tutored me in the art of confession. First, in Psalm 32, King David reflects on an experience of doing wrong, refusing to admit it for a time, and then finally confessing his wrong and receiving forgiveness. It seems to have been written as was Psalm 51, in the aftermath of a sordid period in David's life that began with an act of adultery. Adultery would be transgression enough, but the man whose wife David has taken has been one of his most trusted colleagues, a general in David's army. So David's adultery is also a betrayal of friendship and collegiality. Worse still, when David finds the woman is pregnant, he conspires to cover up the affair by having the general come back from the front lines to have relations with her, in hopes that the husband will think the child is his own. When the general's loyalty to his troops frustrates David's cover-up plan, David conspires – successfully – to have the general sent to the front lines where he will be killed. Then he takes the woman as his wife, and his cover-up appears to have worked perfectly.

Until, that is, a pesky prophet comes and exposes David's unconscionable behaviour.[4]

So, David has experienced the great grief of exposed wrongdoing and the even greater relief of coming clean. 'Happy are those,' he says, 'whose transgression is forgiven, whose sin is covered.' By covered, he doesn't mean *kept in secrecy* – because he then contrasts the happiness of coming clean with the misery of living in secrecy: 'While I kept silence . . . My strength was dried up as by the heat of summer' (32:3–4). The energy required to cover up, to broadcast a false, inflated image, David suggests, depletes the soul, creating a sick internal environment, a kind of moral HIV. Ironically, when he stops covering up his sin, his sin is covered – like a bill, like a debt, like an enemy attack – as if God says, 'Don't worry. I've got you covered,' covered by mercy, covered by grace.

If one manages to maintain the cover-up and keep broadcasting the fraudulent image, one becomes, if not acutely feverish, at least chronically numb – *calloused* is an image often used in the Bible, or *stiff-necked*, or *hard-hearted*. The projected image (what psychologist Paul Tournier called the *personage*) becomes disconnected from the inner person, the appearance from reality.[5] No wonder the ancient Hebrews had a proverb that said, 'Keep your heart with all vigilance, for from it flow the springs of life.' (Prov. 4:23) No wonder they were taught to pray,

> Search me, O God, and know my heart;
> test me and know my anxious thoughts.
> See if there is any offensive way in me,
> and lead me in the way everlasting. (Ps. 139:23–24, NIV)

No wonder they built into their annual calendar holy days of repentance, when all members of the community of faith would pause to examine themselves, acknowledge their faults, individually and as a community, and come clean. No wonder they practised elaborate rituals of sacrifice through which they dramatised the brutality of sin by sacrificing an innocent animal, which then became the main course in a ritual meal of reconciliation.[6]

The conscience is like a moral nerve for the soul. It's like a pain receptor that warns us of moral danger. Self-examination keeps our moral nerves from going numb; it keeps our moral skin sensitive and not calloused. 'Something is wrong!' our conscience shouts. 'You're burning yourself morally!' it screams. 'Your integrity is being bruised or broken!' it cries. 'You're feverish, infected, unwell!' it shouts. The pain of a sensitive conscience finds relief when we stop, self-examine and say the same thing about our wrong that God would say. By awakening us to the moral danger of what we are becoming, confession allows us to choose a better path of becoming.

True, the conscience can become hyperactive, obsessive, self-destructive, like a watchdog that turns on its master with the same fury it has been trained to focus upon an intruder. Just as we need to be protected *by* our conscience from integrity loss and character decay, we need to be protected *from* our conscience at times, from the destructive self-flagellation and the simmering self-hatred it can foster. The practice of self-examination and confession provides a way of calling off the guard dog, dealing with the danger, silencing the conscience's alarm bell, and moving on.

What applies to us as individuals applies to us in groups too, because not all of our faults and wrongs are simply personal. Sometimes they are transpersonal or social, not just embedded in the habits of individuals, but ingrained in the patterns of church, denomination, tribe, nation, or civilisation. Personal actions like lying, breaking marriage vows, dishonouring parents, coveting and stealing, seeking revenge and all our other personal sins, can combine to create social weather patterns from which new categories of evil emerge – tornados of social injustice and economic oppression, hurricanes of racism and class or caste consciousness, heatwaves of homophobia or patriarchy, blinding blizzards of systemic evil. These social weather patterns can last for generations, in turn creating personal behaviour patterns in millions of individuals who have no idea they are being controlled or possessed by invisible forces larger than themselves.[7] We see these systemic problems identified in another instructive moment of confession from the Bible. It comes in the aftermath of an invasion of the Israelite homeland that occurred about 586 BC. To understand the moment, let's imaginatively enter it.

Chapter 11

Sorry! Unleashing Our Own Becoming

> Jokingly but with a great deal of seriousness, [Father Damascus would] say, 'Don't worry about purifying your motives. Simply know that they aren't pure, and proceed.'
> Brother David Steindl-Rast[1]

The Israelites were in a terrible situation. Decades ago, a brutal enemy destroyed the defences of their capital city. An invading army captured and deported the 'best and brightest' of their people. Since then, under occupation, they had struggled against forgetting their history, losing their identity and being assimilated into the enemy culture. For decades, their once-glorious capital city has remained desolate, looted, in ruins.

Then in 444 BC, one of the deportees gained permission to organise a rebuilding team and return to the capital city. They arrived in the city and assessed the damage. It was extensive. But the team leader realised that there was even more damage than met the eye. He knew that you can repair walls externally, but you must also heal the people internally. You can rebuild physical infrastructures, but you must also rebuild internal structures of character and identity, the social structures of justice and trust. The experience of conquest, occupation, exile and domination had broken the people, and the visible ruins of the city are in many ways a metaphor for their damaged inner identity – not just as individuals, but as a people, as a community. Their corporate soul lies violated and in ruins just like their capital city does.

So, as the city was physically restored brick by brick, wall by wall, and street by street, their leaders gathered the people together in a solemn assembly. The day began with exactly the kind of invocation, thanksgiving and worship we have already considered, and then it moved to confession.

As the day progressed, their leaders retold their story, beginning with their ancient ancestor Abraham. They recounted the various episodes of their journey as a people, from God's calling of Abraham to his settling in a new homeland, from the first exile and enslavement in Egypt to the exodus from wandering in the wilderness to resettling in their homeland. In each episode, God was with them, faithfully helping them survive and thrive.

And then came the word *but*. God had done so much for them, *but* they had failed to live as they should. And so they confessed their sins to the Lord (Neh. 9:6–37).

How different is this kind of public acknowledgement from what normally happens in our communities and nations as we recount our past! We typically shrink our faults to invisibility and inflate our virtues to grandiosity in a public orgy of religious supremacy, patriotic nationalism and corporate denial. But on that day of solemn assembly, it was different: the ancient Hebrews, under Nehemiah's leadership, came clean about their faults and did not indulge in self-defence, self-flattering excuses or saving of face. Yes, they had a glorious past, *but* their history also had a dark side. Thankfully, there was a second *but* after the first one, creating a compound syntax that seems perennially essential for public mental and moral health: God blessed them, *but* they were repeatedly unfaithful, *but* even then God remained gracious, forgiving and compassionate to them. The only reason they survived was the compound grace of God that contradicts even our own contradiction of God's original grace. A portion of their corporate confession reads:

> But they, our forefathers, became arrogant and stiff-necked, and did not obey your commands. They refused to listen and failed to remember the miracles you performed among them. They became stiff-necked and in their rebellion appointed a leader in order to return to their slavery. But you are a forgiving God, gracious and compassionate, slow to anger and abounding in love. Therefore you did not desert them, even when they cast for themselves an image of a calf and said, 'This is your god, who brought you up out of Egypt', or when they committed awful blasphemies. (Neh. 9:16–18, NIV)

The symmetrical pattern of infidelity, forgiveness and new infidelity repeated itself, not just once more, but again and again. But it was bracketed by an even larger symmetry: *the people were consistently unfaithful to God but God was utterly faithful to them. They abandoned God, but God did not abandon them.* The people gathered in Jerusalem that day define for us the essence of social confession. They came out of the closet as a people, told their true story, and came clean about their history – the glorious parts and the shameful parts, the grace of God and their own repeated shabby and disgusting betrayal of that grace. There is no sugar-coating here: the document has the feel of business memo or legal brief, seeking to tell the truth, the whole truth, and nothing but the truth. Just as David was honest about 'I' and 'my sin', they are honest about 'us' and 'our sin' over many generations. This balance is important for us, especially us in the West where centuries of social and theological individualism have blinded us to many of the realities of social sin, from the historic social sins of our forbears to the contemporary sins of the ecclesial, economic and political systems in which we are all complicit to some degree.

This blindness (itself a kind of social sin) explains why in many churches in my childhood, people could passionately confess certain personal sins (within polite categories) – dishonesty, greed, jealousy, and so on – but remain absolutely oblivious to our racism, anti-semitism, Islamophobia, environmental irresponsibility, homophobia, nationalism and denominational pride – not to mention the sins of our ancestors that created structures of privilege that we took for granted. If Nehemiah's contemporaries were leading us in prayer today, imagine the issues and groups they would name in American history: ethnic cleansing of Native peoples and enslavement of kidnapped Africans; discrimination against Irish and Italian Catholic immigrants and Jews; group profiling of Germans, Japanese and now Latin Americans and people from the Middle East; McCarthyism and segregation; deaths of civilians in Hiroshima and Nagasaki; denial of the vote to women and tolerance for domestic violence; mountaintop removal and climate change; oil spills and toxic waste; corporate plunder; the disproportionate recruiting for military service among the poor; pre-emptive and elective wars. What would corporate repentance for these kind of sins feel like? What effects would flow from it?

There is, to be sure, an opposite kind of blindness, where people freely confess social sins of racism, chauvinism, homophobia and consumerism, but keep their personal sins in the closet – whether it's a cruel way of treating one's spouse, neglect of one's children, drinking too much, sexually harassing subordinates, or whatever. And to be sure, nearly all of us are willing to confess sins in general; after all, who wants to appear so arrogant as to claim perfection? But we hesitate a bit more when things start getting specific – socially or personally, when we feel that the real 'me' or the real 'us' may be brought out of the closet and into the light – exposing us as less holy than we normally try to appear.

Now I'm not a great fan of airing one's dirty laundry in public. I've been in so-called revival meetings where people were pressured or cajoled into a kind of lurid self-exposure that I think was both psychologically damaging and spiritually oppressive in the long-run, even if it was cathartic in the moment. I have no desire to hear – or remember – the details of anyone's drunken orgies, private sexual behaviours or long-standing personal grudges. But I do believe we all need to be completely candid with God in private. And sometimes, whether it's with a trusted priest, spiritual director, sponsor in a recovery programme, or a circle of close friends, we need to bring other human beings into our secrecy too. 'You're only as sick as your secrets,' they say in the world of recovery from addiction.

Sharing our secrets with another human being as well as with God helps us in several ways. First, until I dare to share with you some secret, I am certain that I'm the only person so twisted and crooked and pathetic. But quite often, after I share my secret with you, you will tell me that you have the same problem, that you've made similar mistakes, and in our shared confession, we both learn that we truly are not alone. We're all a mess, and honesty, like misery, loves company. Second, when I dare to share and you dare to respond with compassion rather than with judgement and rejection, your mercy and continuing acceptance can make visible for me the good news that previously seemed beyond belief for me. Experiencing mercy and grace from you – someone both present and visible to me, I can believe in mercy and grace from God – who is present but not visible to me. I realise I am in a safe presence, a presence in which I don't need to pretend because I am accepted by grace just as I am: in your gracious presence, I experience God's gracious presence.

And then, third, comes the great surprise: in an environment of grace – human and divine – I find myself free, free to continue failing if I must, but also free to start doing better if I can. I am no longer expending the energy of broadcasting a false image; I am no longer being drained by the constant anxiety of possibly being exposed for what I really am. That previously wasted energy can now be redirected into actually living a better, fuller life.

This pretence-free environment of grace strikes the *coup de grâce* to our furtive and pretentious patterns of behaviour. In it, we are freed from being focused on what we are trying to escape or avoid. Graceless environments say, in essence, 'Don't even *think* of the number thirteen.' But inevitably, the harder we try to avoid thinking about the number, the more we do it. So imagine the tense teenage guy, infused with hormones, thinking, 'I have to avoid lustful thoughts. I have to avoid thinking of cleavage. I have to avoid thinking of slender legs. I have to avoid ...' You know exactly where this commuter

121

train of thought will lead the poor guy. But in an environment of grace, avoidance of sin stops being the focus, and other things – generosity, creativity, fun, learning, whatever – can occupy our attention so we sin less by thinking about sinning less. We can now yield to the good temptation of better things.[2]

Being able to be frank with God and others about our wrongs, failures, sins, faults and other shameful secrets does justice to the nature of the universe we live in, a place where good things can quickly become perverted or polluted, and where evil things can be healed and restored. Through confession, we stop deluding ourselves about being cosy residents of a status. In a status mindset, we say 'I'm a good person.' This can be a pretty slippery place to stand, because it can lead us to say, 'I am very proud to be a good person,' which can then lead us to become proud, which generally means we are no longer such a good person. And sadly, we are generally the last to know because we are still enthusiastically congratulating ourselves – against increasing evidence – on our status as a good person.[3]

Confession replaces a status mindset with a becoming mindset, a way of thinking that proves much less susceptible to self-delusion and self-limitation. Tutored in the simple word *sorry*, I remember that whatever I was yesterday, I could be something different tomorrow, for better or worse. When I habitually confess my secrets and express my regrets to God over things I have done, I am able to cut the umbilical cord between the me who confesses and the me who did the thing I'm confessing. I'm acknowledging that I am already different from that person, because I am not denying what I did, and I am not defending it or excusing it. I'm saying, 'I no longer want to be the kind of person who does those things, nor do

I want to be the kind of person who covers up doing those things. I want to become a different kind of person.'

So let's bring all this down to street level. Someone hurts you. Someone does you wrong. No doubt about it. They were wrong.[4] So what do you do? You start holding a grudge. You feel bitter and rehearse their hurt and nurse your wound. You feel superior. You refuse to forgive. Your inner ecology begins to change; your inner climate warms in some ways and cools in others. And slowly, evil gets its hooks in you; you're becoming a worse person than you were before. Outwardly, everything's OK and nobody notices. But inwardly, the metal of your character is rusting. The wood of your personality is rotting and termites are tunnelling. Slowly, subtly, something in your inner being is being weakened.

But then through the regular practice of self-examination and confession you do an internal home inspection. You realise what's happening and you express regret. What the other person did was indeed hurtful, but your response to the wound has also been unwise: rather than disinfecting the wound, you've been careless and allowed it to become infected. The wound wasn't your fault, but the infection is. The simple word *Sorry* opens the way for you to interrupt and reverse the moral decay underway within you.[5]

Just as sin is social as well as personal, so communities need to practise spiritual home inspection just as individuals do. Think of a religion or denomination that becomes preoccupied, as so many do, with the doctrinal errors in other religions or denominations. Soon they are congratulating themselves for their purity and correctness. Then they are going out of their way to attack others whom they judge as heretics or infidels. They suspect and reject people and wound or ruin their reputations in the inquisition process. Sometimes, their slanderous words lead to cruel and even murderous actions. If you've never studied the history of religious torture, you should, for it will help you see that a religious status mindset can lead to horrific atrocities done in the name of God. Without the discipline of communal confession, religions can switch sides as Peter did in the Gospel story (Matt. 16:13ff.), speaking through the inspiration of the Holy Spirit one minute, and through an unholy spirit the next, being called a rock one minute, and a stumbling-block the next. What's true of religions or denominations is equally true for nations: how often do our nations practise the self-delusion of exceptionalism rather than self-examination and confession?

So confession, because it is directed first and foremost towards God, helps us affirm the truth of our own becoming – helping us become better and sweeter and humbler, not worse and bitter and more arrogant. And no less important, it also helps us affirm the truth about God: that God is gracious and compassionate, slow to anger and abounding in love, full of mercy, faithful and just, forgiving sin and cleansing us from all that is wrong with us, eager to lead us from darkness into light.

The power of confession surges in a stunning scene near the end of the under-appreciated film *The Big Kahuna*. Danny DeVito plays a character named Phil Cooper. He is far from perfect, but he has learned to acknowledge the truth about himself, keeping intact the vital connection between who he is and who he projects himself to be. Another character, Bob Walker, is arrogantly and naively religious – perhaps we would say he borders on de-ligious. Bob sees himself as a righteous man, free of major flaws and so free of regrets. But Phil sees Bob differently; he warns Bob that until he learns the value of regret, he will always lack true character. Here's their inter-change:

Phil: The question is, do you have any character at all? And if you want my honest opinion, Bob, you do not. For the simple reason that you don't regret anything yet.

Bob: Are you saying I won't have any character unless I do something I regret?

Phil: No, Bob. I'm saying you've already done plenty of things to regret. You just don't know what they are. It's when you discover them. When you see the folly in something you've done. And you wish you had to do over. But you know you can't because it's too late. So you pick that thing up and you carry it with you. To remind you that life goes on. The world will spin without you. You really don't matter in the end. Then will you attain character. Because honesty will reach out from inside and tattoo itself all across your face.[6]

I mentioned my friend Carlos earlier. Phil's words help me understand one of the things I respect so much about him. He has regrets, but he has held them up to the light, and honesty has tattooed itself all across his face. The simple word *sorry* helps us carry our regret in the presence of God, where it will not destroy us but will become an essential nutrient in the growth of true character. Pity the soul who never learns – or refuses or forgets how – to say *sorry*.[6]

The word *sorry*, I'm aware, can quickly feel used up and cheap.[7] So as part of my practice of confession, I try to name my wrongs in a single, simple, specific, direct word: pride, lust, resentment, defensiveness, unkindness, harshness, bitterness, greed, revenge, passive aggression, passivity, exaggeration, lie, half-truth, cowardice, avoidance, and so on. In this way, I've learned to hold open my regret in God's presence, slowly lifting my wrongs up from the shadows into full exposure, as it were – not running from them, denying them, minimising them or making excuses about them. I discover two things as I do so. First, I see why God's presence is described as light, and why God is even identified with light (1 John 1:5). It is only in the light of truth, honesty, justice, integrity, holiness and purity, that my wrongs are fully exposed. But thank God, there is more: the light of God is not only true and just and holy: it is also infinitely gracious, kind, merciful.[8]

And that's another alternative word that helps me in the practice of confession: *Mercy*. If I name my wrong as I exhale, I can hold the word *mercy* as I inhale. Breathing out regret, breathing in mercy ... this is the life-sustaining rhythm of naked spirituality – stripping away my spiritual costume so I can stand before God as I am.

I obviously have a lot to say about confession. Sinner that I am, I can't live a moment without it. The fact that this is one of this book's longest chapters tells you something important about me – as does the fact that the subject of confession will spill over into the next chapter. Do not be impressed if I have spoken eloquently and at length about confession. Just know that I am more like you than you might imagine. Together, let us sinners confess our wrongs to the Lord. *Lord, have mercy.*

Chapter 12

Help! Spiritual Jiu-Jitsu

The Practice of Expansion and Petition: Strengthening Through Weakness

Alternative words: Guidance. Strength. Wisdom. Patience. etc.

> The acknowledgement of our weakness is
> the first step in repairing our loss.
>
> Thomas à Kempis[1]

In the previous chapter, we saw how through self-examination and confession, we can sabotage our failures, sins, weaknesses and wrongs before they sabotage us. When we confess our sins, we reconnect with humility and honesty – 'truth in the inward being' as David put it when he confessed his sins (Ps. 51:6). We have lost some innocence, but have at least gained some humility and honesty ... and, one hopes, some compassion too, since we are now more likely to be sympathetic to others who blow it in their lives as we have in our own. Perhaps humility, honesty and compassion constitute a kind of second innocence, an innocence without naivety, you might say.

The grace of God works on our failures like jiu-jitsu, a weaponless martial art that turns the force of the attacker back on the attacker. In so doing, grace connects us with God and others more powerfully than untested innocence ever could have done. Instead of being connected to God through performance – *look how well I am doing!* – confession connects us to God through God's grace – *look how much I've been forgiven!* It's hard to imagine a more powerful word than *sorry*.

But *help* comes close. Our next spiritual practice, centred in this simple plea, works with a similar kind of jiu-jitsu. When we call out for help, we are bound more powerfully to God through our needs and weaknesses, our unfulfilled hopes and dreams, and our anxieties and problems than we ever could have been through our joys, successes and strengths alone. Because this practice involves expanding our resource base beyond our own limited capacities, we can call it *expansion*. Because it involves making a plea to God for help, we can call it petition as well. Whatever we call it, *help!* represents a move from self-reliance to God-reliance, and that's a step in the right direction.

Now petition means, in the most general way, prayers addressed to God by me and for me. This may sound selfish, and sometimes, it is; there is an immature kind of petition that renders God my personal assistant or fixer or genii, the omnipotent enforcer of my will on earth. This immature petition can become a parody of the Lord's prayer: *May my will be done in reality as it is in my selfish fantasies.* This immature kind of petition is to be expected from immature people – who we all are in many ways: we want God to adjust and remake the universe for our convenience and benefit. A large percentage of my petitions are of this sort:

> I'm running late, most often due to bad planning on my part, and I petition God for good traffic or a close-in parking space.
>
> My wife is angry or disappointed with me about something, so I pray that God will change her heart – that way, I won't have to deal with whatever it is in me that's bothering her.
>
> I'm afraid to confront an interpersonal problem, so I pray that God will solve it for me.
>
> I've said yes to too many things, so I ask God for extra strength to accomplish all of them.

I'm sure God understands these requests, and I think that some of them are mercifully granted. But I'm also sure that God is not interested in enabling me to stay immature forever by rewarding my bad planning, or my insensitivity to my wife, or my conflict-aversion, or my inability to set priorities and stick with them. As I mature, I notice that my prayers shift more and more in this direction:

> 'Lord, I'm running late again, and once again, it's because I thought I could get just two or three extra things done. Please, Lord, help me develop wisdom so that I won't be so prone to tackle too much in too short a time. And when I walk into the meeting late, help me not make any excuses but take full responsibility for inconveniencing my colleagues.'

'Lord, my wife is upset with me. Please help me to understand what's bothering her and to respond with compassion and love. And please help me learn to anticipate and meet her needs rather than frustrate her, as I so often do.'

'Lord, I have a problem with Sam. I need to speak frankly with him about it. Please help me to tell the truth, and not hold back, but help me to do it cleanly, without bitterness or hurt.'

'Lord, once again I've taken on too much. Now I'm exhausted. Help me, Lord, to remember that you are the God who created Sabbath, that you want me to live a life that balances good work with adequate rest. Please liberate me from the fears and insecurities that are like a slave-driver, always demanding more of me, never letting me say "no, I can't". Help me to settle into the healthy rhythm that you set for me, for your yoke is easy and your burden is light.'

I'm sure you see the difference. Immature petition tries to convince God to remake the world in our image for our convenience and ease, but mature petition asks God to remake us in God's own image so that we can expand our capacity to respond to the world as it is. Immature petition asks God to give us an easier world with fewer annoying jerks to contend with, and mature petition asks God to help us become stronger, kinder people – and less annoying to our neighbours.[2]

Now someone is probably asking, 'Well, if you want to be a stronger, kinder person, why ask God? Why not just buck up and be more independent? Isn't the very act of petition a kind of surrender to weakness?' I'm sure, for some people, that may be the case. But there are at least two problems with this independent approach.

First, what happens when we really are floundering in water over our heads? Do we proudly pretend we're stronger than we actually are? Doesn't it make sense to cry out for help? Isn't it better to be humbly dependent and survive than to be proudly independent and drown? And second, what happens when our independence becomes pathological? Couldn't it be that life is engineered to be so hard that we eventually have to admit our helplessness and ask for help beyond ourselves – help from others, help from God? Could it be that the old Beatles song was right – that it's immature to never need help in any way? Couldn't independence be, not the ending point, but an adolescent transition period between childish dependence and mature interdependence? If we succeed in being independent, never needing God's help, couldn't that simply mean that we haven't tried anything very significant or challenging? Could it mean that we've never experienced the miracle of synergy with God, where we find God's strength flowing through us?

Most of the anxiety we face can be reduced down to this fear: *maybe life will bring us more than we can handle.* Maybe we'll fail, or if not fail, at least embarrass ourselves on the way to a second-best success. Maybe things we can't control will sneak in and control us. And maybe, as a result, our lives will not have a happy ending.

Sooner or later we need to accept two truths that both the book of Genesis and the theory of evolution teach us: *Life isn't supposed to be easy, and struggle can lead to growth.* In Genesis, God creates a universe characterised neither by fully ordered stasis nor by complete chaos, but rather order and chaos in dynamic tension. In that matrix, we experience the same stresses of struggle, change and competition that challenge us to evolve, to grow, to become.

Consider what's missing in the good creation of Genesis 1: the earth is not fully populated; the Creator leaves room for procreation by all creatures. The creatures of earth are not named: God gives human beings the honour of naming things. Animals wait to be domesticated and bred for undiscovered traits. Crops wait to be discovered and planted. Seas, mountains, deserts, glaciers and forests wait to be explored. Music and city life, dance and technology all wait to be created. The stresses of change, struggle and competition draw us to seize all of these possibilities and thus develop new strengths. So again and again we are told in Scripture, in dozens of different ways, that the hardships which life throws at us are not intended by God to destroy us, but to strengthen us.

The apostle Paul says that we celebrate our sufferings because they produce in us endurance, which in turn produces character, which in turn produces hope, which in turn makes us receptive to the outpouring of God's love in our hearts (Rom. 5:3–5). He says that the weaker we become outwardly, the more we can be renewed inwardly, and that our struggles – which he describes as light-weight and temporary – produce in us a durable glory – which he describes as weighty and eternal (2 Cor. 4:16–18). He calls suffering a privilege (Phil. 1:12ff.) that allows us to have more and more of the 'mind that was in Christ Jesus' in us (Phil. 2:5).

The apostle James, as we have seen already, says we should receive trials into our lives with joy because, again, trials work like a fertiliser for the growth of character (Jas. 1:2–3). Without trials, we would be morally sterile, lacking qualities like endurance, maturity and wisdom.

The apostle Peter sketches out a similar process. In Christ's suffering, Peter says, we find an example for enduring our own (1 Pet. 2:21–25). Without having to survive life's struggles, we would miss a critical chapter in the overarching story of our spiritual development, which he describes as a cumulative process that begins with faith, and then adds goodness, then knowledge, then self control, and continues through endurance – which presupposes trials – and culminates in godliness, mutual affection and love (2 Pet. 1:3–7).

There are days, of course, when we wish there could be some other system. We wish there could be a way of developing patience without delay, courage without danger, forgiveness without offence, generosity without need, skill without discipline, endurance without fatigue, persistence without obstacles, strength without resistance, virtue without temptation, and strong love without hard-to-love people. But it turns out that there is no other way. The Creator has created the right kind of universe to produce these beautiful qualities in us creatures. And among these beautiful qualities is interdependence – the ability to reach out beyond ourselves, to ask for help – from others and from God, and to offer help as we are able. The whole shebang is rigged for mutuality, for vital connection.

The theory of evolution teaches the same lesson. If survival were easy, species wouldn't develop new adaptive features. If survival were stress-free, there wouldn't be twenty thousand species of butterflies, nor would there be three hundred species of turtles, nor would there be 18,937 species of birds (at last count). In fact, there would be no butterflies, turtles or birds at all, because it was stress, struggle, challenge and change that prompted the first living things – slimy blobs in a tide pool somewhere – to diversify, specialise, adapt and develop into the wonders that surround us and include us now. Seen in this light, evolution isn't a grim theory of 'nature red in tooth and claw'; it depicts the planet as a veritable laboratory for innovations in beauty and diversity, fitness and adaptability, complexity and harmony.[3] It renders the earth a studio for the creative development of interdependence in ecosystems or societies of life. Put beauty, diversity, complexity and harmonious interdependence together and you have something very close to the biblical concepts of glory and *shalom*.

So both science and faith tell us that we find ourselves in a universe whose pre-set conditions challenge us to ongoing growth, development and connection. The cry for help, I propose, is what keeps us in the game. When we cry out for help, we reach out for resources and capacities we don't yet have. We dare to desire strength sufficient to meet life's challenges, instead of wishing for the challenges to shrink to our current levels of capacity. By crying *help!*, we choose expansion rather than contraction, advance rather than retreat.

Clearly, we could make the opposite choice: to contract and opt out of our challenges entirely. If the challenges were to get too great for our taste, we could roll over and die – quickly, through suicide, or more gradually through addiction, despair, capitulation or escape. We could refuse to develop the virtues that life's challenges evoke from us, and instead choose vice as our coping strategy. If the test is hard, we could cheat instead of study. If the truth is unpopular, we could cover it up or twist it rather than tell it straight. If a colleague is unkind or incompetent, we could hate and reject instead of forgive and understand. If our neighbour is ignorant, we could mock instead of gently instruct. If a nation is different and non-compliant with our nation's wishes, we could dominate or exterminate rather than negotiate and reconcile. If a vow becomes inconvenient, we could break it rather than keep it. If people stand in the way of our ambition, we could crush them rather than respect them. If people oppose us, we could run and hide rather than stand and face them with courage.

We can and often do choose the shabbier of these options. But even when we degenerate instead of evolve, even when our hearts have contracted into an angry, ugly little fist, even then it's not too late. We can still have a change of heart. We can feel, from our place of contraction, a higher call to a better, more expansive way of life. Through confession (*sorry!*) we can reverse our current trajectory and then through petition (*help!*) we can expand and grow again. Through that single simple word, we can partner with God to turn each challenge into an opportunity for growth.

We see this growth in the life of Jesus.[4] Shortly before his arrest he is at the most stressful moment of his life to date, and he knows that one fork in the road will take him to even greater agony: torture, mockery, rejection, crucifixion and death. So he goes to a garden – evocative because it recalls the story of Eden, the scene of the original crime in which humanity contracted rather than expanded. There Jesus cries out in petition (Luke 22:42):

Father, if you are willing, remove this cup from me; yet, not my will but yours be done.[5]

Simple words, a simple petition, but unfathomably deep: I don't want to drink this cup of poison. I don't want to throw myself into a raging current that will dash me upon the rocks of human ignorance, hatred, cruelty and violence. I don't want my thirty-three years of life and my three years of ministry to end like this – sweat, whips, bruises, welts, tearing tendons and laboured breathing and my blood dripping down onto the stones. But if doing so will unleash new possibilities for good, possibilities that you, God, desire to be unleashed in the world, then I will drink the cup and expand to meet the challenge.

Was Jesus' prayer answered? No and yes. The first half wasn't. God did not adjust the world to make Jesus' life more comfortable. But the second half was. God's will was done, and the consequences of Jesus' surrender to God's will that night continue to spread across time and space like ripples across a pond. Jesus did not receive a reprieve, a pass, a 'get out of suffering free' card. Nor did he take the path of independence, shutting God out and choosing his own will instead. No, in weakness, in vulnerability, from the edge of the abyss, he reached out to God for help. And he received the strength to go forward and drink the cup of suffering. This is petition in its most mature and majestic form.

Was Jesus in error to start his prayer with a request for the cup to pass from him? Would it have been better for him only to surrender to God's will? I don't think so, and here's why.

The great commandment, articulated most famously by Jesus but also celebrated in Judaism, Islam, Buddhism, and other traditions, calls us to love our neighbour as ourselves. The command presupposes a right and healthy way of loving ourselves. Petition is essential to this wise and healthy practice of love-for-oneself. Jesus' plea for the cup to pass was an expression of that healthy love-for-oneself. If Jesus had stopped there, yes, he would have fallen short. But he didn't. His prayer beautifully integrated love for himself (may this cup pass from me) and love for God (may your will be done).

This integration isn't as easy as it might at first appear. Many years ago, I had a spiritual epiphany one morning that showed me how far away I was from a proper love for myself. I was jogging – something I do, not for the love of exercise, but to avoid putting on weight. Whenever I jog, my muscles and lungs nag me constantly. They say, 'OK. That's enough of this. You've proven your point. Let's just walk now. In fact, let's go over to Dunkin' Donuts and buy a couple of chocolate cream-filled doughnuts to reward you for your good behaviour.' Not very helpful self-talk!

The best way to distract myself from the chattering voices of my muscles and lungs was to listen to recorded lectures and sermons on my Walkman (an old device you can probably still see in a museum somewhere). Anyway, I was running and listening to a lecture and the speaker quoted Abraham Lincoln who said these words:

> I desire to so conduct the affairs of this administration that if, at the end ... I have lost every friend on earth, I shall have one friend left, and that friend shall be down inside me.

As I heard those words, it was as if the Spirit took them and pierced me to the core with them. Out of that deepest part of me, I felt a sob erupt. I had to stop running for a few minutes, and found myself hunched over in the middle of the trail, feeling that in some mysterious way, God was speaking to me and it was a matter of life and death that I listen.

I realised that down inside of me, I had an enemy, not a friend.

If my friend made a mistake, I would tell him it was OK,

that nobody's perfect. But when I made a mistake, I would constantly beat myself up and mercilessly take myself to task. If a friend was working too hard, I would tell him to relax, to take a day off, to go fishing or play a round of golf. But down inside me was a cruel taskmaster who was never satisfied. If a friend had some weaknesses, I would be gracious and compassionate. But not so with myself. And so that day I felt the Spirit using a quote from Abraham Lincoln (taken completely out of context) to tell me that if I was going to last, I actually needed to follow Jesus' words about loving others as myself, which required me to first be a friend to myself.

Some time later, I came across a quote from St Bernard of Clairvaux, who talked about the three stages of love. In the first stage, we love God for our own sake, for what God can do for us. In the second stage, we love God for God's own sake, for who God is in God's own character and glory and beauty. It's hard to imagine anything better than that, but Bernard said in the third stage, we love ourselves for God's sake. We join with God in seeing ourselves in a gracious and compassionate light.

This is what petition is for. Through the practice of petition, you learn to stand with God and see yourself as needy, weak, limited, imperfect, edgy, stressed, driven, frightened or troubled. But you don't criticise, condemn, chide or reject yourself. Rather, you join God in God's desire for your own expansion and well-being. You join God in wanting the best for yourself, and in that light, you make your request for your friend, yourself.

Chapter 13

Help! Tapping Into the Current of Power

> Prayer is what the brain does or wants to do to transcend the boundaries of the self, to sense a connection with what lies beyond the praying self.
>
> Ken Wilson[1]

Over a decade ago, millions of people bought and read a book that made a bold promise about the value of petition. *The Prayer of Jabez: Breaking Through to the Blessed Life*[2] began like this: 'Dear Reader, I want to teach you how to pray a daring prayer that God always answers.' The book stirred up, along with millions of dollars in sales, a lot of controversy. It pandered, some said, to the name-it-and-claim-it kind of petition often associated with 'the prosperity gospel', a kind of get-rich-quick approach to petition where the only thing keeping poor people poor and sick people sick is their own failure to pray the right formulas with sufficient faith. It reduced God to a kind of genii, some said, forced to do our will by our clever mastery of a magic formula. No, others said: the book is simply a celebration of petition.

The book focused on a marginal character mentioned in

passing in a hard-to-translate passage (1 Chr. 4:7–10). The NRSV renders it like this:

> The sons of Helah: Zereth, Izhar, and Ethnan. Koz became the father of Anub, Zobebah and of the families of Aharhel son of Harum. Jabez was honoured more than his brothers, and his mother named him Jabez, saying, 'Because I bore him in pain.' Jabez called on the God of Israel, saying, 'Oh, that you would bless me and enlarge my border and that your hand might be with me, and keep me from hurt and harm.' And God granted what he asked.

In this case, I think the NKJV has a better – or at least more interesting – translation of the last verse of the passage; it's the one used in the book.

> And Jabez called on the God of Israel saying, 'Oh, that You would bless me indeed, and enlarge my territory, that Your hand would be with me, and that You would keep me from evil, that I may not cause pain!' So God granted him what he requested.

The mini-plot of this mini-narrative seems to focus on Jabez's identity. He is honoured even though his mother dishonoured him with a name meaning *pain*. (We might imagine a mother today naming her child Headache, Nausea or Cramps.) Cursed with this unflattering name – and, we might imagine, not particularly blessed to have a mother who would name her child in this way! – Jabez doesn't want to become a victim of the situation into which he was born. So he asks God to overcome the misfortune of his name.

I don't take this as a selfish prayer: I take this as a liberating petition: *Liberate me, God, from the way I have been labelled by my mother. Liberate me to enjoy life in its fullness.* As is often the case in Hebrew literature, the prayer is rendered twice, in parallel form. First, it is rendered in the positive: bless me, enlarge my landholdings, let your hand be with me. And then it is rendered in the negative: keep me from evil, that I may not cause harm. And this last line, I think, is the key to the whole prayer.

Jabez seems to be saying, 'I caused my mother pain at birth. She named me Pain in response. And that name has hurt me. But I don't want to keep the chain reaction going. I don't want to pay the pain forward and do to others what was done to me. So, God, please bless me and enlarge my borders and let your hand be with me … so that I can stop the cycle of pain. Bless me so that I may be a blessing to others rather than a source of pain to them.'

Seen in this way, Jabez is echoing the primal calling of Abraham and of all people of true faith, recorded in Genesis 12. God says, 'Abram, I will make you a great nation. I will bless you. I will make your name great.' But that's not all: interwoven with these promises of blessing are these parallel promises: 'You will be a blessing. All peoples on the earth will be blessed through you.'

So in petition, like Jabez, we expand beyond selfishness to otherliness, beyond pain to blessing: 'Bless me, not just so I can be blessed, but more: so I can be a blessing to others. Heal me, not just so I can be healed, but more: so I can be a healer for others. Provide for me, not just so that I can be comfortable, but more: so that I can provide for others and bring comfort to them too. Bless me and keep me from harm, so that I will not cause pain to others, but will instead be a source of joy for them.'

With this expanded understanding of petition, I'm not at all discouraging you from asking God for blessings for yourself. I'm encouraging you to do so. In fact, I would say that you have a moral responsibility to do so. Why? Because if you don't, you'll become anxious and preoccupied with your needs and wants. If you feel that all your happiness and safety depends on you, you will be increasingly self-focused. More and more of your energies will curve inward as you become increasingly self-absorbed. The story of your life will shrink to 'me worrying about me for my sake'. But by practising petition, by referring your anxieties to God through the simple prayer *Help!*, your life story will expand to 'me trusting God to take care of me so I can focus on others for God's sake'.

In that light, it's clear why both Jesus and Paul saw anxiety as such a destructive force.[3] Anxiety is the black hole that sucks everything into itself. So, both Jesus and Paul say, 'Don't be anxious', and Paul continues, 'By prayer and petition, translate your anxieties into requests to God. And what will God do? Remake the world according to your desires? No. But God will change you, because you will be invaded – not by what you fear, but by the peace of God, a peace that soars above all comprehension. This peace will be like a border guard securing your hearts and minds, keeping your thoughts in the mature mindset of Jesus the liberating king' (author's paraphrase of Phil. 4:6–7, echoing 2:5).

There's a powerful secret in these words: the very act of translating anxieties into requests serves to disempower our anxiety and empower us. To put it simply: through petition we *reframe the situation* and *rename our need*.

How do we reframe the situation? Anxiety tempts us to catastrophise, to inflate every risk into a potential cataclysm. Soon, surrounded by possible catastrophes on all sides, we shrink into what author Parker Palmer calls the primitive mind. We sink into reptilian scripts that limit our options to three: fight, flee or freeze.[4] Through petition, we reframe our anxieties into opportunities for growth, calling to mind the joint lesson of Genesis and the theory of evolution from the previous chapter.

This reframing enables us to rename our need. For example, the reptilian brain might shout that we need to fight: 'I must vanquish all who oppose or threaten me!' But we can instead request *compassion* to understand our antagonists, *mercy* to forgive them, *wisdom* to communicate with them, and *determination* to work toward reconciliation with them. The reptilian brain might scream that we need to flee: 'This situation is stressful! I need to get out of here!' But we can instead request *patience* to endure the situation, *insight* into why we are so reactive, and *creativity* to transform our response into something more productive. The reptilian brain might whisper that we need to freeze: 'Somebody is mad at me. I'd better keep my head down, lay low, and stay out of sight.' But we can instead request the *courage* to stand tall, the *humility* to accept being misunderstood, and the *resilience* to get back up again after being knocked down.

Anxieties can grey the whole sky like cloud cover or descend on our whole horizon like a fog. When we rename our anxieties, in a sense we distil them into requests. What covered the whole sky can now be contained in a couple of buckets. So when we're suffering from anxiety, we can begin by simply holding the word *help* before God, letting that one word bring focus to the chaos of our racing thoughts. Once we feel that our mind is out of the frantic zone and into a spirit of connection with God, we can let the general word *help* go, and in its place, hold more specific words that name what we need; thereby condensing the cloud of vague anxiety into a bucket of substantial request. So we might hold the word *guidance* before God. Or *patience*. Or *courage*. Or *resilience*. Or *boundaries, mercy, compassion, determination, healing, calm, freedom, wisdom,* or *peace*.

For me the fog of anxiety is sometimes so thick that I can hardly concentrate enough to go through this reframing and renaming process. That's one of many reasons I often find it helpful to write my prayers.[5] The act of writing helps me concentrate so I don't drift from the road of petition back onto the shoulder of worry or over into the ditch of catastrophising.

When I write my petitions, I often find it helpful to separate them into minor and major leagues.[6] Sometimes, I'm so preoccupied with little things that I miss the big things, and sometimes, it's the reverse. So I often take a page in my journal (or on my laptop) and write (or type): LITTLE THINGS in big letters across the top. Then I'll list every little frustration or problem that comes to mind, leaving some space between each one. Then, I'll go back to each item and write a prayer starting with the word *help*. My page might look like this:

Meeting with my boss: Help me, Lord, to focus on his feelings and not react, whatever he says. Help me draw out his concerns and practise active listening.

Finances: Help me, Lord, to put that money I wasted on that lawn maintenance service behind me, and help me make some good decisions about decreasing our monthly expenses. Especially help me be firm when I call the cable company and reduce that bill.

Weight: Help me, Lord, to get back on track with my diet.

Help me throw out that bag of crisps, even though it's only half-empty. I don't need the rest of it!

Car: Help me, Lord, to stop worrying about that funny sound in the rear tyres. Help me make the call today to schedule getting the brakes checked.

Once I've cleared away the little frustrations and anxieties that are nagging at me, on another page, I'll write BIG THINGS. On this page, I'll try to get to some of the broader and deeper issues that are causing me stress. My page might begin like this:

Schedule/Priorities: Help me, Lord, to be less driven by the need to say yes to every request that comes my way. Help me be a good manager of myself. I would never keep piling more and more duties on an employee, but this is exactly what I do to myself. Help me get to the root of why I keep doing this. Is it the fear of disappointing other people? Is it a need to be liked, or a fear of being criticised if I say no? Help me, Lord, to stop being a slave to the opinions of me held by other people, and help me to discern and live by wise priorities instead.

Office: Help me, Lord, to understand and respond to the tense feeling in my office these days. Help me not to blame my boss or co-workers, and help me not slip into the 'fix it' mode without first getting to the real issues. It feels like we go in cycles, and here we are again. Help me …

Resentment: Lord, I notice a growing resentment in my heart towards Bernard. I realise that I'm still feeling wounded by what I was told that he said about me last week. Help me to see him as a critical friend, not an enemy.

Anxiety isn't the only struggle that drives us to petition. We also need to practise petition when we're hurt or wounded by others. In a way, this is the flip side of confession; confession deals with the times we do wrong to others, but hurt-related petition deals with the times others do wrong to us. I've noticed that many churches have a prayer of confession each week, but I have never (yet) heard a regular prayer of woundedness in a church, a prayer by which we acknowledge and process the pain of being hurt, insulted, taken for granted, presumed upon, inconvenienced, betrayed, or otherwise mistreated by other people. Since being wounded or sinned against is a terribly common experience, I suspect we need to pay it more attention. In fact, being wronged is directly linked in the Lord's prayer to the reality of doing wrong: we pray, 'forgive us our sins *as we forgive those who sin against us*'.

Fr Richard Rohr says it well: *Pain that isn't processed is passed on. Pain that isn't transformed is transmitted.*' So we need to process our woundedness with God, and that processing begins by naming our pain and holding it – as we've been holding each of our simple words – in God's presence:

> Betrayed. Insulted. Taken advantage of. Lied to. Forgotten. Used. Abused. Belittled. Passed over. Cheated. Mocked. Snubbed. Robbed. Vandalised. Misunderstood. Misinterpreted. Excluded. Disrespected. Ripped off. Confused. Misled.

It's important not to rush this process. We need to feel our feelings, to let the pain actually catch up with us, to drop out of the rat race of hurt-suppression and denial. I've found that it takes less energy to feel and process my pain than it does to suppress it or run away from it. So, just as through confession we name our own wrongs and feel regret, through petition we name and feel the pain that results from the wrongs of others. And just as we rename our anxieties as requests to God, we translate our pain into requests:

Comfort. Encouragement. Reassurance. Companionship. Vindication. Appreciation. Boundaries. Acknowledgement.

It's important to note that we are not naming what we need *the person who wronged us* to do for us. If we focus on what we wish the antagonist would do to make us feel better, we're unintentionally arming the antagonist with still more power to hurt us. Instead, in this naming, we are turning from the antagonist to God, focusing on what we need God to do for us. We're opening our souls to receive healing from God's ever-present, ever-generous Spirit.

Along with anxieties and hurts, we also bring our disappointments to God. If anxieties focus on what *might happen*, and hurts focus on what *has happened*, disappointments focus on what *has not happened*. Again, as the saying goes, revealing your feeling is the beginning of healing, so simply acknowledging or naming our disappointment to God is an important move. This is especially important because many of us, if we don't bring our disappointment to God, will blame our disappointment on God, thus alienating ourselves from our best hope of comfort and strength. Again, if we condense our cloud of disappointment into a name and a request, we take a step forward in maturity and faith:

I didn't get that job, and I was really hoping for it. Now I'm *crushed* with *disappointment*. But I'm not giving up.

I'm still trusting in you, God. Something else will come my way in time. Help me persevere.

I had hoped this was the relationship that would lead to marriage. But now we've broken up, and I feel *heartbroken* and *deflated*. I bring my pain to you, God. Help me heal.

I was hoping this treatment would kill the tumour, or at least shrink it. But the reports say otherwise, and I'm deep in a pit of *despair*. Help me accept this *shattering blow*, Lord, and not be wiped out by it.

Whether we're dealing with anxieties, wounds, disappointments, or other needs or struggles, there is enormous power in simple words – the words by which we name our pain and then translate it into a request to God. *Help!* is the door into this vital practice of petition, through which we expand beyond our own capacities and resources to God's.

Sometimes we experience dramatic answers to our prayers for help. I think of one of the worst days of my life, when I was visiting the girl I loved and to whom I was engaged. When she told me she wasn't sure about our relationship and wanted to break the engagement, I was so broken-hearted that I simply walked out of her house. With nowhere to go, I walked the streets of her city, knowing nobody, feeling utterly alone and dejected. I could muster little more – to be honest – than a string of cursewords, not cursing her, but cursing my terrible situation. But sandwiched between my muttered profanities, I also managed to send up the simple word *help*, hoping Somebody would hear.

After walking for what seemed like hours, and having left my watch at my ex-fiancée's home, I asked a man doing his garden if he knew what time it was. After telling me, he then asked, 'Are you OK? Do you need to talk?' When I fumbled for the right words, he said, 'When I saw you walking along, I felt like God was telling me you needed a friend.' And so a few minutes later, I was sitting at his kitchen table having a cup of coffee, pouring out my heart to a perfect stranger. I felt – and still feel – that God had directed me to him, just as I have felt on other occasions that I have been the stranger to whom a person in need has been directed. I was still heart-broken, but the kindness of a stranger told me that I wasn't as utterly alone as I had felt a few minutes before. I felt as the Psalmist did (34:6): 'This poor soul cried, and was heard by the Lord, and was saved from every trouble.' (And yes, eventually Grace and I did get our problems worked out, and after thirty-one years of marriage, I think it's going to last.)

Other times, it's much harder to know whether our cry for help has been heard at all, as things go from bad to worse to even worse to worse still. But imagine if instead of naming our anxieties, needs, wounds and disappointments, and turning them into requests to God, we let other forces take control of our inner world: self-protection instead of guidance, revenge instead of patience, panic instead of courage, retreat instead of resilience, placating instead of setting boundaries, self-hatred instead of mercy, blame instead of compassion, fantasy instead of determination, despair instead of healing, bitterness instead of peace, resignation instead of resilience. Imagine the change in our inner ecology after ten minutes, or ten days, or ten years of living without the expanding influence of petition. Where would we be, and who would we be if we couldn't turn outside ourselves, direct our needs to the living God, and cry *Help!*

Through this practice of expansion and petition, we discover something priceless: the sacred connection can grow stronger through, not in spite of, our anxieties, wounds, disappointments, struggles and needs. The Compassionate One is our gracious friend, and we don't have to earn anything, deserve anything, achieve anything, or merit anything to bring our needs to God. We can come just as we are. If it takes our weaknesses and disappointments to teach us this truth, then may our weaknesses and disappointments be blessed, just as the apostle Paul said:

> If I must boast, I will boast of the things that show my weakness ... [The Lord] said to me, 'My grace is sufficient for you, for my power is made perfect in weakness.' Therefore I will boast all the more gladly about my weaknesses, so that Christ's power may rest on me. That is why, for Christ's sake, I delight in weaknesses, in insults, in hardships, in persecutions, in difficulties. For when I am weak, then I am strong. (2 Cor. 11:30; 12:9–10, NIV)

So now, it's time to put this book aside again and perhaps to take out a piece of paper or open up a new page on your computer and condense your anxieties into a list of little requests and big requests. It's your opportunity to scan your soul for wounds, worries and weaknesses. It's your opportunity to ask God for help in transforming your pain so you don't transmit it. It's your opportunity to stand with God and see yourself from the vantage point of a friend, speaking kindly and compassionately to God on your behalf. You are loved, so you deserve this opportunity. You really do.

Chapter 14

Please! At Least Two Hearts Care

The Practice of Compassion and Intercession: Strengthening Through Empathy

Alternative words: Mercy. Bless. Peace. Grace.

> Our prayer is public and for all, and when we pray, we pray not for a single person, but for the whole people, because we are all one. The God of peace, the teacher of harmony, who taught us unity, willed that each should pray for all, according as he carried us all in himself alone.
>
> St Cyprian[1]

As you know from my story about being tracked down in the woods of Pennsylvania, one of our children is a cancer survivor. About midway through Trevor's three-plus years of daily chemotherapy, I was standing in the kitchen one afternoon, sorting through mail. I came to the monthly newsletter from a support group for parents of kids with cancer, and something happened to me as I read through it.

First, tears began streaming down my face, and soon I was

so overcome by emotion that I found myself bent over the kitchen counter, head in hands, tears now running down my forearms. But I wasn't exactly sure why. They weren't simply tears of grief for our still-precarious situation that moved me that afternoon. No, by then the actual and potential losses that go along with a cancer diagnosis had become the new normal for us, part of our daily routine. It was something else, something I had seldom felt at such a profound level: a rising feeling of connection with every other family with a sick child.

After months of having to hold our son while he received painful spinal infusions or bone marrow aspirations, after months of having to live with the daily danger of relapse and never knowing if we would end the day at home or in the hospital, after months of fatigue bordering on exhaustion, my heart was strangely warmed, enlarged and invigorated with empathy and compassion. My broken heart was becoming a broken-open heart.[2]

So far, we have considered the role of five simple words in the spiritual life. First we considered three words of simplicity: *Here. Thanks! O!* (spiritual practices through which we present ourselves to the Presence, thank God for life's innumerable gifts, and joyfully celebrate God's unfathomable wonder and goodness). Then we turned to words of complexity ... words that grapple with life's difficulties. We reflected on *sorry*, the vital connection of confession, the practice that sabotages our failures by drawing us beyond denial or despair to honesty, humility and grace. Then we turned to *help*, the prayer that uses our own weaknesses and needs to strengthen the vital connection. Now we move beyond our weaknesses and needs to those of others, from *help!* to *please*. The traditional name for this spiritual practice is intercession, a word whose Latin roots suggest going between (*inter*- meaning *between*, and -*cede* meaning *go*, as in 'proceed' or 'exceed'). Through intercession, we offer ourselves as a bridge between the needs of others and the love and comfort of God.

Wisdom, in whatever small ways I've experienced it, has involved learning the advantages of disadvantages and the reverse as well. As I learned that afternoon in my kitchen, when we experience the downsides of pain and struggle, we can also experience the unexpected upside of increased compassion for others. It doesn't always work this way, of course: sometimes our pain overwhelms us and we plunge into the vortex of inwardness. But if we experience some degree of sacred comfort in our own pain, we eventually find ourselves empowered to turn outward in sacred compassion toward others.[3]

When we practise compassion through simple words of intercession, we affirm two profound truths: first, that God cares for all who suffer and are in need, and second, that we care too. If we didn't believe God cared, we wouldn't turn to God, nor would we do so if we ourselves didn't care. When we call out *Please!* on behalf of someone else, we make a vital connection between our compassion and the compassion of God. We say to God and ourselves, 'Someone is suffering, and at least two hearts in the universe notice and refuse to turn away – God's heart, and my own.'

The simple intercession we utter to God on behalf of someone in pain or need – *Please!* – is required equipment in a complex world where all is not as it should be. Those in pain need to receive our compassion, of course, but no less do we need to extend it. To understand why, try this thought experiment. You are watching the news on TV, or reading the news in print or online. You learn about another war in another troubled corner of the world, or maybe it's another ecological disaster or outbreak of bigotry, or another famine or epidemic of a terrible disease, or another species threatened with extinction. Hearing this news about your fellow creatures in some terrible predicament means that you now are also in a predicament of your own. Consider your options.

You could just change the channel or click over to a new site – there must be a game show or sitcom or something that will not be so disturbing. But what kind of person are you becoming if you routinely practise pain-avoidance and habitually choose ignorance about the suffering of your fellow creatures?

You could keep watching, and gradually become overwhelmed with all the evil and suffering in the world, slipping deeper and deeper into depression, cynicism, paralysis, despair. If that's the case, haven't you become another casualty added to the catastrophes you have seen? Haven't you been sucked into the problem instead of becoming part of the solution to it?

You could become so accustomed to tragedies and atrocities that they no longer bother you. You could call that lack of concern realism. But wouldn't that mean that you have also become less compassionate, maybe even less humane and human?

You could find someone to blame for the suffering and feel, instead of compassion, fury and self-righteousness as you identify the villains behind the victims. But is a blaming, furious, self-righteous version of you a step upward?

You could rage at God for allowing these things to happen, or maybe even decide to stop believing in God. But does that increase the likelihood that you will sustain sufficient faith, hope and love to get involved in a constructive way?

Clearly, then, the suffering of others invariably puts each of us in a predicament of our own, a moment of choice. Will we, in our chosen response to the suffering of others, become more calloused, uncaring, embittered or overwhelmed? Or will we strengthen the sacred connection with God and others, feeling compassion and desiring relief for our fellow creatures in pain? This choice screams out the reason compassion matters so much in the spiritual life. If we don't strengthen the vital connection of compassion, we will slide toward the tragic disconnections of apathy, self-distancing or despair.

In confession, I courageously face the painful truth about my moral faults and failures and those of my nation, party, religion, tribe or family. In petition, I courageously face the painful truth about my weaknesses, wounds and worries. Through the practice of compassion or intercession, I courageously face the pain in the world. Through the simple word *please* – or related words like *mercy, bless, peace* or *grace* – I choose connection over disconnection, compassion over apathy, commitment and expansion over constriction and contraction.

This choice helps explain why we are in some sense better off *not* having satisfying answers to vexing intellectual questions about why suffering, evil and pain exist in the world.[4] If we can say, 'Oh, there's a clear reason for this', we can remain aloof, safe in the cool and lofty realm of impersonal logic in relation to human suffering. We can explain instead of empathise, theorise instead of pray, and answer instead of act. But in the absence of a satisfying logical explanation for human suffering, we must descend from our brains into our hearts, and respond to the suffering of others with tears and action, not just words and more words.

So, we practise compassion and intercession not because we have fully satisfying answers to explain the suffering of others,

but because we don't. The practice of compassion or intercession, in this light, is not just a response to the agony of
another in pain; it is also the response to our own agony of
not having answers about why anybody is in pain. It is a way
of saying, 'For a fellow creature to be in pain and without help
in God's universe is simply unacceptable to both God and me.
So I will go in between the two. I will grasp the hand of God
with one hand and grasp the hand of my neighbour in pain
with the other. I will join God in willing comfort, blessing,
peace and grace for my sister or brother in need.'

Now the word compassion has come up for us again and
again. I think if you asked most people these days, 'What is the
religion of compassion?' their first answer would be Buddhism,
because the *dharma* (teaching) of Siddhartha Gautama truly
does emphasise compassion in an exemplary way. Meanwhile,
many other religious communities – especially monotheistic ones
– have been putting their least compassionate feet forward lately,
distinguishing themselves as the religions of stridency and
violence more than compassion. That's why I believe all of us
must help convert our religions towards compassion, following
the good example of the best Buddhists.[5]

To Muslims, for example, one of the most revered ways to
refer to God is as 'The Compassionate, the Merciful'. Similarly,
Judaism associates compassion with God's deepest identity by
linking it with God's name (Exod. 34:6, NIV): 'The LORD,
the LORD, the compassionate and gracious God, slow to anger,
abounding in love and faithfulness...' And for Christians, Jesus
was undoubtedly a man of compassion. Compassion is, again
and again in the Gospel narratives, the way Jesus sees.[6] When
he looks over a crowd of people, he doesn't see a 'damned
crowd that doesn't know the Law' as some of the religious

leaders do, but he sees people who are 'harassed and helpless, like sheep without a shepherd'.[7] He looks at a woman caught in adultery and sees, not someone to be executed by her so-called 'righteous' accusers, but rather someone to forgive and give another chance. He sees that woman at the well with compassion, not condemning her for her long string of lovers, but offering her a taste of living water.[8]

When a woman with a notorious reputation crashes a dinner party being held in his honour and makes a potentially embarrassing scene, he sees her, not with revulsion, but with compassion. When he sees a physically short, socially unpopular enemy collaborator named Zacchaeus perched in a tree, he doesn't see him as a bother, but as a brother. When he sees a gaggle of kids looking for hugs, when he sees a blind beggar or group of despised lepers calling out beside the road, when he sees a widow who has recently lost her son to an early death, even when he sees the Roman soldiers gathered around the foot of his cross casting dice for the robe which they have stripped from him, he sees with compassion.

And if the apostles are to be believed, and I believe they are, when people saw this compassion in the eyes of Jesus, they somehow knew that God was compassionate in the same way. Jesus taught this in word just as he embodied it in example: *God's perfection is a compassionate perfection.* Compassion is inherent to all God is and does, extending even to people deemed antagonistic, ungrateful and evil.[9]

Even the way Jesus died revealed to them the degree to which God joined them in their suffering. The political 'powers that be' claimed – as they almost always do – to represent God or the gods, embodying the divine bias for law and order. But in their brutal treatment of Jesus, the powers-that-be overreached.

The cross, intended to expose its victims as weak and defeated by the superior power of the state, ended up exposing the state itself. The cross exposed Caesar and his system as brutal and heartless, quick to judge, condemn and resort to violence to keep the oppressed in line. So in his suffering and dying Jesus embodied for his followers God's solidarity with the crucified not the crucifiers, with the downtrodden not the oppressors, with the meek not the mean.[10]

And the leaders of the religious establishment were exposed just as the political leaders were. They didn't have a monopoly on God as they pretended to do. In the end, their moral bankruptcy was exposed when they rejected the leadership of Jesus and affirmed the ways of Caesar.[11] So through Jesus' life, sufferings, death and resurrection, the early disciples came to believe that God does not stand aloof to condemn us for our weaknesses and wrongs, but rather that God compassionately enters and shares our pain and shame, taking even our failures up into God's own life where our evil is overcome by God's goodness, our ugliness is overwhelmed by God's beauty, and our sickness and toxicity are overwhelmed by God's vitality.

Reading that newsletter in my kitchen that afternoon, and many times before and since, I've felt that I was rubbing up against the deep, deep current of compassion that flows from God's heart and flows through creation. Like a nail rubbing against a magnet, I think each exposure has been changing me.

Because my transformation is so far from complete, and because the needs around me are so great, I am eager to strengthen this vital connection.

Chapter 15

Please! Bearing the Stretcher

> At its best, my prayer does not seek to manipulate God
> into doing my will – quite the opposite. Prayer enters the
> pool of God's own love and widens outward.
>
> Philip Yancey[1]

I was in Capernaum recently. It's a beautiful little town on the
north-west shore of Lake Galilee in Israel. As I sat by the shore
and watched the sun glisten on the water, as I listened to the
waves lapping against smooth shoreline stones, I felt myself
transported back in time to the days when this was Jesus' home
town. I could picture him looking out over the water just as I
was, watching fishing boats rock on the waves, seeing a storm
cross the mountains beyond the lake to the east. I could imagine
him observing sheep and wild flowers on nearby hills, or
listening to crows and sparrows in the scrubby bushes and trees
scattered around. And I could picture one dramatic day when
a large crowd gathered in a home not far from the shore to
hear him teach. As Mark tells the story (2:1–12), the crowd
filled the available space inside and spilled out the open door
into the street.

There was a man in Capernaum who had been paralysed,
and whether he persuaded his four friends to do so or they

thought of the idea, they carried him on a stretcher toward the house, hoping Jesus would heal him. But the crowd was impenetrable, and there was no way in. What would they do? I imagined one of them coming up with a crazy proposal. Climb up on the roof – whether it was thatched or tile, I don't know – and open up a hole through which they could lower the man on his stretcher so that he would bypass the crowd and land right smack in front of Jesus. It was a crazy scheme, but bold, and it just might work, and there were no other options ... so they gave it a try.

And when they did, Mark says that Jesus was impressed by *their* faith – not just the faith of the paralysed man, but that of his friends as well. And so Jesus pronounced forgiveness and healing on the man, and *their* faith – which had already opened a hole in the roof – opened new possibilities for the man. He walked out, Mark says, carrying the stretcher on which he had been carried. I can only imagine how the awe-struck crowd parted to make room for him to leave in a way they hadn't been willing to do when he arrived.

Those four friends, I think, dramatise our sixth simple word, *please*, and the spiritual practice of intercession to which it points. They literally carried their paralysed friend; they let the weight of his condition become their burden to bear, and let his problem create problems for them. In a sense, his paralysis became their paralysis, and their ability to move became his ability to move. Whether or not the man had faith, they did, and as a result, a miracle happened. When we practise compassionate intercession, we become the stretcher-bearers for others in need. Whether or not they have faith and hope, we put our faith and hope to work on their behalf.

There is a Christian doctrine that is intended, I think, to

embed this reality in the heart, but too often it remains only an item of doctrinal controversy: the priesthood of all believers. The doctrine was originally articulated as part of a Protestant critique of Catholicism. It affirmed that every Christian was free to approach God without a priest serving as intermediary. Others took it further, saying that the doctrine intended to obliterate the clergy–laity distinction so that all people could perform priestly duties in church – preaching, baptising, administering the sacraments. Few, though, understood the doctrine to suggest that the priesthood of all believers meant primarily that all the faithful were to function as priests for their neighbours outside the church – to carry their stretcher, to bear their burdens, to supply faith where faith was lacking. Seen in this light, the doctrine isn't primarily about what happens in church; it's about what happens in the neighbourhood, at the workplace, along the road, on the pavements, at the edges of crowds. It's a call for people of faith to bear to God those without faith, and simultaneously to bear God to them. It's not about esoteric controversy in the religious subculture, but rather about practical compassion in the world at large, about being the vital connection between the religious and non-religious, the faithful and the sceptics, the spiritual and the not-so-spiritual.

Our neighbours lack faith for many reasons: intellectual scepticism, bad experiences with de-ligion, simple spiritual laziness, being overwhelmed by the manure that life's proverbial fans widely spread. Our job isn't to criticise or scold people for their lack of faith: it's to carry the one whose faith has been paralysed, to keep faith for them, and to see carrying them not as a burden but as our calling.

Back in Capernaum the day of that roof incident, the religious experts had a front-row seat to the whole story, but they remained critical rather than compassionate to the end. They suffered, it seems, from their own kind of paralysis. Today, both groups – the stretcher-bearers on the one hand and the religious experts on the other – still beckon us to join them. Which group will we join? Will we sit comfortably inside the house with front-row seats to unbeatable religious programming, oblivious to the people who suffer on the margins of the crowd outside? Will we intellectualise about the suffering of others, theorise about how somebody should help them, criticise those who try for not doing better? Or will we join the stretcher-bearers, feeling the pain of a fellow human being and making it our own, so that we carry *our pain* – their pain together with our pain for them – to the One we name the Compassionate?

The word *mercy* again serves as a good substitute or supplement to *please*, even more so in Latin or Spanish. *Misericordia* or *conmiseración* suggests that the sufferer's misery strikes an empathic chord of solidarity in the heart of God and a compassionate neighbour. Sometimes, I find myself praying *Lord, have mercy on us all*, because in compassion, the distinctions between my pain, your pain, our pain, his pain, her pain, its pain and their pain disappear. I find myself appealing to God's *misericordia* and *conmiseración* for the whole of humanity, the whole of creation.

It's worth adding here that sacred compassion doesn't stop with human beings. The ancient psalmists knew that God's compassion extends to every created thing (see Pss. 145:9; 104:10–27), and Jesus didn't doubt that God's concern included the sparrows and wild flowers (Matt. 6:25–30). So our compassion, if it is to join with God's, must include all the animals, all the plants and all the ecosystems that connect them to one another – and to us. The compassionate Spirit of God, Paul claims, helps us feel the groaning of all creation, a groaning for release from evil, decay, futility and abuse. The trees groan as forests are destroyed by human greed. The seas groan as its fisheries are depleted and toxins accumulate due to careless human behaviour. The forests and jungles groan as species disappear, victims of our failure to be wise stewards of God's good world. Even the winds groan as the earth warms due to human haste, waste and greed. Creation's groaning becomes part of our groaning, and it is all taken up into the Spirit of God who in some way brings all of our intercession into God's own heart.[2]

I felt this with unusual intensity one summer day as I was driving along a country road beside the Potomac River in Western Maryland. I came across a wood turtle. Of all turtles, wood turtles are my favourites – intelligent and inquisitive (for a reptile), with a lot of personality (for a reptile). A brown shell on the edge of the tarmac ahead of me caught my eye, and I pulled over and walked up the hill towards it. As I came closer I realised it had been hit by a car just a matter of minutes before I came along. On the hot black roadside, with little bubbles of tar forming on the surface, a dark red, almost purplish, pool of blood now the consistency of pudding was drying in the sun. Just uphill from the pool, there was this beautiful animal – sculptured shell with yellow flecks, bright orange limbs, coal-black head and a golden circle around the pupil of each eye. To my surprise, she was still alive.

I knew she was female by the more slender shape of her head, and the flatter contour of her carapace. I counted seven broken fragments of her upper shell, and I could see the pouch of her body cavity expanding and contracting between the shards. She was alert, and watched me approach, seeming neither afraid ('Oh no, what next?') nor relieved ('Help coming?'). My first thought was to rescue her, to take her home and try to glue her shell together and give her some antibiotics and tender treatment so as to rehabilitate her. But she was gasping for breath, and I realised that since her lungs had been punctured, she could not survive.

My next thought was to finish the job, to put her out of her misery, to euthanase her. But I couldn't, not because I lack the nerve, but because of the way she looked at me with her gold-rimmed eye. I cherish no illusions about the mental capacities of reptiles, but I imagined, if she could think and speak, she would be saying something like this:

So, here you find me in my final predicament. Those cars come so fast and I had no idea that I was in danger until … Crack! … and now I feel my blood draining out of me. Please don't disturb me. Don't try to tip me over to see the condition of my underside. It's no use. It's too bad for that. I have just a few minutes left. Are you thinking about putting me out of my misery? Please don't – I'm not in too much pain, really. In fact, before you walked up, I was thinking that I have never felt the pleasure of life as fully as now. And neither have I noticed how green my world is, how utterly alive, how bright and strong is our sun, how warm is the ground heated by it, how privileged each creature is to be able to move even an inch, which I have tried to do once more, just to savour the feeling and freedom of movement one more time.

So please, stay here with me if you'd like, and think

these thoughts on my behalf, but please do not touch me, and please do not try to help me by putting me out of what you might suppose to be my misery. Because in spite of my horrible wounds, I am not miserable. In fact, no breath of air ever felt so sweet or precious or fresh as the breath I won during that last gasp. I want to enjoy each remaining moment of this sweet life, each breath, each view of those green bushes there across the road, the movement of that butterfly there. If the only moments I ever experienced were ones I now savour, then I would have reason enough to celebrate. True, I am dying, but at this moment, I am living. That is very good.

So kneeling there with her for a few minutes, I witnessed her waning life and waxing death, living myself in a new way somehow in that bright sunlight blazing from above and that heat rising up from the tarmac beneath. When she breathed her last, I removed her body from the roadway and buried her under some fertile forest topsoil. As I returned to my car and drove away in a kind of holy hush, I thought about the Creator, about the Spirit of Creation who knows every sparrow that falls to the ground and every wood turtle who breathes her last. I pondered the magnitude of God's heart, who in some way witnesses every breath of every creature, from first to last, with perfect, infinite compassion. For a few moments, I felt that I had somehow joined God in God's love for one of God's creatures.[3]

Since that afternoon, although I know some might find this laughable, I find myself whispering blessings on trees, praying for threatened wetlands, watching birds in flight as if I were saying goodbye to friends, because in a real way, I believe I am. In noticing, knowing and loving a stream, a dolphin, a butterfly, a mountain range, a tiny salamander or songbird, I am making a vital connection with the Creator who notices, knows and loves each one too. God, recall the Psalmist saying, has compassion on all God has made.

And if this is true regarding non-human creatures, how much more true it is in relation to every person, whatever their age, race, gender, orientation, religions, status, or capacity. God's loving kindness, another Psalmist says, never runs out.

Just as in the prayer of petition, sometimes the best simple word to add to *please* is the one that names the need of the other: *peace, protection, strength, hope, comfort, stamina, patience.* And sometimes the prayer whispered to God becomes a blessing spoken directly to the person in pain. So, 'Please grant her peace, Lord,' becomes 'Peace be with you, my friend'. 'Please, Lord, courage,' becomes, 'Courage, my brother'. Some of us have experienced this kind of blessing – both on the giving end, where we pronounce it, and on the receiving end, where it is pronounced upon us. We know that something powerful happens in a blessing spoken by a believer-priest.[4]

One of the highest and most powerful forms of compassion flows when we learn to pray for those who persecute us, when we dare to bless even our antagonists and enemies.[5] A white South African once told me about a time when he was on the receiving end of such a blessing. During the apartheid years, he believed what he was told by white authority figures, namely, that those working against apartheid were evil: trouble-makers, rabble-rousers, communists, heretics. Chief among the trouble-makers was an activist Anglican priest named Desmond Tutu. Once, walking through an airport, this large white man saw Tutu coming towards him. Overcome with rage, he moved toward Tutu and roughly, intentionally bumped him as he walked by. Tutu, much smaller in stature, fell back on the ground, landing on his backside with a thud. When Tutu opened his eyes, angry blue eyes glared down at him with a sneer of obvious disdain, only to see Tutu's shocked and dazed face gradually focus and form into a smile. 'God bless you, my child,' Tutu said, his brown eyes gleaming with an impossible mix of compassion and mischief.

The man stomped away, infuriated all the more that Tutu found a way to transcend his act of hatred. Over the hours and days that followed, the words of blessing echoed in his memory, and gradually, that big, proud, white man was brought to repentance by a simple, spontaneous blessing. Tutu's non-violence, that moment showed, wasn't simply a political strategy: it was a spiritual practice. It was rooted in this practice of intercession. The only way we will learn to respond to violent actions with non-violent actions is by learning to respond first with non-violent words – words of blessing not cursing, words of prayer not revenge, words of compassion not retaliation.

When we are wounded by others, we're tempted to dehumanise and demonise them by labelling them with words like communist, imperialist, evil, insane, heretic, fundamentalist, liberal or infidel. Ironically, by turning them into subhuman monsters in our own minds, we also empower them, making them larger than life, and intensifying our own anxiety about them. No wonder Jesus taught that our first response should be instead to pray for them and to bless them. In so doing, we turn them back from threatening monsters into what they really are: little human beings like us, human beings with a problem – fear, rage, hate, anxiety, ignorance, misinformation, misguided values, inappropriate habits, harmful training, insecurity or whatever. By praying for them, by blessing them, we look beyond their fault and see their need, and we seek to help them with their need. Rather than getting caught up ourselves in the deadly cycles of violence and counter-violence, we join Desmond Tutu and many other courageous spiritual leaders on a better path, the path of peace and reconciliation.

At the heart of the prayer Jesus taught his disciples, we find a call to this path. When we pray, 'Forgive us our trespasses as we forgive those who trespass against us', we transcend the normal cycles of offence and revenge that tangle and tear the sacred web of life.[6] We divest from the bankrupt economy of eye for eye and tooth for tooth. We invest in the grace economy that returns kindness for cruelty and blessing for cursing.[7] By walking this better path, we render ourselves open to better possibilities, and we make those possibilities more likely to happen.

But is that likelihood mushy and uncertain? Will praying for our enemies really make a difference? In response to our prayers, will God intervene and work miracles? Will our prayers do the trick, get the job done, flip the switch, close the deal, guarantee results, be effective? Will prayer change things? You may have already noticed that until now I've largely left these questions unasked, much less answered.

Questions like these tap us into a whole range of theological assumptions that we are largely unconscious of, assumptions about God's nature and power, God's agency and desired relationship with the universe, God's ability to enforce God's will – and God's ability to limit God's will to make space for the will of other creatures. Others have written brilliantly about these questions.[8] And less brilliantly, no doubt, so have I.[9] But oddly enough, I don't feel a book like this one is the best place to address them.

Here's why: I'm writing about the summer season of complexity in the spiritual life as someone who has already passed through it a time or two; I've gone on to survive some autumn and winter seasons as well. These experiences have changed me. Yes, I still remember how in my first encounters with complexity, questions about divine agency were terribly serious and important and I demanded answers. Firm answers. Black and white answers. Simple yes or no answers. And I got them. But they haven't stood the test of time. As a result, back then I would have had a lot more to say than I do now about 'getting answers to prayer' or 'praying effectively' or 'claiming your miracle' and so on. But from where I am now, with some autumns and winters under my belt, I actually think a better way to deal with these questions is to say,

> Yes, think about these questions. And certainly form and hold and share your opinions in response to them. But don't pretend you have solved them once and for all. Because later on, you'll be seeing things from a different perspective, and from that perspective, much will change. What seems like a problem now won't be so problematic then. And what seems like an answer or solution now will seem like a problem then. The important thing both now and then is to keep praying, whatever answers come or don't come, whatever opinions you hold about how prayer works. Because however much or little prayer changes *things*, prayer certainly changes *you*, and you need to be changed. Remember that you still have a long way to grow, and the best way to grow is to keep praying, to keep strengthening the sacred connection.

In life's summer-like seasons of complexity, if we do not practise confession, petition and intercession, we will not keep
growing and learning in the sacred connection. If we do wrong,
then denial, pride or shame will cause us to disconnect. If
we're in need or pain, then exhaustion, anxiety or disappointment will cause us to disconnect. And if we're faced with
the suffering of others, then we'll succumb to the temptation
to disconnect through apathy or despair or self-distancing. As
a result, our hearts will contract, not expand. And as a further
result, the world, deprived of stronger compassion in people
like us, will inevitably grow worse and suffering will increase.

But if through confession, petition and intercession, you and
I strengthen the sacred connection in the midst of life's
complexities, what will happen then? Won't we become – habitually, radically, truly – more aligned with God's compassion,
more empowered by it, more resonant with its holy frequency?
And won't more of us who are more filled with God's compassion help make a better world?

Imagine a world filled with people who are practising compassion for themselves and others. Hungry stomachs will be filled.
War zones will be invaded by peacemakers. Abused victims
will be rescued and cruel victimisers will be confronted. Tears
will be dried. And God's compassion will be behind these
wonders … God's compassion alive in our hands and eyes and
voices, as we bear stretchers and defy crowds and open holes
in roofs and become more part of the solution and less part
of the problems in the world.

So my suspicion is that if you stop now and open your heart,
you'll realise that just outside the front door of your consciousness there are some needy people. A relative or co-worker. A
neighbour or friend. Someone you heard about on the radio,

read about in the news, or saw on TV. If you slow down for a few minutes, there will be other neighbours – non-human ones – that will also come to mind – endangered species, threatened ecosystems, plundered landscapes. And now is your chance to enter into their pain.

Now is your chance to bear the stretcher by feeling its weight and carrying it to God, sharing it with God, joining God in the vital connection of compassion, generosity and kindness.

> Christ has no body here but ours, no hands or feet here
>   on earth but ours.
> Ours are the eyes through which he looks on this world
>   with kindness.
> Ours are the hands through which he works. Ours are
>   the feet on which he moves.
> Ours are the voices through which he speaks to this
>   world with kindness.
> Through our touch, our smile, our listening ear,
> Embodied in us, Jesus is living here.
> So let us go now, filled with the Spirit, into this world
> With kindness.[10]

Three
Perplexity: The Season of Spiritual Surviving

Perplexity

You are alone. Even God seems to have abandoned you. Here in this bitter space, answered prayers of the past seem like ironic coincidences, a cruel joke. You're like a gambler, who after a string of gambling wins is tempted to risk everything on rolling the dice for a seven. But you roll a two and a four, and now, you've lost everything you previously gained. You're not just back to where you started. You're worse off, because when you started you had hope. You felt lucky. Now you feel abandoned, cursed.

In simplicity we reach out to God in happiness. We see the world as it should be. God is with us here, and through invocation we acknowledge God's *here-ness*. God blesses us, and through thanksgiving we pour out our gratitude to God – *Thanks!* God is wonderful, and through worship we overflow in wonder that can't be contained in normal speech – *O!*

In complexity, we reach out to God in struggle. We cry *Sorry!* as, through confession, we refuse to deny, cover or excuse our wrongs and we instead name them, express regret and receive mercy. We cry *Help!* as, through petition, we turn our anxieties into requests, and we learn to share our needs and burdens with God so we will not be preoccupied with ourselves. And we cry *Please!* As, through intercession, we respond to the needs and pain of others by joining our compassion with God's. In each case, a spiritual practice has provided us a way of coping and surviving – and more, of overcoming and thriving, of *winning*.

But sometimes, there is no winning. There are no solutions or answers or consolations in sight. The spring of simplicity and the summer of complexity slip away, and now the autumn winds of perplexity blow in a biting cold rain. Now, what matters most to us – more than being right, more than being effective – is being honest, authentic, even brutally so. We've moved from a dualistic and pragmatic mindset to a relativistic and critical one. Leaders we once admired as correct authority figures and confident coaches we now suspect of being frauds – pretending to know more than they do, proclaiming their opinions as facts, misleading and manipulating the naïve for their own selfish purposes. Life itself is no longer the simple war or the complex game it used to be for us. On our bad days it's a joke, and on our good days it's a quest, and most days it's a bit of both.

We've grown beyond being dependent infants who look to their leaders for everything, and beyond being somewhat independent children who boast, 'I can do it myself!' Now we have become counter-dependent – perhaps like adolescents who find our identity among a small band of similarly alienated friends. If we acquired our faith in Simplicity or Complexity, we will probably doubt it now and may even abandon it for a while. At the very least, we will need to add margin for mystery and unbolt some of the structural elements of our faith that have been until now tightly fitted together. Our faith becomes less the nest and more the quest at this stage, and God evokes feelings of ambivalence. It's a great season for honesty and for digging deeper, but not so great for commitment, energy, or enthusiasm.

For all its angst, there's beauty in perplexity, the autumn blaze of colour between green and gone. There's the strength of ruthless honesty, the courage of dogged endurance, the companionship of the disillusioned, the determination of the long-distance runner who won't give up even though he's exhausted. In that act of not giving up, there is faith too, and hope, perhaps the most vibrant faith and hope of all.

There's a special catalytic moment that comes late in the season of perplexity. Having practised critical thinking about the thoughts and beliefs of others, thinkers turn their critical eye on their own thinking. They become sceptical about their scepticism and cynical about their cynicism. And in so doing, they begin to push themselves beyond perplexity. But it's a long, hard road between here and there.

Chapter 16

When? How Long Can I Last?

The Practice of Aspiration, Exasperation and Desperation: Surviving Through Delay

Alternative words: How long? Where?

> Whenever I get depressed by a lack of spiritual progress,
> I realise that my very dismay is a sign of progress.
>
> Philip Yancey[1]

I began writing this chapter in the days after a catastrophic earthquake devastated Haiti, and continued writing as a catastrophic oil spill devastated the Gulf of Mexico. I've heard one question again and again over these months: how long? How long until help comes? How long until the spill is contained? When will things be made right?

When news of the earthquake broke, death projections started at 10,000 and quickly went to 50,000. Then they rose to 100,000, and then the estimate doubled again. When the count reached 230,000, I read an article about all the ways God was being brought into the tragedy. One televangelist said God was punishing Haiti. Another preacher said that it was all part of God's plan, even though we can't understand it.

Another said it was a sign of the end times. Their words felt like sand in my mouth. Even though I am a believer in God, I felt more in sync with a young person being interviewed on the street of Port-au-Prince who said he no longer could believe in a God who would crush babies, children and the elderly between slabs of concrete.

When the death toll was still at 50,000, I received this email from my friend Kent who has lived and worked in Haiti for many years. He helped start an NGO to make a difference there and he knows and loves Haiti in a profound way.[2] My soul finds comfort in his words, something that tastes real and right, though I'm not sure why:

> I believe in the God who multiplied fish and loaves to feed the hungry. I believe in the God who says I'm always with you. And right now, it's achingly clear – heartbreakingly, angrily clear – isn't it, that we who believe also believe in the God who is hidden sometimes, sometimes when we are most in need, to whom the Psalmist cried out, 'How long, oh Lord, how long?'
>
> How long?
>
> Too long. There's no other answer right now. People are being rescued, but too many aren't, and 50,000 never will be. There will be other answers in the weeks and months ahead, but right now the only answer is, too long.

Too long. Those words often apply to things within our control – our procrastination in working for needed political reform, our delay in turning from dirty to clean energy, our slowness in preventing preventable diseases and in acknowledging personal and social addictions, our failure to resolve conflicts and address the problems we love to complain about.

Sometimes, those words apply to things beyond our control, like earthquakes and God.

In the spiritual spring of simplicity, life is a gentle river in which we flow merrily and prayer is the song we sing in joy. Everything feels under control. Then, in the spiritual summer of complexity, life becomes a stretch of rapids we must run, a game that we think we can win or a challenge we think we can master, and prayer is a key element of our strategy. Through prayer we often shoot the rapids, win the game, master the challenge, regain control. Often, but not always.

Just as simplicity once gave way to complexity, now complexity gives way to perplexity. Things are out of control and we can't get them fixed anytime soon. After an earthquake, after a phone call from the police, after a psychiatrist's or oncologist's report, after a letter from the Board of Directors, after an explosion or collapse or meltdown, the coping strategies that carried us thus far stop working.

For example, in confession, what happens when our faults overwhelm us? What happens when we have sabotaged our success and wounded others we love through our stupidity? What happens when being forgiven is simply insufficient consolation, because we need more than relief from guilt: we need to stop doing what we're doing and change for the better? What happens when, pray as we might, vicious cycles spin and spin, gears grind, and we go nowhere?

In petition, what happens when we're praying, praying more fervently than we ever have, but the wisdom we need is not forthcoming, the self-control we seek is deteriorating, endurance has blinked out like a spent candle, and hope stopped singing hours ago? We've faced a long string of calamities, and each time we prayed the very opposite happened – what then?

Or in intercession, what happens when the death toll keeps doubling, and the oil spill keeps gushing, when the suffering seems so great that we begin losing our ability to sustain belief that God is compassionate or that compassion matters? What happens when the score is suffering 142 to compassion zero, and we have despaired of compassion ever even scoring, much less catching up? What happens when we do all in our power to help those in need, yet God seems well-meaning but impotent, or distant and unwilling to help, or blankly, frankly non-existent in the face of a rising tide of pain? What good is all this sentimental rhetoric about naked spirituality when death and evil seem to be winning by a landslide?

If the season of simplicity is like smooth sailing and complexity is like running rapids, sooner or later you smash on some rocks, you get swamped, you lose buoyancy. Your little boat of faith springs one leak, then two, then five or seven, and no matter how hard you bail through confession, petition and intercession, you have to acknowledge that the water level is rising and your boat is going down, and the roar of more rapids awaits you downstream.

Maybe you've never experienced the kind of spiritual sinking we're going to explore in the coming chapters. Maybe you believe you never will. Maybe, in fact, you are angry with anyone who would dare doubt that God will solve all problems and keep us afloat if we simply work the confession, petition and intercession programme according to the sermons of well-meaning Stage Two preachers. Maybe you will be able to maintain this illusion until you die. But maybe you should take these chapters seriously anyway, just in case, just in case you aren't as smart and invulnerable as you think you are at this moment.

I remember the first time I entered the spiritual autumn of perplexity. I was in college. I had learned the arts of invocation, thanksgiving and worship. I was well-versed in confession, petition and intercession. I frequently experienced dramatic answers to my prayers, and I regularly experienced powerful 'touches' of the Holy Spirit – what some would call baptisms and others would call fillings and still others would call anointings or movings of the Spirit. I was working the programme – praying, reading my Bible, experiencing fellowship, witnessing to my faith and leading others to Christ – but then the programme stopped working.

It wasn't just that I no longer felt the warm summer breezes that I had grown accustomed to. I had experienced down times, dry times, flat times before, when God's presence wasn't as present or perceptible to my soul. This time was different because day after day, week after week, I felt the cold, damp, grey absence of God. Positive, palpable absence, not just the lack of presence, became the elephant in the room. And in the chilling bluster of that naked absence, all of my previous experiences of God seemed utterly inaccessible. Yes, I remembered they happened, but I doubted they had ever been real.

I wondered if maybe it had all been a kind of psycho-spiritual illusion, a mirage conjured by heatwaves rising from a summer highway. When I prayed, I thought, 'I'm just talking to myself – there's nobody really there to listen, much less answer.' When I read the Bible, I thought, 'This seems like a bunch of legends and mythology. And a lot of it is pretty barbaric.' When I attended church, I thought, 'These people are deep into a kind of social make-believe, a hyped-up group-think, a choreographed role-play. They're like little boys playing army or little girls playing house. It's just a game of pretend – pretence manipulated through the tradition and hierarchy of a priestly class that's making a good living.' I didn't want to think these things. But I couldn't help it.

At first, I felt sad. I grieved my loss of feeling God's presence. But the grief was nothing compared to what came next: fear.

The fear ran along these lines: what happens if the feeling of God's presence never comes back? What happens if my simple, strong, confident faith never returns? How long can I last in this wasteland? How long before I die of thirst in this scorching desert, or freeze in this cold rain that is fast changing over to sleet?

How long will this dry season last? When will this cold emptiness end? When? When?! That is the question of the first prayer in the season of perplexity. I want to call it the prayer of delay, fear or frustration, but there is a slightly more hopeful term that has found a place in spiritual theology, largely thanks to the Wesley brothers, John and Charles, and their early Methodist hymnals: *aspiration.*

Aspiration has two meanings. More literally, aspiration means inhalation – breathing in. More figuratively, it means any abiding hunger or thirst – the intense, persistent desire to receive something you don't have, to become something you are not yet. Put the two together, and you get close to what I'm describing here: a breathless, gasping longing, a life-and-death thirst, a deep and passionate – even desperate – desire to survive and thrive as a person of authentic faith.

John Wesley taught the early Methodists that a higher form of Christian living was possible – a state which he described as entire sanctification.[3] When people believed him – and millions did – they had to acknowledge that their actual lives of semi-sanctification, pseudo-sanctification or faux-sanctification fell far below the standard of entire sanctification they now believed was possible. The gap between the desired possible life with God and the possessed actual life found expression – not in polite, genteel, restrained, refined classical music – but in the passionate songs and choruses of spiritual *enthusiasm*, a term that carried a sense of condescension or even derision in those days. Here is an example:[4]

> Drooping soul, shake off thy fears,
> Fearful soul, be strong, be bold;
> Tarry till the Lord appears,
> Never, never quit thy hold!
> Murmur not at His delay,
> Dare not set thy God a time;
> Calmly for His coming stay,
> Leave it, leave it all to Him.

One feels the tension – the desire to receive all that God offers immediately, yet the frustration, the 'drooping', at what seems like a delay. A similar hymn asks, 'Why not now?'

> Why not now, my God, my God!
> Ready if Thou always art,
> Make in me Thy mean [humble] abode,
> Take possession of my heart?
> If Thou canst so greatly bow,
> Friend of sinners, why not now?

184

Another hymn wonders if the time of waiting for 'full redemption' has ended, and captures the tension of aspiration in the gap between 'dying, if thou still delay' and 'enter now ... now':

> God of love, if this my day
> For Thyself to Thee I cry;
> Dying, if Thou still delay
> Must I not for ever die?
> Enter now Thy poorest home,
> Now, my utmost Saviour, come!

Early aspiration is fervent, eager, positive – grasping for more and better. Eventually, though, unsatisfied aspiration becomes frustration and then exasperation, as the gasping soul grows impatient, oxygen-starved, parched and famished, and desperate for something – a touch of grace, a feeling of assurance – to conquer an invasion of doubt and despair, before it's too late.

As time goes on, *When?* and *How long?* give way to *Where?* Where have you gone, God? Where are you? *When? How long? Where?* These prayers of aspiration, exasperation and desperation groan out from our souls as we hope against hope that an answer will come before too long.

Chapter 17

When? Survival Is Under-rated

Step 1: We admitted we were powerless over our addiction
– that our lives had become unmanageable.

Step 2: Came to believe that a Power greater than ourselves
could restore us to sanity.

> The Twelve Steps of Alcoholics Anonymous

You can feel aspiration morphing into exasperation and desperation in a song lyric written almost three thousand years before
the hymns of early Methodism. In Psalm 42, the poet moves
from a tender image of thirst to the urgent question *when?*

> As a deer longs for flowing streams,
> so my soul longs for you, O God.
> My soul thirsts for God,
> for the living God.
> When shall I come and behold the face of God?

The psalmist's thirst, it turns out, has been mockingly quenched
– not with fulfilment of 'flowing streams', but with his constant
flow of salty tears. Just as his tears mock his thirst, so others
mock him for his spiritual depression: shouldn't his God be

meeting his needs? Their words, he says later (42:10), are like a mortal wound to his body:

> My tears have been my food
> day and night,
> while people say to me continually,
> 'Where is your God?'

One senses the bitter contrast between the delayed presence of comfort and the constant presence of unfulfilment. Meanwhile, each good memory of joyful times – those bright days when he felt spiritual fulfilment together with his peers – now only darkens his long nights of alienation and pain.

> These things I remember,
> as I pour out my soul:
> how I went with the throng,
> and led them in procession to the house of God,
> with glad shouts and songs of thanksgiving,
> a multitude keeping festival.

Then comes the refrain:

> Why are you cast down, O my soul,
> and why are you disquieted within me?
> Hope in God; for I shall again praise him,
> my help and my God.

The *why* of this refrain – addressed to his own soul – is mirrored by another even more disturbing *why* question, addressed to God (v. 9): 'Why have you forgotten me?'

187

All these questions go unanswered: When? How long? Where? Why? Yet above the prayer of aspiration a tattered flag of faith and hope still flies: 'Hope in God, for I shall again praise him.' That simple word *again* – vague and undefined, but real – seeks to answer the painful question *when*. It doesn't dare claim 'soon'; instead it more modestly claims 'someday'.

You ask 'When? How long?' because you know – or at least you believe – or at least you hope – that your panting, gasping, famished feelings of unfulfilled longing, abandonment and confusion won't go on forever. A sense of peace and fullness will come *again*, *someday*, like spring. And so, as you wait … in the meantime, in the October of loss, through chilly November, into December with its cruelly short dim days and cruelly long cold nights. You talk to yourself: 'Why are you cast down? Hope in God.' And you talk to God: 'Why have you forgotten me? My soul longs for you!' And like a beginner repeating a mantra, or like a cheerleader trying to rouse a weary team – When? Again! When? Again! When? Again! – you survive, one day, one moment at a time.

Many years ago I came across a sturdy old poem by Annie Johnson Flint, called *What God Has Promised*. It's the kind of poem one might find on a greeting card or wall plaque, but it begins with a rather surprising dose of honesty:

> God has not promised
> Skies always blue,
> Flower-strewn pathways
> All our lives through.
>
> God has not promised
> Sun without rain,

Joy without sorrow,
Peace without pain.

Then comes the affirmation:

But God has promised
Strength for the day
Rest for the labour
Light for the way;

Grace for the trials
Help from above
Unfailing sympathy
Undying love.

Beneath the sing-song rhythm and greeting-card rhymes hides a poem of disillusionment. The blue-sky flower-strewn illusions of false faith must be sorted from the realities of good faith – complete with rain, sorrow, pain, labour and trials. And that process takes time. And pain. And so, through delay, through frustration, through hardships that we feel can't be endured another minute, our desire is tested and stretched almost to the breaking point. Day after day we express desire – for 'full redemption', for 'entire sanctification', for 'a more perfect union', for an end to a season of spiritual depression and dryness, for the gap between our dreams and reality to be narrowed. In so doing, we keep our desire alive. Alive for one more day. One more step. One more moment. For this *now* we aren't giving up. And *this* now. And *this*.

'How long, O Lord?' we ask, like children wondering when they will finally arrive at their destination. 'How much longer?'

we ask, like a runner building up aerobic strength, fortifying our faith by pushing it to its limits, yearning for the next milestone, dreaming of the finish line, weary and breathless but refusing to stop.

That might not seem like much. But it is survival, and survival is underrated.

Sometimes survival is a victory in itself.

Now my mind goes back to my friend Kent and his many friends in Haiti. How long before they receive water and food? When will medical care come? How long will they feel abandoned and vulnerable? How long until Haiti sees better days? Where was God when the earth shook? Where is God now?

And now my imagination travels down a mile below the Gulf of Mexico, where again today, 60,000 to 100,000 barrels of oil are surging into the ocean, creating catastrophic consequences that we can't imagine. When will it be stopped? How? Where was God when politicians cut deals with corporate executives, careless of their impacts on dolphins, sea turtles, seagulls and millions of people? How long will this kind of greed-driven exploitation continue? When will answers come? When will new technologies be discovered? When will we convert from dirty to clean energy? When?

Things may be going just fine for you right now, smooth sailing, everything under control. But beneath a calm exterior, pressure may also be mounting. Unfulfilled aspiration may be fermenting into exasperation, and exasperation boiling into desperation. Counsellors tell us that if we don't find healthy ways to express this rising emotional pressure, it will turn inward and become depression – sometimes manifesting in a slow burn-out and sometimes in a fast flame-out. As with an earthquake or an oil spill, the results can be catastrophic.

So now is the time to put this book aside and acknowledge the growing pressure hidden beneath the surface. Now is the time to listen to the impatience growing within you and to express it, not just to yourself, but to the Spirit. It might feel like a groan: *When? How long?* It might feel like an accusation: *So when, then? How much longer then?* Its tone might be eager, frightened, fatigued, or even angry. Whatever it is, rather than letting the pressure build to unhealthy levels, how about learning to express it through this practice of aspiration, exasperation and desperation?

Hold your *when?* or *how long?* or *where?* before God. Make space for your disappointment, frustration and unfulfilment to come out of hiding and present themselves in the light. Don't rush, even though you'll be tempted to see these times of spiritual dryness and aspiration as a mistake, a sign of failure you want to put behind you. Instead, slow down and hold this moment as an opportunity to express and strengthen spiritual desire. Realise that the Spirit doesn't want to shame you for groaning for fulfilment and release: the Spirit wants to join you, to empathise with you, to intensify your desire, not deny it.

So feel it; don't fear it. Just as the only way to stretch or strengthen a muscle is to bring it to the point of ache, the only way to strengthen a desire is to stretch it, to draw it out, to force it, through unfulfilment, to last longer. And that hurts. So it's OK to let it out like an 'ouch': *This hurts! How long must it last? I don't like this! When will it end? I can't last much longer. Where are you?* If it helps, you might think of yourself as complaining to God, letting God know that you aren't satisfied and you won't just go away. You're banging on God's door and won't give God any rest until your thirst receives some satisfaction. Things will either get better or worse. If they get better, you'll appreciate the relief all the more because of the intensity and persistence of your holding your *when?* or *where?* or *how long?* before God. If they get worse, your refusal now to be satisfied will only strengthen and energise you for what's to come later on.

This space of unfulfilment is a kind of void. And since the time of the Roman philosopher Lucretius, insightful thinkers have seen in a void something more than absence.[1] A void creates, in fact, a kind of power. Without a void within it, a sponge would lose the power to absorb moisture. Air would lose the power to transmit sound or scent. In fact, nothing could move if there weren't space – a void – into which it could pass. Here's how Lucretius said it:

> But now through oceans, lands, and heights of heaven
> By divers causes and in divers modes,
> Before our eyes we mark how much may move,
> Which, finding not a void, would fail deprived
> Of stir and motion; nay, would then have been
> Nowise begot at all, since matter, then,
> Had staid at rest, its parts together crammed.
> Then too, however solid objects seem,
> They yet are formed of matter mixed with void.[2]

Through the autumn-like season of perplexity, the void expands. Unfulfilment grows. And this is in no way pleasurable. But as Lucretius realised, the creation of empty space makes way for movement, for new potential, for new empowerment.

But sadly, none of that is visible now.

Chapter 18

No! The Void Expands

The Practice of Rage and Refusal: Surviving Through Disillusionment

No Alternative Words.

> If you have a false idea of God, the more religious you
> are, the worse it is for you – it were better for you to be
> an atheist.
>
> William Temple[1]

Sometimes, I think most times, the prayer of aspiration works
like a long doorless passageway. You keep trudging along, on
and on, until finally, when you are about to collapse on the
floor in fatigue or boredom, you come to a door. You turn the
latch and it clicks and the door opens and suddenly you're
outside.

Or it's like a song you keep singing through the long dry
season, day after day, sweating and surviving, trying to keep
the tune of faith alive on your lips or in your mind, humming,
How long? How long? And then one afternoon as you're
humming the tune, off in the distance you hear thunder, and
you see the hump of a grey cloud rise on the horizon, and

soon on your sunburned skin you feel a breeze with a certain moist scent you can barely remember. And then, before you know it, you are standing, laughing, dancing in a downpour of joy. The presence of God again baptises you. Your season in the wilderness ends. *When?* gives way to *again*. You break through.

Usually. But sometimes it doesn't go that way.

Sometimes the passageway goes on and on and when you come to a door and open it, it's a dark, damp closet that leads nowhere. Or the rains don't come, the crops wither in the fields, the herds start dying and you lie down on your bed and wait to die too.

What do you do now as aspiration sours into exasperation? What word forms in your soul as you curl up in a foetal position in the closet, or as you lie back on your bed as if it were a cross? The merciful parts of me hope that you never have to find this out, that you'll never need to know what I'm about to tell you. I hoped I would never need to know it. But here it is, just in case.

In these moments, you raise your fists and you rage at God. *No!* you shout. *No!* you scream. *No!* you groan. Curse if you must and cry if you can. But whatever you do, don't be silent. Don't let your fury and disappointment harden and die into a cold, silent ice of bitterness in you. Keep it hot. Keep it fermenting, churning, restless, unwilling to be denied. Keep shouting, *No!*

This practice of refusal may sound like unbelief. It may sound like blasphemy. But don't be fooled. Those who rage at God believe there is a God who is willing to be raged at. That belief is a quivering spark that can again be fanned into flame. It's those who have stopped raging and have lapsed into a frigid, rigid silence whom you should pity and for whom you should grieve. The ragers' fury and apparent unbelief signal a deeper faith that still survives: that a God worth believing and loving should not have let things go this way. The fact that things have gone this way – that things have ended up like this – may lead them to believe that God has failed. And so, they may punish God with fury and insult, blasphemy and invective, mockery and derision.

Reactive believers may try to silence them: 'Don't talk that way!' they'll say. They might even threaten with damnation those who rage. But what they don't see is this: the god the angry are punishing deserves to be punished. Beneath or behind that failed god is another G-d, one whose higher standard exposes the false, failed god as a fraud. The rage wouldn't exist if some vision of the truer-God-behind-the-false-god didn't remain. Perhaps by his raging against the failed image of God, it will fall, and behind it the truer G-d will appear, the truer G-d to whom Meister Eckhart prayed, 'God save me from god.'

This is why doubters, atheists and sceptics have an important place in the community of faith.[2] The acid of their critique flows – even though they may not realise it – from their sadness that a truer, brighter, bigger, better God isn't showing up, but only a second-rate imposter god. And their *No!* is a dual rejection: first, it is a refusal to accept the second-rate imposter god's presence, and second, it is a refusal to accept the true and living G-d's absence. Can you see the remarkable faith and virtue disguised in that *No!*?

It is here, in this moment of rage and refusal, that most of us have to face more directly a thousand-and-one thorny intellectual questions about God, prayer and the spiritual life. We have kept these questions at bay for months, years, even decades.

These simmering questions, pushed to the back burners of our mind, now begin to boil over. We wonder: If God is all-good and all-powerful, why wouldn't God have already chosen to aid a needy person apart from our intercession? Does God lack goodwill without our coaxing? Why has God allowed this person or group – or me – to suffer in the first place? How could God create a world where lovers are separated, where precious little girls are raped, where mothers send their sons off to war to be killed or to kill the sons of other mothers, where parents give birth to children with severe diseases, or children nurse their parents through years of mental illness or dementia in its varied forms? Was it a lack of effective advanced universe-planning? If God's goodness and compassion would never plan for suffering, and if God's wisdom and power would never allow it to go unchallenged, how can it exist – and not only in rare instances, but pervasively, horrifically, enduringly?

This rolling boil of intellectual questions leaves us with four logical options:

Either A) there is no suffering and there is no God, or B) there is no suffering and there is a God, or C) there is suffering and there is no God, or D) there is suffering and there is a God.

If suffering didn't exist, we wouldn't have a problem, so we know that A and B aren't true. That leaves us with C and D. If C is true, there is no intellectual problem, but neither is there a source of spiritual resources to deal with suffering. (Actually, there is an intellectual problem: why does it bother us to accept as a fact that suffering is pervasive and mean-ingless?) If D is true, there is an intellectual problem, but there is also a source of spiritual resources to deal with suffering.

If we're left with a choice between C and D, D seems to be

the most hopeful choice, but it leaves us in tension. We don't deny the reality of suffering on the one hand, nor do we deny the possibility of God on the other.

Again, this acknowledgement certainly does not constitute an answer to the intellectual problem of pain. I believe there are answers on a certain level. But even the best answers are terribly unsatisfying, and they work better in a classroom than in a hospital room, earthquake aftermath, or crime scene. They provide only cold comfort to a person in agony, and often, as they solve one intellectual quandary, they create twenty-two more. As C. S. Lewis famously and wisely stated, the best answers don't do as much good for a person in pain as a dose of courage does.[3] So to pray on in the face of outrageous suffering, it seems to me, is at heart a choice of courage and hope, even if the prayers sound like blasphemies to observers.

So we shout, *No!* No – I will not reject God! But no, no, no, neither will I deny my questions either! *No!* I will not cave into despair, but no, neither will I be pacified with unsatisfying answers or superficial comfort! *No!*

Interestingly, the Scriptures are less shy about raging spirituality than we typically are. Consider these agonising opening words of Psalm 77:

> I cried out to God for help;
> I cried out to God to hear me.
> When I was in distress, I sought the Lord;
> at night I stretched out untiring hands... (NIV)

And what comes next? 'And God answered my prayer and comforted me?' No! The psalmist rages, '*... and my soul refused to be comforted*.' Did thoughts of God bring peace? No! The psalmist laments, 'I remembered you, O God, and I groaned; I mused, and my spirit grew faint.' The more I think about it, he says, the more drained I feel! And then, as if to refuse to let us move forward to quickly seeking some relief, he adds, 'Selah', which is either a call to pause and ponder, or a signal for a pensive musical interlude to be played, or more likely, both.

The Psalmist (identified as Asaph) continues to feel his spiritual agony. God keeps his eyes from closing. He is speechless with pain. He wonders if God has decisively rejected him forever, if God will never be gracious again, if God's so-called unfailing love has failed, if God's promise has turned out to be a bitter lie, if God has got amnesia and forgotten how to be merciful and compassionate. Then, he turns his thoughts to the stories of long ago – the epic stories of God's faithfulness in the past, and this seems to bring him some comfort.

But even if Asaph in Psalm 77 can come to the ledge of rage and then back away, the Korahites in Psalm 88 cannot. Their poet-protagonist begins by begging God – 'the God who saves me' – to hear him, and things go downhill from there.

'My soul is full of trouble,' he says. 'I feel like hell … my strength is gone. I'm forgotten by you and cut off from your care. You've thrown me into a deep pit of depression. Your anger batters me like a cold and bitter surf, and I'm drowning. You have turned my friends against me. They now are disgusted with me because of you. You've trapped me in a cramped cell and I'm going blind with rage and despair.'

Even though he calls out to God, even though every day he spreads out his hands in sincere petition, God doesn't answer. Questions beseige him, questions echoing in an empty room. 'The God who saves me' has in fact destroyed me, he says

(v. 16). A tsunami of terror has swept him off his feet and he is now absolutely helpless, carried away by a roiling flood of despair. And in contrast to Psalm 77, here there is not even a faint whisper of hope at the end. Feel the crushing bleakness of these final words:

> You have taken my companions and loved ones from me;
> The darkness is my closest friend. (NIV)

Can you dare to feel this abandonment? Can you dare to pray this kind of raging prayer and hold open this feverish void?

Can you see the faith in it? Can you see how, no less than Psalm 23 with its green pastures and still waters, this prayer of raging despair is also a prayer of faith, because 'the valley of the shadow of death' is for this psalmist not just a possibility, but the actual Death-Valley geography from which he prays? Can you see the primal, indestructible diamond of faith being formed under the unfathomable pressures of feeling utterly abandoned and betrayed by God?

This daring word *No!* has more holiness to it than it gets credit for. Through it, we refuse to let God off the hook. We demand not to be abandoned. We reject the status quo, deny its status as acceptable. We stamp our foot in God's presence, no, more, we raise our fist and say, 'I will not accept this!' And at the same time, our *No!* is directed at unbelief: we obstinately refuse to let life with God degenerate into life without God. No!

We've come a long way from that simple word *here*. Now God appears to be *nowhere*. That doesn't seem like progress.

Chapter 19

No! Mad With God

The best way to pray is: stop. Let prayer pray within you, whether you know it or not. This means a deep awareness of our true inner identity. It implies a life of faith, but also of doubt. You can't have faith without doubt. Give up the business of suppressing doubt. Doubt and faith are two sides of the same thing. Faith will grow out of doubt, the real doubt. We don't pray right because we evade doubt.

Thomas Merton[1]

When we think of a fist raised in rage against God, we think of poor Job. But I must admit, I struggle with the structure of the book of Job. I often feel that the deep middle of Job has been betrayed by the addition of a shallow preface and dishonest epilogue. It's as if Job's comforters, whom God silences as a bunch of pious ninnies at the end of the middle section, sneak back and add a preface and epilogue, in order to get the last word after all. But however one reads the beginning and end, the middle of Job rings with Job's refusal to wallpaper over the ugly cracks in reality. For him, better to see the ugliness than to cover it with an insipid, sentimental flowery print of pretentious pseudo-piety.[2] And scandalously, God agrees with Job.

Consider how scandalous it is: here is a document declared to be part of the canon of inspired Scripture. But perhaps sixty per cent of it – or whatever the exact portion uttered by Job's so-called comforters might be – is called a gust of hot, empty air, first by Job and then by God (16:3; 38:2)! And their puerile chatter contains – again, we have to face it – exactly the kind of sweet, simple logic we find in Deuteronomy and Proverbs, and in the preface and epilogue of Job itself: bad things happen to bad people and good things happen to good people. How do we reconcile this tension?

Of course, the answer is, we don't reconcile it. We don't say, 'There is no justice in the world.' But neither do we say, 'There is a simple, clear, black-and-white justice in the world.' Instead, we do what Job does, and what the Bible as a whole does: we live with the tension and we feel its pain, and we let the discomfort churn within us. We abandon hope of an explanation that will let us happily and easily accept reality as it is. And something happens when we make this move: when we refuse all easier alternatives, we find our hearts being strangely empowered. We grow resolute, determined to throw our lives into the cause of justice, comfort, compassion and healing, aiming our *No!* at all that is hateful, unjust, false, foolish. And whenever the pain proves unbearable, we shout to God in the prayer of rage and refusal.

Things are not as they should be in our world. Nor are things as they should be in our own lives – in our emotions, in our thinking, in our behaviour, in our relationships. *No!* is the response to all that is unacceptable. It is a refusal to accept the unacceptable. The descendants of those who gave us Psalms 77 and 88, the book of Job and the rabbi Jesus know this refusal too well.[3]

In 1953, the Israeli Parliament created a solemn day of commemoration called Yom Hashoah to memorialise the Holocaust of the previous decade. The day was set aside to mourn the lives of six million killed by the Nazis between 1938 and 1945. More recently, the Conservative Jewish movement created the first formal liturgy for use on Yom Hashoah, entitled *Megillat Hashoah*, meaning 'The Scroll of the Holocaust'. It is, my wise friend Duane Shank explains,

> ... built largely around first-person testimonies. After an opening chapter that gives a searing overview of the victims' suffering, it offers composite sketches of a Christian journalist observing life in the Warsaw Ghetto, a Jewish woman in a work camp and a Jewish youth who was forced to pull out the teeth from his brother's corpse and shove other dead bodies into ovens. A fifth chapter consists of a eulogy for those who died in the Holocaust; the final chapter recounts the efforts to rebuild Jewish life after the war ended.
>
> It is also intended to address some of the theological questions raised by the Holocaust.... The overriding theological message of the *Megillat* [Scroll] is that human beings have a right to question the divine, but they cannot expect answers – and that even without answers, the Jewish faith in God endures. The *Megillat* ends with the exhortation: 'Do not mourn too much, but do not sink into the forgetfulness of apathy. Do not allow days of darkness to return; weep, but wipe the tears away. Do not absolve and do not exonerate, do not attempt to understand. Learn to live without an answer. Through our blood, live!'[4]

No! isn't a rejection of God: it's a refusal to accept unsatisfying attempts to let God off the hook. And it's a parallel refusal to give up hope altogether. Perhaps you can see how the post-Holocaust cry of 'Never again' is an alternative expression of the *No!* of raging prayer. Perhaps, when you look into the abyss of human suffering and evil, you can see how desperately we need this painful, heroic, faithfully doubting spiritual practice. Otherwise, it's too easy to sink 'into the forgetfulness of apathy'.

Our outrage is addressed to God, but it isn't aimed at God, or at least not at the G-d we hope exists. We may be furious with the disappointing god who apparently exists, but our *No!* faithfully calls out to the better G-d who we hope exists. We aren't mad at *that* G-d, though in our pain we may express it this way at times. Instead, we are mad *with* G-d – *with* G-d raging *against* the monstrous false god who appears to rule in these outrageous circumstances. We share our outrage with G-d – the real and hoped-for G-d, and we express it in the presence of G-d – in confidence that this 'most high' G-d will understand our disappointment with the mid-level pseudo-gods we inherited. G-d won't be made insecure by our honesty, we realise, and G-d can handle it. After all, we believe that G-d, of all beings, is the one most incapable of accepting the unacceptable or being apathetic in the presence of evil and injustice and pain. *No!*, then, is actually a *Yes!* to a deep and pure belief – that G-d, if G-d exists, would rather us be honest doubters than hypocritical believers, and that G-d, if G-d exists, is even more implacably opposed to and heartbroken about the status quo than we are.

But the practice of refusal doesn't feel like a *yes* most of the time. It feels like death.[5] And then it gets worse.

The most powerful dramatic moment possible in Greek theatre, according to Aristotle, is called *peripeteia*. The agony of *peripeteia* brings a complete reversal in a person's understanding of his life. Think of the moment in Sophocles' *Oedipus Rex* when the protagonist discovers that he has killed his own father and married his own mother. Everything that seemed true about his life is shown to be false, and what seemed false and impossible is shown to be true. Such a moment of breakdown might be called a paradigm crash, and it plunges one into the deepest kind of pain imaginable. In the face of *peripeteia*, one can only cry, groan, shout, rage and cry some more: *No!*

Oedipus Rex ends with Oedipus being led away to exile beyond the borders of his beloved Thebes. He has blinded himself as a kind of self-punishment for failing to see the truth. His daughters, born of his unintentional incest, have been brought to say a tearful goodbye. He begs that they be allowed to accompany him, since they have nothing to look forward to in Thebes except shame and rejection. But his pathetic plea receives this stern answer, the tragedy's penultimate lines: 'Crave not mastery in all, for the mastery that raised you was your bane and wrought your fall.'

Job reaches a similar tragic moment in his story. Job's wife, you may recall, offers Job a way out of his pain: 'Curse God and die,' she says. Her words may be a euphemism for suicide, or they may imagine Job so angering God that a lightning bolt will come and put him out of his misery. Whatever her words intend, they suggest an end to the rage and refusal. *Get it over with*, they say. But Job, like the *Megillat Hashoah*, refuses to get it over with. He refuses both the false comfort of his friends and the false escape of his wife. Through his refusal he chooses to live, but to do so loudly, shouting his fury to the end.

After Job vents his fury, Elihu, a young man filled with the arrogant, angry piety of the stupid, self-assured zealot, explodes 'like bottled-up wine' because he is 'full of words' (32:18–19). Full indeed, full of something, for he blusters on for six long chapters. As he does, apparently, a storm approaches, which he describes in great detail, and it is out of that storm that the voice of the Lord finally comes. And the voice of the Lord comes, not with answers, but with a tornado of questions.[6] And in the face of those questions, Job feebly replies, 'How can I reply? I will say no more.' Another torrent of questions deluges him, and he replies similarly, in resignation, 'Surely I spoke of things I did not understand, things too wonderful for me to know.'

And here, it seems, we come to the end of refusal: to the point where we simply say, 'I don't know. I don't understand.' And after that, we are silent. That silence is painful. And golden.

Could it be that here the Greeks and the Jews agree – that a tragic thread runs through every life, and it unravels in the end in an agonizing *peripeteia*? That life conspires to bring us to the realisation that, contrary to everything we have known or hoped, we actually have no control, no mastery, no explanation, no argument, no understanding? That we stand (as songwriter Bruce Cockburn said it), in front of all this beauty – and agony – *understanding nothing?*[7]

Perhaps there hides in our shout of *No!* a defiant denial, a remaining shred of mastery and control, a lingering refusal to accept the truth of our smallness. Perhaps we refuse to the very last moment to accept the truth: that we are not in fact kings and masters of our destiny; that we are not good men and women who have things figured out. But rather that we all, even King Oedipus and righteous Job, are small, frail, contingent creatures. Could this be the tragic moment towards which our lives inevitably run like water towards the lowest point – the moment when our *No!* sheds that last shred of self-delusion? Can there be, beyond the *No!* of rage with all its ambivalence and tension, a *No!* of recognition? Could our rage and refusal exhaust itself so that our *No!* changes in tone from fury to lament?

We will never know if we try to rush the process, if we try to avoid *peripeteia*, if we refuse refusal. And so we must let this horrible moment crash upon us like a merciless wave, wash over us in all its grinding power, pull us down, push us down, hold us down and threaten to drown us.

If you are in the zone of *peripeteia*, you'll face any number of temptations: to distract yourself from the pain by thrashing about in mindless activity, to numb yourself with routine, to anaesthetise the pain with drugs or alcohol, to seek to return (in bad faith) to an earlier zone when life was simpler and easier, to turn the pain into anger and vent that anger at yourself or others. You can cause a lot of damage to yourself and others in the process. The only sane alternative is to hold the pain, to feel it, to in a sense stretch yourself out on the cross of it, to lie down in front of it and let its pain crash upon you, and as you do, to voice your protest, disappointment, rage and refusal with *No!* – shouted, screamed, groaned, whispered, whatever.

You may find it helpful to translate that single word into many words: to write your own poetry of lament and fury or, if that feels too demanding, you could simply begin to list, memo-style, your grievances against reality, spirituality and the Almighty. What is it that you refuse to accept? What is it that enrages your heart? What in you stands up and will not sit down, speaks up and will not be silent, acts up and will not behave? Can you see how important it is to let what is trying to rise up within you be allowed to do so?

If you aren't there in that raging void, you can't really practise this posture. But you can, perhaps, recall encounters with it in the past, and you may be able to acknowledge the pre-labour contractions that are with you even now. Where are you still seizing control, claiming mastery? What are you most afraid to lose? Where are you demanding an answer that empowers you with explanations? Can you dare imagine the rage if you had to lay those explanations on the altar? It's OK if your answer is *No! No!* In fact, that's exactly the point. It's only by refusing until you can refuse no more that you will ever come to that quiet, naked, tender moment beyond refusal.

Your *No!* exhausts itself. Your furious exclamation breaks open, and from it emerges a tender question.

Chapter 20

Why? When You Come to Zero

The Practice of Lament and Agony: Surviving Through Abandonment

No Alternative Words

> And the waves of pain did wash over me with a rhythmic quality. Ebbing and flowing. Coming and going. I felt I needed to lie completely still so as not to be swept away.... There was no escape, no way out except to go all the way through it. In time – a couple hours I think – the waves of grief subsided. It's hard to describe what happened after that.... I felt empty and spent, but I also felt comforted by God's loving presence.... Nothing was fixed, but I was okay. I had not been swept away.
>
> Ruth Haley Barton[1]

One of my mentors once told me that in the school of faith, we first take the test and then we learn the lesson. He could just as easily have said that we first *fail* the test and then learn the lesson, because in my experience, failure is what makes me more ready to learn than anything else. In fact, failure is itself the lesson. Once you admit that you are a failure, you are, strangely, free. Once you admit that you don't know, that you can't know, you know something you previously refused to know. Everything is possible again when you have fought and struggled and been defeated, when you have come to zero.

If faith shoots up in the springtime of simplicity, and if it branches out and grows robust in the summer of complexity, it appears to fade and fall like leaves in the autumn of perplexity. It falters in the impatient *When?* of aspiration, and then it falls to pieces in the *No!* of rage. The furious *No!* of raging prayer leaves one spent, exhausted, feeling blind and exiled like tragic Oedipus, feeling stupid and ashamed like honest Job, and strangely quiet. And in that quiet, in that hush and stillness of exhaustion, a subtle turning occurs, a turn from *No!* to something beyond it. It's the beginning of a kind of surrender, in a way: we say, 'OK. Life hasn't gone my way. My expectations are shattered. I have no mastery, no control. Why must it be this way?'

Do you see the subtle but real shift? One minute, you are yelling, 'No! It can't be this way'!' and then you are whispering, 'Why? Why must it be this way?'

That *why?* – the prayer of lament – is the kind of prayer you offer on the longest night of the year, the night autumn ends and winter begins. Long ago, your *When? How long?* turned into a raging *No!* Aspiration gave way to exasperation, desperation and then a raging refusal because *how long?* had become *too long*! Having spent your rage, having lost your hope, you now sink into a kind of resignation, a release of all mastery, an acceptance that life is beyond your control. Now, with a feeble voice, you turn toward God, whispering, *Why?*

The prayer is profoundly ironic, isn't it? It acknowledges, 'I don't have answers,' but it still dares to hope that there is an answer, so it asks. This is seasoned faith at work, chastened faith ... faith humbled by a season of perplexity, hunched over, holding one's head in one's hands, as the *peripeteia* does its disorienting work.

We should beware of theologies formed in times of prosperity and comfort, theologies formed on college campuses among undergraduates who are living on their parents' allowances and their professors' patience, theologies defended by seminarians who are young Elihus, reading and theorising about other people's agony but not yet knowing their own. We should be politely aloof in the presence of theologies created and debated by scholars with secure tenure, safe in their bubbles of ease and isolation, lecturing on like Job's friends as they keep their neat theories sequestered from their messy, grubby real lives. We should beware of springtime theologies and even summertime theologies that haven't felt the burn of numbing cold winds and the sting of icy rains that soak and chill to the bone. Those who haven't felt the pain of loss or the agony of disappointment can only teach us so much. But those who have come to this point, who have groaned or shouted or spat out the prayer of *No!* and have spent themselves to nothing in the process ... only they can teach us about a faith that endures when faith has failed, a hope that endures when hope has died.

And yes, you have every right to wonder if I know what I am talking about, if I've walked this road myself. And of course, if I haven't, it would be fruitless to try to convince you that I have, just as it would be unnecessary if I have.

The Bible looks different once you've survived the autumn. It's no longer a repository for theological abstractions that can be organised into a tidy fortress called a 'Christian world-view' or 'orthodoxy'.[2] It's no longer a wallet full of credit cards that you can slap on the table to pay every bill. It's no longer a weapon by which you vanquish those who don't have the good fortune of sharing your approved opinions. No, for an autumn-humbled seeker, the Bible is the living legacy of people who have lived in the real world, a diary of complexities and perplexities survived and reflected upon. It's the family album that carries the memories of ancestors who managed to keep their faith, hope and love alive in a world that shocked them, rocked them and mocked them. When you're in springtime, you love the Bible for the affirmation of the goodness of life that it offers. When you're in summertime, you love the Bible for the motivation to stay in the fray that it offers. But in autumn, you love the Bible more than ever, now for the honesty it offers – honesty about the death of naivety, the falling of all green leaves.

With this perspective, it's no wonder that one of my favourite theologians is Walter Brueggemann[3]. In his lectures and books you encounter a weather-beaten soul who knows what it means to survive 'in hope against hope', which means 'through disappointment after disappointment'. When he reads the Bible – and in particular the Psalms – he sees three kinds of prayers.

First are **prayers of orientation.** These are the spring and summertime prayers of people who have never asked why, because God and the world make sense to them. Take Psalm 1, for example. In the simple summer world of Psalm 1, the good guys are blessed with good, and the bad guys get what they deserve.

Blessed is the man
who does not walk in the counsel of the wicked

or stand in the way of sinners
or sit in the seat of mockers.

But his delight is in the law of the LORD,
and on his law he meditates day and night.
He is like a tree planted by streams of water,
which yields its fruit in season
and whose leaf does not wither.
Whatever he does prospers.

Not so the wicked!
They are like chaff
that the wind blows away.
Therefore the wicked will not stand in the judgment,
nor sinners in the assembly of the righteous.

For the LORD watches over the way of the righteous,
but the way of the wicked will perish. (NIV)

The good prosper. The wicked wither. Prayers are answered. Disasters are averted. So all's right with the world.

I remember reading someone's story in the days after the September 2001 attacks in New York City. On his way to work that day, he had prayed in the train and felt extra close to God. He was high in World Trade Center when the planes had hit. Somehow, he was able to break through a wall that trapped him in rubble and he escaped. He and his family rejoiced, and I rejoiced with them. But then I thought about the woman in the next office, and the guy in the one after that. Did God love them less? Was their demise their own fault because they didn't pray as much as this man did on the train that morning? Ask those kinds of questions, and your spring and summer world of integration starts to unravel, and you move to Brueggemann's second kind of prayer, **the prayer of disorientation**.

If Psalm 1 conveys orientation, the lament that begins in Lamentations 3 conveys disorientation. 'I am the man who has seen affliction,' the poet begins, because he has been stricken by God's angry rod. God makes him 'walk in darkness rather than light'. He complains, 'Indeed, God has turned his hand against me again and again, all day long.'

The poet describes in painstaking – and painful – detail how he feels because of God's displeasure: old, besieged, surrounded 'with bitterness and hardship', walled in, trapped, weighed down, shut out, barred from progress, lost in a maze. God has become, he feels, like a vicious predator: 'Like a bear lying in wait, like a lion in hiding, he dragged me from the path and mangled me and left me without help.' (This is in the Bible!) If that's not bad enough, God is like a sniper, and has done target practice on his heart. His litany of grievances against God ends like this:

> He has filled me with bitter herbs
> and sated me with gall.
> He has broken my teeth with gravel;
> he has trampled me in the dust.
> I have been deprived of peace;
> I have forgotten what prosperity is.
> So I say, 'My splendour is gone
> and all that I had hoped from the LORD.' (NIV)

Is the Bible telling the truth about God and life here? Has God indeed done all of these things to him? Is this the way we should truly feel about our hardships – that they are evidence of the unkindness of God? After all, this is in the Bible.

Here's how I would respond: The poet is not telling the truth about God and life, but he is telling the truth about how he feels about God and life, and we should feel free to tell the truth about how we feel as well. But as we do, we need to remember that our current feelings about God and life, as painfully true as they are to us right now, may not be the ultimate explanation of reality. They're the truth as we see it, but not the truth, the whole truth, and nothing but the truth.

The prayer of lament takes a brief hopeful turn as the poet tries to encourage himself, but again descends into grief, and finally ends in a question, repeated twice:

> Why do you always forget us?
> Why do you forsake us so long? (Lam. 5:20, NIV)

Why? is the final prayer of disorientation, the prayer beyond aspiration and exasperation, the prayer beyond refusal and rage. The world doesn't make sense any more. Our old answers don't satisfy. God seems to be our enemy, not our friend. We have raged about how utterly unacceptable this is. We have faced the option of walking away and saying, 'Case closed. I am now an atheist', or '&#$$% God! I'm on my own now!' But we have refused even that refusal. After all, where else could we go, once we acknowledge that we don't understand, if we foreclose on the possibility of help beyond our understanding? So we choose to keep the question open: *Why?*

Think of the autumn of perplexity as a tunnel with two ends. At the front end of the tunnel, we are quite sure that our easy answers will start working again after this brief delay is over.

It's just a matter of time, we say, praying, with intensifying anxiety, *When? How long?* As we wait, we extract promises from the Bible and rub them like magic lamps. We focus on Proverbs, Joshua and Matthew – places in the Bible where life makes sense and chaos is contained; we avoid Ecclesiastes, Job, Judges, Psalm 88 and Lamentations, because they scare us. We build theologies of forced naivety, celebrating the passages that comfort us and explaining away or ignoring the ones that bother us. We package these reassuring theologies in books and sermons. These books sell amazingly well in bookstores, and they elicit generous donations in religious broadcasting, because we want to believe them. Paying for them, we hope, will demonstrate our investment in them. But the farther we go into the tunnel, the less we can believe them. We feel we're being dishonest unless we let out our rage and tell the truth about how insane life feels, how cruel and uncaring God seems to be.

So in the middle of the tunnel, where it's the darkest, we assume the worst, and we rage about the unacceptability of our lightless plight, shouting *No! No! No!* But then, if we keep groping in the darkness, stumbling one foot after the other, still unable to see anything, we begin to reopen the question: maybe there's a reason or purpose after all, maybe there's hope after all, maybe God hasn't disappeared or failed us after all – it's just our illusions and partial beliefs about God that have failed us.

So we ask *why?* And as we do, a glimmering pinpoint appears off in the distance. At first, we rub our eyes, sure we're imagining it. But we move toward it anyway. Where else can we go?

As we stumble forward, we experience what Walter Brueggemann calls **prayers of reorientation.** Lamentation now moves to this new space:

215

Yet this I call to mind
and therefore I have hope:
Because of the LORD's great love we are not consumed,
for his compassions never fail.
They are new every morning;
great is your faithfulness.
I say to myself, 'The LORD is my portion;
therefore I will wait for him.'
The LORD is good to those whose hope is in him,
to the one who seeks him;
it is good to wait quietly
for the salvation of the LORD.
It is good for a man to bear the yoke
while he is young.
Let him sit alone in silence,
for the LORD has laid it on him.
Let him bury his face in the dust
there may yet be hope.
Let him offer his cheek to one who would strike him,
and let him be filled with disgrace.
For men are not cast off
by the Lord forever.
Though he brings grief, he will show compassion,
so great is his unfailing love.
For he does not willingly bring affliction
or grief to the children of men. (Lam. 3:21–33, NIV)

At this far end of the tunnel, we add to our honesty about our pain a new honesty about our hope. But this is not the naïve hope of a fresh-faced child. This is the tested hope of a leathery elder, whose eyes have seen disappointment, whose heart has been broken by tragedy and whose faith, hope and love have endured the test.

I think of such an elder, an old man who knew a lot of pain. He had been misunderstood by those he respected. He became the object of threats and plots to kill him. Still he kept on serving God, trusting God, loving God. He kept taking risks, knowing they would lead him to suffer still more: betrayal by friends, rumours from competitors, false accusations, long periods of imprisonment, beatings and the daily pressure of concern for those he loved. He wrote: 'I consider that our present sufferings are not worth comparing with the glory that will be revealed in us.'[4]

These words would sound trite and cheap if someone who suffered less had said them. But this scarred man dared to believe that from every anguish, glory could be born, that each pain could become a labour pain, giving birth to glory: 'We know that the whole creation has been groaning as in the pains of childbirth right up to the present time.'[5] Then he sees even deeper into the heart of things, that our groanings, our when's and no's and why's, are actually a sharing in the groanings of the Spirit herself, for she is the mother giving birth. Similarly, Jesus said, in the unique pain of a stupid, rebellious, runaway's father we can see the love that groans in the heart of God (Luke 15:11–24). Jesus himself imaged that pain as he wept in a garden, as he bled on a cross, as he prayed forgiveness for those who mocked and crucified him. And so the cry of God becomes our own. Can this mean that the practice of lament is not simply humans crying to God, but God crying through humans? Could it be that through our compounding, agonising autumnal tragedies, we in our own small way connect and tap into the pain that lies in the heart of the Creator?

As we've seen, there are many ways we can back away from this mystery. We can try to turn our pain into anger by blaming someone, even God. We can take the drug of retaliation by scapegoating, by finding someone or something on whom to vent our pent-up anger.[6] We can construct elaborate theodicies – theories that explain and justify how evil has a right to exist, how it is in fact right for evil to exist. These approaches retrieve us from the void; they're attempts to return from autumn to Indian summer.

But if we don't turn back, if we allow ourselves to go naked into the void, we render ourselves vulnerable to a strange discovery: that we exist, that God has given us space to exist – even when God does not seem to exist. To be abandoned is to find out how real you are. God has made you so real that you exist even when alone. Yes, this can be terrifying: there is something in us that is still very infant-like, terrified of being alone. But along with terrifying, this realisation can be electrifying, an awakening, an enlightenment, a kind of shock therapy that makes a new state of being possible. It is the terror and wonder of realising more fully the significance of the gift we have always had: the gift of being, of existing, of standing out of the void, of being alive.

If we dare to persevere, if we dare to keep holding our *why?* of lament through the longest, darkest night of the year, morning will come. And when it comes, we will carry a new gravitas, a new substance, a new reality worthy of that word 'glory'. We will find the new day is a moment longer, and the next night a moment shorter. And the turning of a season will have begun, even though the cold of winter hasn't yet begun to show its full force.

Chapter 21

Why? Holding the Question Open

All that I'm now going through
Will make me better or bitter
Break down or break through
Learning this patience – it takes so much patience.
It's a great education,
But why is the tuition so high?
Why, God why?

When I was a pastor, many people in my congregation worried about me (just as some of my readers do now). Why wasn't my theology as plain and simple as the famous preachers on religious radio and TV? For those notables, everything was clear. There was an easy formula for everything, a simple black-and-white explanation or equation, a 'biblical' solution, and no *when, no* or *why*. I would try to explain to them that life on this side of the microphone where we live isn't that simple. Even though radio-orthodox faith-formulas might bring in donations, sell lots of books and give a certain kind of comfort to people at a distance, I would say, such a formulaic faith doesn't work so well at close range, where life is lumpy, messy, ragged, chipped and torn.

In fact, the same formulaic, easy-answer faith that fills some people with confidence fills others with dread and despair. It turns *why* into a weapon. It isolates the person crying in the hospice, or grieving at the graveside. *Why didn't you have enough faith?* It heaps more guilt on the person in the psychiatric ward. *Why don't you just pull yourself together?* It blames the parent at the PFLAG[2] meeting, not to mention what it does to the son or daughter in question. *Why can't you see what's black and white and conform to what's right?* It mocks the person sitting on the back row of the empty church who is experiencing *peripeteia*, or the person who won't even dare come that far inside. *Why don't you just believe?* Honest pastors who live on the same side of the microphone as their people can't wield *why* as a weapon. They can't simply broadcast the springtime and summertime faith of integration 24/7. No, on this side of the microphone, we must all go through disintegration together, so together we can discover reintegration on the other side.

And that's what we find in one of our most cherished psalms, Psalm 23 – not a formulaic faith, but a faith that has walked through the dark valley and come through on the other side.

> The LORD is my shepherd, I shall not be in want.
> He makes me lie down in green pastures,
> he leads me beside quiet waters,
> he restores my soul.
> He guides me in paths of righteousness
> for his name's sake.
> Even though I walk
> through the valley of the shadow of death,
> I will fear no evil,

for you are with me;
your rod and your staff,
they comfort me.

You prepare a table before me
in the presence of my enemies.
You anoint my head with oil;
my cup overflows.
Surely goodness and love will follow me
all the days of my life,
and I will dwell in the house of the LORD forever.
   (Ps. 23, NIV)

Yes, thank God, in this life there are green pastures, still waters, overflowing cups, laden banquet tables. But there are also valleys of the shadow of death in which evil lurks and enemies wait for a misstep or mistake upon which to pounce. To sustain us through those dark valleys, we are given simple words of aspiration, refusal and lament: *When? No! Why?*

   The most powerful dark-valley-prayer in the Bible, I believe, is also the shortest, uttered by Jesus as he hung on a cross: 'My God, my God,' he cried, expressing the tattered remains of faith: doesn't that simple word *my* express some hold on God, some claim, some relationship? But then comes, 'Why have you forsaken me?' Could there be a more naked expression of doubt than those words? The forsaking is in the present perfect tense, meaning that it has already happened, it's a done deal, and is at this moment ongoing. Abandonment is the splintered, brutal reality to which Jesus is nailed as he says these words. He is suspended and stretched spiritually just as he is physically, crucified between the *my* of faith and the *why* of abandonment. This is his *peripeteia*, if you will, the moment at which everything he has trusted has collapsed under him. But even in that moment of total darkness, could the word *why* still hold open a crack in the door, a hope against hope that there is some reason for this madness?

Now that word I just used, *reason*, is problematic. If by it I mean *explanation*, I don't think it's helpful, because as we've seen, offering an explanation for evil, abandonment, or suffering creates as many problems as it solves. If *reason* means *plan*, we're equally in trouble: do we really want to say that God happily engineers earthquakes, rapes, crashes, murders and childhood diseases all as part of a pre-ordained plan? (Yes, I know this rape is unpleasant now, and yes, this genocide is quite frightening now, and yes, that fire is quite hot and that collapsing ceiling is quite heavy and starvation is a tough way to die. But don't worry. It's all part of a plan.) Is it possible to save that kind of God from being a heartless puppet-master?

Both explanations and plans put us in a determined universe, a mechanistic universe, a universe without real freedom, an engineered, rat-in-a-maze universe. Explanations do so by telling us something about the present: *in the nature of things, this is inevitable; it must happen, must be this way, because this is just how the gears turn, and this is how the engines fire.* Plans reach back into the past, telling us that the present explanation isn't a design flaw but is actually pre-engineered intentionally: *all this was preordained, written into the script by God, designed in every detail so that every nerve ending would burn with exactly this excruciation at this moment. Not to worry.*

But there's another possible meaning for that word *reason*, a meaning that together with the word *why* can liberate us from a determined, mechanistic universe. Instead of saying, *What plan in the past predetermined this suffering and therefore explains it in the present?*, we could ask a very different question: *What possible good in the future can be brought out of this tragic suffering in the present?* This question makes no assumption that the present moment is inevitable or intentional. But it also makes no assumption that the present moment is meaningless. It holds open the possibility that some future meaning, some future value, some future good could be wrested from this present tragedy and loss. Ultimately, this is what we all need when we suffer: not explanations or reasons, but meaning.

The *why* that seeks an explanation and a plan looks backwards; the *why* that seeks meaning by bringing some future good out of this agony looks forward. The former invites passivity and resignation. The latter seeks a new creative possibility, even at the nadir of hope, at midnight on the longest night of the year. It says, 'Well, the worst has happened. There it is. It's all in ruins, all a loss, a complete failure and disaster.' But instead of saying, 'I'll just curse God and die,' it dares ask, 'What good can we pull from this mess? What meaning can we make of this madness?'

It's dangerous to try to psychologise Jesus, I know, but let's go back once again to the night before his crucifixion. Jesus has a sense of where things are going, and so he goes to pray in an olive grove called Gethsemane. Matthew and Mark speak of him feeling 'great sorrow', being 'overwhelmed', even 'to the point of death', so much so that he doesn't want to be left alone (Matt. 26:38; Mark 14:34). At this moment, if Jesus lived in an explanation-driven, plan-driven universe, we would expect him to pray, 'I know this can't be avoided. I know it's part of your plan. So give me the strength to go through with it.' But that's far different from what he says: 'If it is possible, may this cup be taken from me ...' That word *if* tells us something terrifyingly significant: at this moment, Jesus doesn't have clarity about a pre-determined, set-in-concrete plan. At this moment, he wonders if there can be some other way. But *if* not, he says, 'Your will be done.'[3]

To go through with a plan is one thing. But to step into the abyss of *if* is another thing. And I sense a powerful resonance between this *if* in Gethsemane and that *why* on Golgotha: Jesus isn't trusting a plan; he is trusting God. He believes that whatever happens, God can turn it for good. I have tried, but I have never succeeded in imagining a trust more naked and pure than this.

In uttering that question *why?*, Jesus validated that pain, abandonment, doubt and despair are indeed part of the human condition, and they are even part of a life well-lived. But they are not the last word. They can be questioned. Jesus thus comes out in solidarity not only with faithful people, but also with doubters, questioners and sceptics everywhere. He sustained both *my God* and *why God*, naked faith and naked honesty.

Do you see what this means for us? When we are in the middle of the tunnel, at the low point of the valley, on the longest, darkest night of the year crying *Why? Why? Why?* in the void, we are both alone and not alone. Jesus is with us, and through him, God is with us, even as we declare our doubt and faith in the same agonising cry. Now here I am being transparently Trinitarian, and some may not be able to go here with me. But for me, as I seek to enter that moment and ponder it from the inside, here's what I see:

224

God isn't above all this, looking down with the divine clipboard on which sits the divine checklist, checking off achieved divine objectives on the divine plan as they occur. Whipping, check. First nail, check. Second nail, check. First pint of blood, check. And so on. Neither is God apart from this, somehow at a distance, uninvolved. No, G-d is a part of this, in it, fully crucified in the agony of this personal, historical, political, social, spiritual, finite, infinite moment. In Christ, G-d is godforsaken. In Christ, G-d hangs without a script or skyhook, without an escape clause written into the contract, without an explanation or plan, without a reason in that sense, and without a prayer, except that simple word *why?*[4]

And in that simple, painful word is found all the hope that exists in the universe: not a hope that reaches backwards for an explanatory plan, but a hope that reaches forward, into the darkness, saying, 'Can we work any good from this?' And whatever resurrection means, however we conceive of it, it must mean that yes, even in this, even in the worst, even in the end, even in *peripeteia*, good can be willed or sought or hoped for. Good can be worked. Good can rise again.

So even now you can dare to hold the simple word Why? before God. As you hold it, first imagine yourself alone. Alone you feel your own pain, your own unanswered prayers, your own exhaustion and disappointment. Don't rush away from it: let *why* be a container and let it fill with all the pain you've kept at bay. If tears come, let them. If they don't, it's OK.

Still alone, now you expand your circle of empathy, thinking of others you know, bringing their agony into your own: *why?* Alone you feel the suffering that nobody is doing anything

225

about, and you cry *why?* Alone you feel the utter unaccept-ability of an unjust past and an unjust present, and you hold your *why* in your soul before G-d and the universe, on behalf of everyone whose hopes have been mocked by bitterness. Remember, you are not seeking an easy explanation that will make injustice acceptable rather, you are refusing all such expla-nations. As they present themselves, you dismiss each one with another *why?* If no one else in the universe raised the ques-tion, you would raise your *why* alone.

Now imagine yourself being joined by others, or rather, imagine yourself joining them, because millions were in this place of agony and lament long before you knew it existed. So imagine yourself now joining the countless people whose company you have tried all your life to avoid: the forgotten and the despairing, the suffering heroes and the uncelebrated martyrs, the losers and the failures, the mystified and the bewil-dered, the wannabe's and the has-beens. You've always sought a place among the successful elite in the winner's circle, the inner circle, but you now find yourself nowhere, in darkness, with so many others. Their lot is yours now; you are identi-fied with them in the 'we' who suffer. And with them you cry *why?*

After this identification has settled in, it's time to let your *why* lean forward. You have questioned an unacceptable and unjust past and present; now you must tilt your question toward the future. Perhaps now your *why* becomes a *why not?* Why not a better future? Why not more compassion, more justice, more harmony, more connection, more vitality, more beauty, more truth, more grace? Why not? Let your *why* and your *why not* hold open the possibility of a future where things are not perfect, but are at least moving in the direction of hope, of light, of life. In this way, your *why* gradually can become an expression of will: you choose to will future good in the midst of present evil, to will future light in the midst of present darkness, to will future resurrection in the midst of present death. Hold that *why* as an act of will.

If this is difficult for you, it may help you to turn your *why* against something: Why should I *not* give up hope? Why should I *not* become cynical, jaded, despairing? Why should I *not* lose faith? Why should I *not* just seek to save my own skin, and say to hell with everyone else? Implicit in your question will be the answer: *so that some good may come.*

Here in this willing, I believe, you will sense G-d is present already ... forever willing goodness, truth and beauty, and waiting for others to will it too. If you sense that Presence, simply will with it, letting that will say, in essence, *here's why.*

When you practise lament, when you are stretched and suspended on the cross of abandonment, you do not feel heroic. You do not feel like a runner about to cross the finish line. You do not feel that a hopeful Sunday is coming after a nightmarish Friday and a blank, lifeless Saturday. You feel exhausted and finished. You feel as though you're fading, dying, letting go. And so you do. Having kept the question open as long as you can, you let go.

Dare you do so now? Dare you drop, crying why, falling not from the God above you, but into the G-d below you?

Four

Harmony:
The Season of
Spiritual Deepening

Harmony

You never knew you were capable of feeling, much less surviving, such pain. You felt that you were about to break open, that all your blood and all your insides, would explode out of you if the pressure lasted for one more second. It couldn't get any worse, you thought. But then it did. Contraction after contraction. Worse, and worse, and worse still. And then, grunting, panting, sweating, screaming, you took a deep breath and pushed once more, feeling it was futile to do so but doing so anyway. Suddenly ... it was hard to believe ... suddenly there was this gush and the feeling of something slipping between your thighs and the midwife picked up your daughter and lifted her to your breast. A gasp, a cry, a beautiful cry. Tears – yours, your husband's, even the midwife's. Clean towels, warm blankets, a camera flash, and there in your arms is your little girl, and it's happening without you trying, without her trying: you are bonding to one another, sweaty maternal skin to slippery infant skin, in a bond that can never be broken.

Harmony. It comes through pain, after pain. The artist agonises, and finally, no not yet, no not yet ... yes, yes, at the finally after finally, beauty comes. The team struggles, defeat, defeat, defeat, and then victory. The struggle for liberation faces setback, betrayal, duplicity, more betrayal, hope, disappointment, more setbacks, vicious lies, humiliation, defection, despair and then, almost as an afterthought because it has come so much harder and later than expected, breakthrough.

There are joys in simplicity. There are victories. There are joys in complexity too, and even certain satisfactions in perplexity. But there is a quiet fullness of joy that comes after perplexity. We might call it humility, even maturity, or better, harmony, because it not only transcends the previous stages, but includes them. It integrates simplicity, complexity and perplexity and more into a rich, dynamic four-part harmony. It's a clear and open space, a quiet time and place that makes room for new melodies to take shape and find voice. There is nothing like the life that is born through the hard labour of becoming, enduring, never giving up, never letting go ... and then, paradoxically, letting go ... and then receiving all you had hoped for and more.[1]

When Stage Three perplexity gives way to Stage Four harmony, there is a quiet transcendence – a transcendence that brings along or includes the previous stages rather than leaving them behind. So the right-versus-wrong dualism of Simplicity and the effective-versus-ineffective pragmatism of Complexity and the honest-versus-dishonest relativism of Perplexity are taken up and expanded into something bigger in the Harmony of Stage Four.

The first black-and-white simplicity now fills out into a second simplicity that is full-colour and alive. If first-simplicity truths were bold, judging and exclusive, second-simplicity truths are no less bold, but they harmonise, integrate and reconcile. You can feel this grand second simplicity glowing in elegant, harmonising words like these:

I desire compassion and not sacrifice. (Matt. 12:7)
Seek first God's reign and God's justice, and everything
    else you need will come to you in time. (Matt. 6:33)
Love God with all your being and love your neighbours
    as yourself. (Matt 22:36–39)
Faith, hope and love abide, these three, but the greatest
    of these is love.[2] (I Cor. 13:13)

If in Stage One we knew that everything was knowable, in Stage Two we knew that everything was doable, and in Stage Three we knew that everything was relative, now we in some way come to know with the old sage that 'everything is beautiful in its time' (Eccl. 3:11). We can finally begin to accept that all our knowing, past and present, is partial (I Cor. 13:12).[3] Harmony requires this posture of humility, which allows us to finally see authority figures neither as god-like (as in Stages One and Two) nor as demonic (as in Stage Three), but rather as human beings like us, often doing the best they can and even then making plenty of mistakes along the way. This new-found humility also allows us to find our identity in a new way in relation to others: not in Stage One dependence, and not in Stage Two independence, and not in Stage Three counter-dependence, but in the more mature inter-dependence of mutuality.

And what happens to our view of God in Stage Four? In some ways, this is the stage when faith takes off its dualistic, pragmatic and relativistic clothing and seeks to encounter God nakedly. Of course, in Stage Four we know we must use words just as we have in previous stages, but we also know that our words conceal as they reveal. Similarly, we must celebrate the rich heritage of our religious traditions, but those traditions are now the foundation on which we build, not the ceiling under which we are trapped. Stage One orthodoxy now morphs into what some have called paradoxy – the realisation that every true statement about God (including this one) cannot fully contain the true majesty and wonder of God. This humility before God helps create harmony among all of us who believe in God, making it harder for us to maintain the old us-versus-them dualisms that have so often animated religious conservatives and liberals alike. (For this reason, Stage Four people will often react against this four-stage framework itself, feeling that it separates them from others to whom they want to be connected and with whom they want to be identified.)

And where from here? Is this the pinnacle? Have we now arrived?

As you might expect, this season of harmony opens into a new simplicity. This new second-simplicity eventually matures into a new season of higher complexity, and so on, in an ascending spiral of growth and discovery that continues as long as life itself. Far from feeling we have finally arrived, in Stage Four we finally begin to understand that arrival has never been the point.

Chapter 22

Behold: The Emergence of the Meditative Mind

The Practice of Meditation and Wonder: Deepening by Seeing

Alternative words: Indeed. Amen. See. Eureka. Maybe. Ah.

> Wonder is the alpha and the omega of the human mind.
> It stands at the beginning and end of our quest to under-
> stand ourselves and the world. Aristotle said philosophy
> begins in wonder. It is the most primal of emotions, at
> once ordinary and disturbing. As the sixth sense, the
> natural religious sense, wonder is the royal road that leads
> us to the other elemental emotions, and thus to a renewed
> sense of the sacred.
>
> Sam Keen[1]

It was Easter several years ago. I had just survived a decade that
had basically kicked the stuffing out of me. I was thinking about
the meaning of resurrection in my life and in the stories of
Lazarus and Jesus. This song took shape over a couple of weeks:

When we think back on our journey over many years,
Nights of joys and laughter, and days of trials and tears,
With piercing, draining sorrows that broke us on our
    knees,
While deep inside hide our regrets that no one ever sees
    …
How can comfort find us locked up in our darkest room?
How can we leave the past behind and escape it like a
    tomb?
Sometimes we feel like Lazarus, buried in our shame,
But the risen Christ is on the move, and we faintly hear
    our name.

From deep fatigue and heartache, we come back full and
    strong …
From guilty isolation, to a place where we belong.
We wonder every springtime when birds are on the wing,
When the forests show a mist of green and the brooks
    and marshes sing,
How can tender life endure the winter's vicious storms?
How can fragile breath survive the freeze 'til April
    warms?
Life keeps resurrecting. How, we don't understand.
But when the risen Christ comes near, spring breaks
    across the land.

I had lost a lot during those years of spiritual deconstruction
and struggle, mostly things I've since been better off without.
But the loss was acutely painful nonetheless. It was especially
tough because I was never sure that anything would replace
the spiritual 'baby teeth' that were loosening and falling out

one after another. As I wrote that song, I remember feeling that at least one new substantial realisation had come: God truly is the God of resurrection. God truly is the one who brings you through the valley of the shadow of death. In the dead of winter, God is the source of a new springtime hope. It was a moment of *eureka! Voila! Indeed! Behold!*

In Maryland where I lived most of my fifty-four years, the birds start singing in late January and early February. Even though it's technically winter, the days are already growing longer. The official beginning of spring on 21 March is still weeks away, but somehow the birds know. And so do the plants, as sap silently surges up the trunks of trees and bulbs bulge in the soil. It's not obvious yet; the ponds may still be ice-covered, and the tree buds are still small, clenched tight. But quietly, life is staging an insurrection against the cold, preparing to emerge again based on a hint and hunch of coming warmth. One morning, there it is: a crocus popping through the snow. A few days later, you hear a V-shaped flock of geese moving north above you. One rainy afternoon, you smell the soil as it unfreezes and releases its subtle, moist scent. Behold!

Behold is our simple word for the practice of meditation. It's a call to notice, not just to glance. It's an invitation to open your eyes, blink, linger and see in a new way. It is to normal seeing what listening is to normal hearing or what concentrating is to normal thinking: *behold* evokes focused attention, a holding of what is seen so it can be slowly savoured. *Behold* is, in this sense, a word uttered first to our own souls: *Look and see,* we say to ourselves. *Notice. Be aware. Watch. Appreciate. Maybe* – just maybe there's more going on here than you've ever seen before.

But *behold* is more than talking to ourselves. As we summon ourselves to attention, we acknowledge to God that what God has been trying to show us is finally coming into focus. So *behold* is a prayer indeed. *Ah, Lord, now I see! It was there all along, but I didn't get it! Wow! Amazing! Beautiful! Wonderful! Behold!*

All of these words arise from what Fr Richard Rohr calls 'non-dual seeing' or non-dual thinking or the contemplative mind.[2] By practising this new way of seeing, we turn the calendar page, as it were, to begin a new year.

In the spring season of simplicity, we see in a dualistic way. Everything we see is immediately categorised in relation to the ego. It is evaluated in relation to self-interest: good/evil; us/them; advantageous/disadvantageous; superior/inferior; cost/benefit; right/wrong; in/out; pleasurable/painful; safe/dangerous; acceptable/unacceptable; winners/losers; ally/enemy, and so on. These comparisons and contrasts are absolute judgments, full stop, period, end of story, case closed.

In the summer season of complexity, we see in a multiplex way. Our dualism begins to break down. We move from black and white to shades of gray. We go from seeing the world in terms of twos to seeing the world in threes, fours, fives, dozens. We go from fixed categories to gradations, spectra and ranges, from bounded sets to centred sets. We move from binary categorisation to sophisticated classification, and so judgment and analysis becomes more complex. In this stage we begin to be able to see some good in what we had previously categorised as evil, and some evil in what we had previously categorised as good.

In the autumn season of perplexity, we see in a relativistic way. We take the scrutiny we have developed to dissect the opinions, perspectives and beliefs of others and we turn that scrutiny on our own opinions, perspectives and beliefs. We self-distance enough to self-examine, self-critique and self-deconstruct. We give everything a second thought; in other words, we repent. Like leaves falling off trees, our previous certainties and judgments fall to the ground, until the only absolute left is that there are no absolutes. And that paradox is chilling, and to hold it feels like dying.

So now, the winter season beyond perplexity begins with a kind of nakedness. Naked trees. Frozen ponds. Hibernation. Starkness. Long, dark, silent nights and cold days blanketed in snow. Autumn exhaustion leads now to winter's rest. That chattering, hyper-vigilant consciousness – that first judged in Stage One, then analysed in Stage Two, and then deconstructed in Stage Three – now goes silent. It takes a breath. When we open our eyes in this space, we begin to see and know with the meditative mind.

What you look for determines what you see. What you focus on determines what you miss. The way you see determines what you are blind to, and what you render invisible. So this meditative kind of seeing accepts the limitations of earlier and noisier ways of seeing, and it practises, in their place, a new vision, a new beholding. When we behold in this new way, we enter a second naivety. We begin to remember what was forgotten when we ate of the tree of knowledge of good and evil in the Garden of Eden story. We learn to behold the goodness in everything, the goodness that the Creator beheld in the freshly made world: *behold – it was very good.*[3]

It's not that *everything* is good. Far from it. Nobody who has practised *when, no,* and *why* would ever say that. It's that *there is good in everything* or *there is potential to bring good out of anything.* It's not that *everything is the same.* Far from it. It's that *everything both differs and belongs*, everything can be redeemed, everything can be forgiven. It's not that *everything is relative*, with no firm or fixed identity, but that *everything is related*, so its identity is bound up somehow with the identity of everything else.

We used to look for evil to judge, evil to name, shame and blame. But that was an easy thing, so easy that we now find the whole exercise rather boring and childish and small-minded. It was also an ego-flattering and prideful thing, placing us in a godlike position. We now wish to see without that arrogance, without that air of superiority or supremacy. Now as we learn to behold the good, the world is bathed in a gentle luminosity of compassion instead of a harsh light of analysis, inspection and judgement. Before we looked for flaws, which gave us an excuse to reject, but now we look for goodness, which give us reason to respect. Instead of looking for dangers to flee and fear, we look for possibilities to pursue and encourage. We turn from evaluating to valuing. We grow from fault-finding to something far bigger and better: beauty-finding, beholding, seeing in love, seeing with God.[4]

This new seeing, of course, includes the way we view other human beings. The Apostle Paul had to learn this. Like many of us, he worked hard to become an angry religious man. He had made a big investment in judging, exposing, imprisoning and even killing, those whom he labelled inferior and wrong.

Notice how he describes the transformation he has experienced 'in Christ' – it is a transformation in seeing or encountering:

> The love of Christ is pressing us toward this realisation: if one died for all people, then all people have died. And if one died for all people, then all people should no longer live for themselves, but for him who died and rose from the dead on their behalf. So now, we encounter every person in a new way. No longer do we encounter them from within a self-centred mindset; that was the flawed, egotistical way in which we once encountered Christ himself. Now, having encountered Christ in a new way, we encounter others: for all who are in Christ, all creation is new! The old things have passed away. Behold! All has become new! (2 Cor. 5:14–17, author's translation)

Last year's sight – the sight of spring, summer and autumn – was the sight of a score-keeper or fault-finder. We stood with the Pharisees, stones in hand, staring at a woman caught in adultery. All we could see was a sinner needing punishment. Now, in the early light of a new year, we stand with Christ, in Christ, beholding a daughter needing love. Last spring, summer and autumn, we stood with the disciples, disgusted by a Gentile woman, an outsider who had the nerve to ask *our* Messiah for help. Now, in the clear cool light of winter, we stand in Christ and behold through his eyes a woman of great faith and great love. Once we stood with Peter, seeing Cornelius and his friends as 'unclean' because they were different from us; now, in the light of a new day, we behold people 'in Christ', beyond the old categories of us/them, clean/unclean.[5] This new way of seeing is so different from our old way of seeing that we now say, 'Once I was blind, but now I see' (John 9:25).

Behold: a new creation! A new reality! A new universe![6] In the old, flawed, egotistical mindset, I used to see some people as my friends and others as my enemies, some as superior and others as inferior, some as clean and others as unclean, some as worthy and others as unworthy, some as 'us' and others as 'them'. I judged their value in relation to me and my safety, my interests, my opinions, my pride, my profit, my lust, my affiliations, my fear. *Behold!* Now I am able to escape the black-hole gravity of my old ego-centric perspective, aptly described by novelist Walker Percy as *the great suck of self*. Instead, we rise to see with the living God, seeing others with the living, loving, holy God's compassionate eyes.[7]

But my renewed vision doesn't stop with the faces of others: it continues when I look in the mirror. Up until now I have seen myself as a mix of good and bad, good I am proud of and bad I am ashamed of – again, seeing myself in relation to my own interests in being popular, powerful, approved, successful. If I'm tempted to self-worship, I live with one kind of blindness about myself failing to acknowledge my character defects. If I'm tempted to self-loathing, it's another kind of blindness, failing to see my worth as God's beloved creature made in God's image.

But now I disconnect from those old viewpoints of myself, and I join God who sees me in the true light of compassion and knows me better than I know myself. My faults aren't excused, but they are swallowed up in love and forgiveness. My weaknesses aren't covered up, but they are not the point. My dark side isn't denied, but neither is it thrown in my face as an accusation. My strengths are neither exaggerated nor minimised: they simply are. And so I join God in seeing me. *Behold!*

But there's still more: my new way of seeing leads me to see all creation differently. I used to look at a forested hillside and all I saw was how many profitable board-feet of lumber it could produce for me, or how many tons of coal I could blast out of it to sell. I looked at an empty field and called it 'undeveloped', oblivious to the beautiful ecosystem that had developed there over millennia. I imagined the profit I could make by 'developing' it with bulldozers and car parks and oil derricks and shopping centres. But that was seeing in the old way.

Now, with Moses in the desert, I see a common bush aglow with a holy non-consuming flame. Now, with Isaiah standing before a forest, I see the leaves in the wind-swept branches shimmering, and for me, they are applauding God. Now, with the Psalmists, I see wild creatures thriving in God's care. Now, the waves roar and lightning pierces the sky in dramatic celebration of God's glorious majesty and splendour. Now, with Jesus, I see the flowers of the field and the birds of the air as God's beloved creatures, each and every thing possessing true and intrinsic value, apart from any price put on it in the meat-markets of human economy. No wonder Martin Luther could say, 'If you could understand a single grain of wheat, you would die for wonder.'[8]

Most wonderful of all, if we dare venture into the new creation, you and I will behold God in a new way. We used to encounter God from our self-serving vantage point – for what God could do for us, advancing our agenda, coddling our insecurities, fulfilling our desires, reinforcing our prejudices. But now, even God shines in a new light. God has been transformed for us – not that G-d has changed in essence or character, but that our concept or image of G-d has changed, adjusted, expanded, been corrected, slightly at least, in the direction of who G-d truly is. *Behold!*

Something happens at this stage that is very difficult to describe: we learn as never before to separate G-d from our God-concepts. We learn that it is one thing to trust our beliefs or believe in our theology or have confidence in our doctrines and creeds about God. But it is a very different thing to trust God directly, desperately, helplessly, nakedly. We believe in G-d-beyond-beliefs as distinguished from the-god-of-my-beliefs. I think this is the distinction people in various twelve-step recovery movements are making – albeit inarticulately at times – when they refer to 'God as we understand him' in steps 3 and 11.[9] The 'Power greater than ourselves' of step 2 obliquely refers to the One we have identified as G-d in these pages. So by referring to G-d as 'God as we understood him', we acknowledge that our best understanding of God is just that: our current best attempt to understand One who by definition, excels, overflows and transcends anything and everything we will ever think or say. When we acknowledge that no word, concept, name, image, temple, system, creed or religion can ever contain G-d, we climb a high mountain with the prophet Isaiah and shout to the valley below, 'Behold your God!'[10] We are reduced to saying, 'I can't tell you in words alone: you have to see for yourself.'

And so we come to this practice of simply beholding, in humble stillness, in wide-eyed awe. And we realise, perhaps with some dismay as well as wonder, not only that the God we now behold is bigger than our previous understandings, but also that this will always be the case. Language fails us at

244

these moments. Our pronouns falter, because God is more than we understand when we say *he, she, it* or even *you*. Our nouns stumble – even revered nouns like power, father, rock, spirit, creator, being, lord, god, God, and even G-d. Even our most paradoxical and mysterious nouns break open — like Trinity or the Divine or the Sacred One or the Holy One – because even they can't fully contain or define the mystery to which they point and ascribe honour. Our verbs point, but even they can't contain, and our best statements stutter, as true as they are. Yes, to say 'God is great' speaks the truth, but it might simultaneously obscure the equal truth that God is gentle and kind, or that God dwells with the lowly. At a moment like this, when we feel that the reality of our Subject over-saturates and bursts every attempt to contain it, we may be tempted just to be silent, to say nothing. But how can we? How can we not speak of a God so wonderful to behold?[11]

I first began to bump up against this paradox in the middle of the difficult years that I described at the beginning of this chapter. I was doubting my beliefs about God, deconstructing my theological system, and questioning my concepts of God. The experience was terrifying. It was terrifying in large part because I was a human being who had become as accustomed to living in my belief system as I was to living in my house, my marriage, my skin. It felt as though my faith-home was caving in with me inside of it. It felt like my faith-marriage was collapsing. I was no longer comfortable in my own faith-skin.

Beyond that, I had the added practical stress of making my living as a teacher of the theological system in which I was at home and to which I was wedded in deep commitment. So it was like my home, my marriage and my career were all simultaneously collapsing. My entire life was being sucked into the vortex of some terrible whirlpool, hurricane, or tornado.

To whom do you turn in such a circumstance? All I can say is that I had no one to turn to, no one other than God, the G-d, that is, who transcended and therefore could be separated from my beliefs, systems and concepts. I can't explain how the transfer of trust from God to G-d happened, only that it was messy, slow, reiterative and terrifying. And wonderful. The process remains unfinished, of course. As it unfolds, there are moments when I find myself in the eye of the storm, and there I can breathe. And behold.

Chapter 23

Behold: Faith Beyond Belief

Truth is there for finding, but the logic that's involved
is a mystery unwinding, not a problem to be solved.

David Wilcox[1]

There is a kind of slow-motion quality to finding yourself in this eye of the storm, and the slowness can only be described as reverent or holy. Beholding is a slow and reverent seeing with God, a slow and reverent knowing with God, a slow and reverent holding of everyone and everything in the light of God ... others, ourselves, all creation, even God. In that suspended moment, we breathe in wonder, and we breathe out *behold*. There are many ways we might try to express this beholding: *Ah, now I see. How did I miss it for so long?* Or *So that's what was really going on when I used to think I understood.* Or *Ouch. I can't believe I was so wrongheaded and ignorant before!* Or *Wow. Maybe there's still more I haven't seen and understood.* Or *Before I had the words but not the meaning; now I have the meaning – but I can't find the words to do it justice.* Or *Beautiful. Indescribable.*

Whatever words best capture the experience, meditation becomes a practice of returning to and holding the wide-eyed wonder of childhood. We don't waste a lot of time upbraiding

247

ourselves for how wrong we've been about so many things. No, we simply let our mistakes fade into the past, and we focus instead on seeing anew, seeing whole, beholding the beauty we missed for so long.

This seeing-with-God is especially precious because we have just passed through the season of *when? no!* and *why?* The pain, the dissatisfaction, and disorientation of that declining season have created the void into which surprise and wonder now silently burst. The aspiration, exasperation, fury, rage, doubt and abandonment now give way to wonder, joy and peace. Sometimes that peace comes to us all at once, in a moment of ecstasy and revelation. But more often, I think, it's like a gradual dawning, as when Joseph looked back over his life with all its betrayal, delay, unfairness and mistreatment, and gradually began to see that: others intended him harm, but God intended his well-being all along. Others did evil, but even from their evil, God created good. (Gen. 50:20)

And to the degree we can maintain the prayerful seeing and insightful prayer of meditation, when new troubles come our way, new threats, we can maintain a kind of peace, a peace beyond understanding, which means that we remain free of turmoil without having figured out what's going on. We can rest in God in the eye of the storm, seeing our difficulties neither as a punishment for some past offence, not as evidence that God's protection has gone off-line, but as an opportunity for God to speak expanding good into an expanding void. This is why this kind of seeing is often associated with the word *wait* in Scripture. Wait on the Lord, we are told. Don't slide back into anxiety and anger. Don't rush ahead in a rush to judgement. Don't demand a quick solution (as you may have done when you were praying *when?*).

Don't assume the worst (as you may have done when you were praying *no!*). Don't presume that an answer is forthcoming (as you may have done when you prayed *why?*). No, just wait. Relax. Rest. Don't feel the situation has to be fixed. Hold on, and keep yours eyes open, and you will eventually behold what you do not see now.

The waiting, the slowing down, applies to our pleasures too. Don't rush through this pleasure, but savour it as a gift from God. Taste it. Enjoy it. Linger here. Join God in seeing what a wonderful thing, what a wonderful moment, what a wonderful gift this is. Often, the gift is an insight. You're reading a book, perhaps even this one, or even better, Scripture itself, and you see something. *Behold!* you say. But rather than rushing on to the next thought, you put the book down; you close your eyes, and you hold the thought in your mind as you might hold a spoonful of delicious ice cream or a sip of extraordinary wine on your tongue. Ah, you say. Mmmm, you say. Delicious, you say. You are speaking the language of meditation. This is what Gregory of Nyssa meant when he said, 'Only wonder understands.' Just to hold an insight in a shared, wondrous *behold* with God – perhaps we need to invent a new word to describe it: *wonderstanding*.

This ability to behold is especially essential when we encounter paradox and mystery. We see things that we can't understand, and we are tempted to shrink them to fit into our existing constructs, paradigms, world-views or thought-systems. We want to explain what we see, to capture it in words, to resolve its tensions, but if we do, we will shrink, flatten or reduce our vision. If we resist that reflex even for a few moments, we can simply stand in silence, in awe, and see – see both sides of the paradox and not need to explain one side away.

Many experiences come to mind when I think of this practice of meditation in my own life, but I'll only recount one. It occurred during that tough season of doubt and deconstruction; it was one of those eye-of-the-storm moments. I was preparing a sermon, a sermon about which, by the way, I don't remember anything. I had my Bible open on my desk, and another book too. I may have just read a quote from St Augustine, but I don't remember the details. I do remember that it was in the afternoon, and as I was reading, thinking, and pondering, I began to sense that something was waiting for me if I didn't rush on to the next thought.

Then, it was as if I broke through to a deeper level, or fell through the floor – that might be a better image for it. I stopped reading. I stopped writing and working on my outline. I just sat there in my chair and closed my eyes. If you had seen me, you would have said, 'Poor guy. He's fallen asleep … he's taking a nap.' And in a sense I was. I was resting, resting in God's presence. My thoughts were like a flock of birds flying overhead. They floated by, floated by, and then they were gone. All I could feel was a joyful stillness surrounding me, a clarity cooling me, a peace breathing into me.

As I sat there, a question formed itself in my mind. I didn't feel as though I had created the question or had to go after it or reach for it. I felt that it just opened up in me, having formed by surprise in my mind. The question seemed to spill from God's mind to my own: 'Is there any thought you can have of God that is too good?' And for some moments, I just sat with that question, and as I did, I received something: a deep and powerful realisation of the goodness of God. I was suspended in that realisation for some time. Other questions slowly presented themselves: Can you accept that you will never, ever,

ever contain God? That you will never, ever capture God in words – even though you are a preacher and writer, working with words? Can you just behold, in silent wonder and reverent awe?[3]

Since that afternoon, meditative seeing – seeing with God, seeing in God – has become a more and more important part of my spiritual life. Every day provides constant opportunities to experiment. Consider these three scenarios that you could try right now:

First, you could go to a public place and practise beholding people with God. You'll no doubt hear your chattering, analysing, critical mind assessing each one in accordance with its own agendas, desires, drives and neuroses: fat, thin, rich, poor, stylish, frumpish, sexually attractive, sexually unattractive, my kind of person, not my kind of person, Christian, non-Christian, and so on. Instead of living within this cramped space of judgement, observe it – behold it from a distance: 'There it goes again,' you might say with amusement. 'My limited human mind is acting as if I were God and I were qualified to judge these people.' Consciously separate yourself from that small mental courtroom, and instead step outside it and above it into God's larger, more gracious space. Allow the Spirit to help you see these people in God's light – each one precious, each one in need, each one at once beautiful and broken and dangerous and dignified. Whenever you find yourself shrinking back into the dualist, courtroom mind, simply observe it, name it and step outside it as you return to a more generous, gracious beholding with God.

Second, you could go to a natural place – anywhere, really, where there's a patch of sky or a blade of grass or some grains of sand – and behold God's creative work. Let your senses wake up – sight, of course, but also smell, hearing and touch – and imagine yourself in an art gallery where every single thing is a work of art, and each work has been placed in relation to others. Again, you'll probably hear your well-exercised critical faculties at work: mosquito – bad, flower – good, weed – bad, lawn – good, and so on. Simply observe your critical observations, and allow yourself to not be limited by them. You may be drawn to one specific thing – a single leaf, a branch, a stone, a patch of sky reflected on water. Pause with it and simply let it show itself to you, with a sense of openness to see God's fingerprints, God's signature, God's glory shining through it. It may help to quietly say, 'Behold' to yourself, and as you do, to invite yourself to see with God. Don't be surprised if you feel a tenderness, a love arising in you. That love is inherent to the way God sees everything God has made.

Finally, you could find yourself in an uncomfortable place – in a dentist's chair, on a crowded bus, in the room next to a couple arguing, in a hospital bed or waiting room. Here again, you will no doubt hear the buzz of anxieties, complaints, arguments and judgements bothering your soul. But again, if you observe your reactions, you can contain them rather than being contained by them, and you can allow yourself to live and breathe, even for a few brief moments at first, outside them. You can open your heart to God (holding the word *here* will help you, as will holding *help*, *please* and *when?*), and gradually allow yourself to see with God: to see the situation in a larger frame of reference, to see the people who may be annoying you, even to see yourself within it. You can let the whole scenario be bathed in God's gentle, gracious light, and in that light, even for a few stolen moments, you can behold.

More and more of our lives can be taken up into this kind of beholding – eating slowly, savouring each mouthful; walking slowly, treasuring each step; reading slowly (as you may have been doing at this moment without realising it), holding each fragment of meaning that accumulates into a larger and larger meaning, a wonder to behold.

This profound and joyful beholding defies all explanations. Like a fragile butterfly, to capture it would be to damage or kill it. And that's how I feel at this moment. After having written all these words, I feel that I have failed to capture it. A few words written by St Augustine – maybe the ones I was reading that day? – seem to honour beholding far better than my many words can:

All shall be amen and alleluia.
We shall rest and we shall see,
We shall see and we shall know,
We shall know and we shall love,
We shall love and we shall praise.
Behold our end which is no end.

Chapter 24

Yes: A Universal Spiritual Vocation

The Practice of Consecration and Surrender: Deepening by Joining

At Plum Village, I teach the young people a simple verse to practice while walking: 'Oui, Oui, Oui,' as they breathe in, and, 'Merci, merci, merci,' as they breathe out. 'Yes, yes, yes. Thanks, thanks, thanks.' I want them to respond to life, to society, and to the Earth in a positive way. They enjoy it very much.

Thich Nhat Hanh[1]

When we speak of joining God in seeing, it is as if, having climbed a long path up a mountain, we reach the summit and gain a view so vast that it takes our breath away. What could be more majestic and inspiring than transcending our normal frame of reference and mounting up with eagle's wings to see from a loftier viewpoint? That's why we must linger here and let the *behold* ring and echo in our hearts, sharing our vision with God. But our journey is not yet finished. We cannot stay on the mountain, but rather, we must descend back to the valley again.

It would be tempting to stay forever on the high ridge of meditation, except that when we see with God, we see with compassion. And just as compassion brings God down to earth to share in our pain and struggle, compassion leads us into downward mobility too. Going down again, down into the valley, will mean distractions, temptations, regressions, misadventures, conflict, struggle. Compassion motivates us to accept these challenges for the sake of others. But it's not just for the sake of others that we must leave the mountains of meditation: it's for our own continuing growth too. God isn't finished with us yet. And so the Spirit of God says, 'Come on. Let's go. Follow me. Follow me down, deeper down and deeper in. For the sake of others. And for your own wellbeing too.' And when our heart says *Yes*, we are entering the next spiritual practice, the practice of consecration and commitment, surrender and submission.

It surprises many people to hear God call them down. We think God is up. We're trained by the ladder of success to think it's for climbing, not descending. But God's mobility is opposite to our own. I'm writing these words at the beginning of Advent, when we Christians celebrate God's downward movement to us, God-in-Christ coming down to a poor and humble woman, down into her womb, down into a stable, down into hay. And that's just the beginning. When Jesus comes of age, he doesn't climb a mountain and live above the fray in a contemplative cave or commune. No, after a brief period in the wilderness (much of which, in that part of the world, is very mountainous and prime territory for lofty, expansive views), he moves continually down into the mess of human history. He moves down into the struggles of human politics and economics, down into the ugliness of human ignorance and misunderstanding, down even into the horror of human injustice and bigotry, even into the tragedy of human violence and murder.

That is the substance of one of the first Christian hymns (Phil. 2:6–11), and it tells us not only that Jesus was humble and downwardly mobile, but more: that God is humble and downwardly mobile.[2] The final vision of the Apocalypse (Rev. 21–22) dares proclaim this same truth: that God's presence, symbolised by a cubical city (evoking, no doubt, the Holy of Holies in the temple), moves downward to be among humanity. So, when we join God on the mountain and see from within a new creation, we shouldn't be surprised that God's next call is to come on down. Will we surrender, yield, commit, submit to that downward call with our *yes?*

In the beginning of our venture with God, we heard our name being called and we said, 'Here I am.' That was the call to communion. But now we have the call of commission. First came the call to transformation – to yield ourselves to God's transforming work in our lives. Now comes the vocation to transforming mission – to join with God in God's work in the world. Having joined God in being together and seeing together, now we agree to join God in serving together – and yes, in suffering and dying together. The call to service is offensive to those who seek fame, comfort, advantage, safety and status. But it is joyful and good to those who seek to put compassion into action.

In my early years as a Christian, this consecrated life of surrender was known as 'total commitment', and I sought it as wholeheartedly as I could (and still do). As we saw earlier, John Wesley called it 'entire sanctification', and his critics derided it as 'enthusiasm', as if someone should be ashamed of being completely 'into God' (which is what *en-theos-asm* actually means). Pentecostals at their best know this is what 'being filled with the Spirit' is all about. It's not just speaking in tongues or jumping and shouting (or planting 'seed gifts' hoping for a big return on investment). Rather, to be Spirit-filled is to be surrendered to the Spirit so the fruit of the Spirit, the power of the Spirit, and the gifts of the Spirit will flow from our lives. Some Roman Catholics tended to isolate this kind of life for 'the religious' and exempted 'the secular' or 'lay people' from it. But counter movements through Catholic history emphasised that all dimensions of our lives may be taken up into God's sacred creative project. This integration later became a hallmark of much of the Reformed tradition in Protestantism. So faithful people from all sectors of the religious world have known in their bones that all of us are called to a consecrated life. All have a divine vocation – whether they are farmers, teachers, lawyers, scientists, homemakers, or shop-keepers. The invitation and vocation are there: we just needed to say yes, to pray and practise *Yes!*

Evangelicals have long understood the need to call people to commitment. For Evangelicals, you're not automatically born into a spiritual life, like being Polish or blonde or left-handed. Rather, the spiritual life is like a marriage, and you must say yes to it. That's why Evangelicals often emphasise that first yes through something called an altar call or a gospel invitation.[3] But just as one 'I do' is necessary but not sufficient for a marriage, so that first 'yes' is essential but requires the follow-up of more yeses. Baptism can serve as a second yes. (For denominations that baptise infants, confirmation can serve as a first yes.) Participating in the eucharist yet another *yes*, as is volunteering for a ministry, or becoming regular in weekly church attendance. But even those yeses eventually become routine and automatic, habits rather than conscious choices. So what after that? Revival services with their special 'anointings', 'movings' or 'blessings' of the Spirit, which periodically challenge people to revive their *yes* again and again.

Whatever our tradition, we eventually realise that our *yes* must become, not simply an event, but a practice. Each of us must learn to hold open our *yes* to the Spirit on a moment-by-moment basis. Jesus used an image for this practice that was both powerful and – to his hearers, anyway – familiar: a branch abiding in a grapevine. The branch can't bear fruit on its own, he said. But if it abides in the vine, it will naturally bear fruit season after season. Yes, pruning will come, and pruning may be painful, but again, if the branch just abides, just stays, just says yes season after season, that pruning will result in ever more fruitfulness as the years go by (John 15:1–11).[4]

Ideally, public gatherings for worship create opportunities for people to reaffirm their *yes* at least weekly. And special holy seasons – Advent, Lent and Pentecost for Christians, Ramadan for Muslims, Passover for Jews, and so on – also build reaffirmation and rededication into the annual calendar. But often, the reaffirmations that count the most come up unexpectedly. A friend in need on a busy day, a stranger in need alongside the road, an enemy or antagonist in need in the middle of conflict ... these 'inconveniences' become opportunities to put our own agendas and comfort aside and say *yes* to abiding in the vine, *yes* to joining God in compassion, *yes* to being God's hands and feet, eyes and ears.

Our *yes* counts most when we receive mistreatment rather than praise for our effort. That's why the theme of suffering for doing good is so central to all our spiritual traditions. To say *yes* to doing good and then be ignored, to say *yes* to doing right and then be misunderstood and criticised, to say *yes* to being loving and then to be vilified and even crucified – this is the territory into which we will all someday be invited. This is the yes of *not my will, but your will be done.*

Chapter 25

Yes: Do You Love Me?

God be in my head, and in my understanding;
God be in my eyes, and in my looking;
God be in my mouth, and in my speaking;
God be in my heart, and in my thinking;
God be at my end, and in my departing.
From a fifteenth-century French *Book of Hours*[1]

Richard Rohr says this about prayer:

Prayer is not primarily saying words or thinking thoughts.
It is, rather, a stance, a way of being present. It's a way
of living *in* the Presence, living in *awareness* of the
Presence, and even of enjoying the Presence. Presence
knows Presence.

The full contemplative is not just aware of the Presence,
but trusts, allows, and delights in it.

All spiritual disciplines have one purpose: to get rid of
illusions so we can *be present*. These disciplines exist so
that we can see what is, see all that is, see who we are,
and see what is really happening right now.[2]

The spiritual life Richard describes is a *yes!* life. In the quiet of winter, it whispers yes to what has been, to what is and to what is to come. This *yes!* of consecration provides the counterpart to the *no!* of refusal; it isn't a mere contradiction, but rather a continuation and completion.

We see exactly this yoking of refusal and consecration in the story of Peter in the Gospels, especially the Fourth Gospel. It's hard to impose traditional storytelling categories on any of the four Gospels. Each has its own unique terrain and structure, reflecting different rhetorical purposes and spiritual insights.[3] There are, it seems, new conflicts and mini-climaxes on every page, and although the resurrection should be a happy ending, it also seems more like a 'to be continued', marking a new beginning.

John's Gospel ends on a shoreline along the Sea of Galilee, far north of Jerusalem. The feel is open and expansive in contrast to the tight, constricted feel of the not-so-holy city. Some days earlier, back in the city, Peter had boasted of his great loyalty to Jesus and Jesus warned Peter that he would deny him three times before the rooster signalled dawn the next day. Determined to live up to his boast, when a group came to take Jesus into custody, Peter demonstrated his loyalty – by pulling out a sword and striking a member of the arrest party. (He thus started two longstanding Christian traditions: first, religious violence, and second, behaving in a manner completely inconsistent with Jesus himself.) Jesus rebuked Peter and healed the victim and then was taken in ropes or chains to the courtyard of Annas the High Priest. Peter and another disciple followed at some distance and eventually managed to gain entry to the courtyard. Seeking to remain inconspicuous, they huddled with others in the evening chill around a charcoal fire (an important detail). In the light of that fire, Peter saw Jesus being interrogated and roughed up by a member of the High Priest's staff.

During that long night, whenever Peter was suspected of being affiliated with the man in custody, he denied their connection. As morning dawned, a rooster crowed and Peter realised he had fallen into exactly the kind of denial Jesus had predicted. He went out, another Gospel writer tells us, and wept bitterly. (Those tears, I suspect, represented his moment of lament, just as Jesus' tears had done the night before.)

As morning dawned, Jesus was convicted of religious blasphemy (claiming to be one with God) and civil treason (claiming to be a king). He was taken by the Romans and tortured, executed by crucifixion and buried. But two days later, Jesus began appearing again to a growing circle of disciples – including Peter. Jesus was scarred on his hands and feet, but to the disciples' unimaginable joy, Jesus was in some real way truly, truly, truly alive.

We aren't told how many more days pass, but (in John's Gospel) Peter and friends go back to Galilee.[4] Peter invites a handful of fellow disciples to join him fishing. Did this represent a sense of closure – the adventure was over now, so they were back to their old way of making a living? Did Peter make the assumption that because of his humiliating denial, he was no longer fit to be a 'fisher of people', so he was demoted back to fisher of fish? Or was it simply the comforting rhythm of the waves, of casting the net and retrieving it, that drew Peter out on the water again? We aren't told his inner motives. But we are told that Peter and friends spend a sleepless night fishing and catching nothing, reminiscent of that recent sleepless night when Jesus had been arrested.

At dawn – recalling both the dawn when the rooster crowed

and the dawn when Jesus was rumoured to be alive again – a voice from the shore tells the disciples to cast their nets on the starboard side of the boat, which they do, only to have a huge school of fish fill their nets. Peter quickly jumps in the water and swims ashore. There he discovers that Jesus has made a fire, and not just any fire, but a *charcoal* fire. The flickering light, the hiss and crackle, and the acrid smell of that charcoal fire, of course, together evoke the bitter memories of that recent chilly pre-dawn darkness when Peter had denied Jesus.

Jesus asks the disciples to bring some of their fresh fish for breakfast, and he provides bread – again evoking that night when, over broken bread, Peter had made his now-humiliating boast. After breakfast, within range of the sight, sounds and smell of the charcoal fire on the beach, Jesus invites Peter for a walk. Some steps away from the fire, he asks a question: *Peter, do you love me?* Three times, perhaps once for each of his recent refusals, he asks him. Peter's reply epitomises this simple practice of surrender: *Yes.*

This would be a happy ending of sorts, a heart-warming moment. But the curtain doesn't fall and the plot takes an unexpected twist. Now Jesus tells Peter that a time is coming when he will be taken forcibly against his will and will in fact die. He will face the boast he made and the test he failed back in Jerusalem, and this time, Jesus says, he will pass it: he will be faithful to the point of death. Then Jesus says, 'Follow me.' Will Peter follow Jesus, knowing that it will mean confronting his greatest failure, his greatest fear?

It would be yet another happy ending if Peter simply said yes. The violins could swell; Jesus and Peter could embrace and face the sunrise, the other disciples could huddle in a group hug of tears and laughter, and the credits could roll. But the

263

opposite happens. The ending remains shockingly open, the question stunningly unanswered, the command – *follow me* – blatantly left hanging. Instead – could there be a more anti-climactic move than this? – Peter points to one of the other disciples and does something so unheroic, so petty, so backward, so untransformed, so cowardly that it is hard to imagine. He evades the question entirely. 'What about him?' he asks.

So as the Gospel ends Peter's future hangs in the balance. Will he say, *Yes, I will follow you, Lord, even to death?* We turn the page, not knowing.

The evangelist's rhetorical strategy isn't hard to guess: the open ending puts each of us in Peter's place. We each know our own false starts, our own foolish boasts, our own abysmal failures, our own pathetic relapses. Will we supply the *yes* that Peter dares not give?

A pious, devotional *yes* is easy to say. But Jesus has pressed the matter further with Peter. He has defined very specifically the terms of re-engagement. First, comes the call to love the one he denied. Then Jesus links Peter's *yes* with a repeated call to join him in mission: 'If you love me, feed my sheep.' And finally Jesus pushes further still: 'If you love me, follow me into suffering, even to death.' The yes that is requested of us can only be requested, never forced, because a forced yes is no yes at all. Will you say *yes* to love, *yes* to service, *yes* to risk, suffering and even death?

You'll notice this essential pattern in the spiritual life. The purpose of the spiritual life is not simply to connect us more deeply to God; it also must connect us more deeply to our neighbour – reflected in Jesus' words, *Feed my sheep*. The *formation* we have experienced through our first ten practices prepares us *for mission* in this eleventh simple word. Through the great joy of springtime practice to the great work of summer practice through the great pain of autumn practice, we now come to the great love evoked in the word *yes*, a love that cannot separate God and others, but rather, that loves God in others and loves others in God, saying to both a single *yes*, even to the point of sacrifice, suffering and death.

Most of us, of course, won't die as martyrs. But all of us will die. And as we approach our death, we will have our walk on the beach, our opportunity to say *yes* to God even in death. We will see that life itself is a gift that we are in the end asked to let go of … for the sake of others. We will relinquish our space here so someone else may fill it; we will vacate our room so someone else may have a place to stay. We do this in love for future generations, just as past generations did for us, trusting that we will receive an even greater gift of an even more wonderful life for having relinquished this one. Will we say yes?

As a child, the thought of death terrified me. It seemed like a nightmare, an eternal falling into a bottomless abyss of the unknown. I remember pushing the thought away, hoping it would become less terrifying as I grew up. And it has. Of course, I don't know how it will be when my time comes, but I wonder if it will come to me as three questions not unlike the questions posed to Peter that morning. Brian, do you love me? *Yes, Lord, you know I love you.* Brian, do you love me even more than life itself? *Yes, Lord, for life is the gift and you are the giver. Without the giver, there is no gift, but with the giver, there is the gift as well.* Brian, will you let go of the life you have known so far, and will you follow me through the doorway of death into a new dimension of life? *Yes, Lord. Yes.* And my *yes* of surrender and trust will allow me to let go of this life and fall – not into a bottomless pit of darkness, but into love, into light, into God, into the company of all our ancestors who are upheld in God's love, into a fullness of life that I cannot even imagine now. That falling will be a rising.

And in a sense, that *yes* will simply be the fulfilment of the *yes* that I began practising in my youth that night under the stars, and that I have prayed morning by morning and day by day ever since, and that I hold even now at this moment, each breath in – a *yes* of grateful receptivity and each breath out – a *yes* of release, surrender, consecration.

The other Gospels begin with Jesus saying *Follow me*, but the Fourth Gospel, fascinatingly, ends with this invitation. When my heart is healthy and awake, when I listen into the silence like a child listening into a seashell, I hear God's voice, calling me into adventure and life … *Follow me, imitate me, learn from me, dance with me, work with me, join me.* And I realise that this is what life is: joining the Life in being alive. This is what holiness and love are: joining the Holy and joining Love in being holy and loving. This is what joy and sorrow and hope and regret are: joining the living God in responses to life's diverse experiences. And this is what death will also be, which removes the sting from death and makes death disappear into life: joining God in a reality we have not yet seen or even imagined.

Episcopal priest Robert Farrar Capon has said that the biblical story starts with a break-up and ends with a wedding, and so the history in between is most truly a romance. Yes, the romance is filled with tragedy and comedy, but it always and at every moment remains at heart a love story, and every moment is a proposal. The gift of every moment is the Holy Spirit's holy seduction, the tender proposal of God: I love you.

Do you love me? Will you join me in at-one-ment, unity, recon-ciliation, reunion, belonging, membership, love? Will you accept my proposal and enter into the vital communion of theosis – union with God? Yes, yes, yes, yes, yes.

In death, with our final *yes*, we turn out the light in our little room and a greater love envelopes us. May this moment of consecration be a practice and rehearsal for that one.

Perhaps now, before turning the page, you will pause to feel the proposal the Spirit is making to you. Whether for the first time or the ten-thousandth, you can reach out your *yes* to the *yes* that extends to you:

Yes, I love you. Yes, I want you in my mission. Yes, I forgive you. Yes, I accept you as you are. Do you love me? Do you want to follow me, to join me in my work of healing, feeding, caring and self-giving? Are you with me, as I am always with you?

Perhaps you can put this book down in a moment, adjusting the rhythm of your response to the rhythm of your breath. God offers you life, grace, love, hope, purpose, mission, mercy, meaning ... and you receive them as you inhale your next breath: *yes*. And as you exhale, you reciprocate, offering your life to God, joining God in God's compassionate mission, joining your full presence with God's presence in this world: *Yes* ... yes. *Yes* ... yes. *Yes* ... yes. *Yes* ...

Chapter 26

[...] Naked, Clothed in Silence

The Practice of Contemplation and Rest: Deepening by Being With

Silence is the language of God, and the only language deep enough to absorb all the contradictions and failures that we are holding against ourselves. God loves us silently because God has no case to make against us. The silent communion absorbs our self-hatred, as every lover knows.

Richard Rohr[1]

We put words between ourselves and things. Even God has become another conceptual unreality in a no-man's land of language that no longer serves as a means of communion with reality. The solitary life, being silent, clears away the smokescreen of words that we have laid down between our mind and things. In solitude we remain face to face with the naked being of things. And yet we find that the nakedness of reality which we have feared is neither a matter of terror nor of shame. It is clothed in the friendly communion of silence, and this silence is related to love.

Thomas Merton[2]

Mature musicians don't rush through each note of a song so they can say, 'Good! Another song completed! Check that one off the list!' No, the best musicians enter into the mystery of music with a sense of wonder and leisure mixed with intensity, the opposite of hurry. They feel, just as experienced listeners to great music do, that music ushers them into a kind of transcendence over time, where past, present and future are taken up into something bigger, deeper and wider: the song itself. They realise that each isolated note, like a word, has meaning within the musical phrase in which it is found. And the full meaning and beauty of that phrase only take shape in relation to the phrases before it and after it, and those combined phrases constitute a movement or verse that similarly becomes meaningful through interaction with the other movements or verses that constitute the song.

And even the song isn't an island into itself; its meaning arises within its genre – the blues, techno, folk music, classical music, tribal music, Irish jig, Latin jazz, whatever. And each of those genres has meaning and identity in relation to one another. And the whole body of music today – you can anticipate this – has meaning in relation to the music of the past, and even in relation to the as-yet uncreated music of the future.

So the master musician brings to each note, to each song, to each genre, and to the whole body of music, some degree of awareness of this infinite regression and infinite expansion of meaning and connection – an awareness that goes beyond conscious thought but is nonetheless real. Something similar, I think, could be said about painters with colour and shape, or poets with letter and word, or storytellers with character and incident, or dancers and actors with gesture and posture.

And spiritual people with spiritual practices. The resonating meaning of the simplest practice – here, thanks, O, sorry, help, please, when, no, why, behold, yes – transcends itself and expands to connect with everything, always. There is another even grander dimension to this resonating, expanding field of meaning, but it's hard to convey.

As musicians draw the bow across the string or blow across the reed or press their fingers upon the keys, they at some level know that silence is the field in which music happens. Without the space or field of silence, there can be no music. Under or around or above or before or after each note or song there is silence, a silence so necessary that we might call it holy.

Painters know something similar about negative space, as do dancers or actors about the empty space of the stage, as do landscapers, farmers or gardeners about the space of the land. Blank canvas, empty space, silence … they are, we might say, good. We might say they are as precious as – perhaps even more precious than? – the colours, actions, words, objects or music with which we fill them, because they create the possibility not only for the actuality of this song, this painting, this poem, but the possibility for uncounted other actualities as well.

And so imagine the musician who loves music intensely, but she also loves silence, the field of absence that makes the presence of all music possible. And imagine the painter who loves colour and shape and line, but also loves the void of negative space for the possibilities it holds. And imagine the dancer who loves movement and also stillness. And now imagine the person who loves God and who therefore loves spiritual practices but who also loves … can I say it this way? Not practising. Being in silence. Being at rest with God with no words at all. This is not the passive silence of emptiness, compla-

270

cency or negation but rather the living silence that is pregnant with infinite possibilities.

And so the last of our simple words is no word at all. The withheld word. The unspoken word. The word that doesn't need to be said. The breath without a sound. If you want to give it a descriptive word, perhaps *be* would suffice, as in, 'Be still and know that I am God. Don't think. Don't speak: just *be*.'

Better still would be the sound of a breath, a sigh of relaxation, an *ahhh* of rest, and the silence that ensues.

There's a story told about Mother Teresa; I don't know if it is true or not, but the story tells the truth whether or not it happened. She was asked by a reporter (the story goes) what she said to God when she prayed. She replied, 'Mostly I just listen.' The reporter followed up: and what does God say to you? 'Mostly he just listens,' she replied. Could it be that the loving, attentive, mutual listening of the soul and the Spirit constitute the greatest expression of spirituality? Lovers know that this is true: they know there is a kind of attention, a kind of 'just listening', that is one of the highest imaginable expressions of love. Holy listening holds space open between beloved and Beloved, the soul and God, and that space, like the silence in which all music happens, holds infinite possibilities.[3]

Although all three of our Stage Four practices could be called contemplation, I am reserving the word for this kind of silent attentiveness, this holy receptivity to possibility, this beautiful, sacred, restful, naked silence.

Part of me hated contemplation in my younger years. I didn't get it, and when others tried to introduce me to it, something inside me rebelled, even if I complied out of a sense of duty. There were tasks to be checked off my to-do list; there were souls to be saved, sermons to be preached, problems to be solved, goals to be achieved and (how arrogant and naïve was this?) the world to be changed or *transformed* in my lifetime. Contemplative prayer felt too much like doing nothing in the midst of such frantic urgency. Frankly, it seemed like wasting time.

Which, of course, was the point. In resting, in quietness, in nothingness, I would have been pratising a kind of trust to which I assented mentally but struggled to actually internalise, trust expressed in biblical passages like these:

Unless the LORD builds the house,
those who build it labour in vain.
Unless the Lord guards the city,
the guard keeps watch in vain.
It is in vain that you rise up early
and go late to rest,
eating the bread of anxious toil;
for he gives sleep to his beloved. (Ps. 127:1–2)

For thus said the Lord God, the Holy One of Israel:
In returning and rest you shall be saved;
in quietness and in trust shall be your strength.
But you refused and said,
'No! We will flee upon horses' –
therefore you shall flee!
and, 'We will ride upon swift steeds' –
therefore your pursuers shall be swift! (Isa. 30:15–16)

I am the vine, you are the branches. Those who abide in me and I in them bear much fruit, because apart from me you can do nothing. (John 15:5)

Perhaps it was seeing how little fruit my fretful activity produced. Perhaps it was simply wisdom gained through experience. But eventually, I began to realise that to be an activist – to get good things done, and done well – meant that I must see contemplation not as a burden, duty, or distraction, but as a gift, as an opportunity, as a joy. This explains why my friends at the Centre for Action and Contemplation, say that the most important word in their name is *and*. Similarly, Jim Wallis, in my favourite of his many good books, says:

> To be a contemplative means to find a motivation deeper than the hope of results. You have to be sustained by more important things ... It is a paradox: to be successful you must finally give up the demand for success and do what you do from the deeper motivations of what you believe is right.[4]

When I first read those words many years ago, I sensed they were right, but I also knew they were beyond me. I could only place *versus* between action and contemplation, and it took a long time to really settle into the wisdom of *and*. For so many years, I was desperate for results – big ones, and fast. I was caught up in words, ideas, slogans and myths, striving to build an identity of importance to prove myself and my worth. All in God's name of course. The result was a cycle of elation and depression, hope and disappointment, furious activity and deflated cynicism. I saw the same progression in my life that Thomas Merton once described in a letter to his friend Jim Forest – from working for results, to working because of the value of the work itself, to working for specific people whom I love, to allowing myself 'to be used by God's love', to being open to God's power working through me, and finally, simply living, which Merton calls 'the great thing'. The progression involves a shift in hope from what I can do to what God is doing. It's a shift from self-consciousness (How am I doing? Am I doing enough?) to consciousness of God – what is God doing? How can I fit in, support, participate? And at the core of that consciousness of God is a quiet attentiveness, an active receptivity, a blaze of listening.

My friend Steve Bell gets this. He is a gifted songwriter and musician. He's done thousands of concerts through the years, but one moment in one concert stands out among them. Here's how he described it for me in an email:

It was toward the end of a concert I was performing in Virden Manitoba. I had my band with me and we were backed by the Winnipeg Symphony Orchestra for the last of what was an eight-concert tour of rural Manitoba. This final concert was in a tiny community theater that seated a little more than twice the number of people in the orchestra who were comically cramped onto the stage behind me.

At one point, Mike, my piano player, was taking a solo; he seemed particularly inspired as the whole evening had a great, almost magical energy to it. I was intrigued by some of the rhythmical ideas he was playing with in his solo and we locked eyes as I dialed into what he was doing by doing everything I could with my guitar to support and accent his ideas. Not always, but often enough, you can get so absorbed by what another player is doing on stage that you almost lose consciousness of yourself as you become absorbed toward the other.

Suddenly, and surprisingly, it dawned on me that as much as I was absorbed in supporting Mike's playing, he was doing the exact thing toward me. I was playing off him, and he was playing off me – neither was leading. We were both 'othering' at the same time. And almost as suddenly as I realized this, the whole scene stopped like a freeze frame, like someone hit pause on the DVD player. And there was a brief suspension in which the voice of God spoke to me and said, 'Pay attention to this Steve. This is Who I am.' And just as quickly, the whole scene was back in full motion, Mike was burning up the piano, and I was so overcome with a sense of psychic vertigo that I thought I might faint.

For weeks afterwards I was a bit of a mess. I was weepy, unable to concentrate, totally overwhelmed by what had happened and equally as desperate to understand. Somewhere in there I came across a book by Rowan Williams called *The Wound of Beauty* and immediately resonated with that title as though I knew exactly, experientially, what that meant.

The phrase that has come to me since is 'mutual-othering'. That the highest moments of human experience and fulness occur when we lose ourselves (or, finally find ourselves) in flourishing the other ... mutually. And this because it is in each rare moment of mutual-othering (inter-being, perichorisis) that we most resemble the One whose image we bear; God, whose oneness is not a numerical oneness, like a tree is one, but a relational oneness – like a forest is one. From here I think I can know that God does not merely endorse, recommend or prefer Love, but rather, God *is* Love.

When Steve's selfless attention met Mike's selfless attention, time disappeared. Everything froze and fell away. The song continued, the exceptional playing continued, but he and the pianist were lost in what a musician might call the infinite groove, what we might call the vital connection.[5] If you've experienced a moment like that – in music, in sport, in conversation, in love-making, or in prayer – you know that this is what it's all about. This is it. And you can say no more, but simply feel the transcending of time in the abundance of holy 'otherly' attention.[6]

This sense of attentiveness is essential to naked spirituality. This is the spirituality of the post-religious and the post-atheist. Literary theorist Mikhail Epstein compares it to a blade of grass daring to rise from a crack in a sidewalk.[7] In that hostile environment, quiet is better than loud. Minimal is better than ornate. The simplicity of poverty is better than the excess of affluence. And silence is better than words – not the barren silence of boredom, but the pregnant silence of listening. Epstein explains:

> It is not the Word which is holy now, but rather Listening and Hearing…. In the post-atheist era, we have begun to understand that God's silence is a way of His listening to us, His attention to our words. Such active silence is necessary for the continuation of dialogue where one speaker alternatively gives the floor to another. After God had uttered His word in the Old and New Testaments, in Scripture and in Flesh, what else could He say? It is time for human beings to reply to God, to respond to His word.

What we seek, he says, is to be 'in the presence of Divine Listening'. Prophets and religions proclaiming the word of the

Lord have their value, Epstein says, but 'hearing is the last realm that cannot be colonised by the reifying force of atheism. God's word, no matter how inspirational and mysterious, can still be reified, retold, reinterpreted, ridiculed, rejected. But ... God's hearing is unsurpassable, it surrounds and encloses our voices like the horizon.' He explains:

> Thus, post-atheist spirituality is neither the religion of God's *voice*, as it was and continues to be in traditional churches and denominations; neither is it agnostic indifference, existential despair or atheistic challenge in the face of God's *silence*. Rather it is a feeling of responsibility arising from the belief that God is silent because He is *listening* to us.

Could it be that the joy we pursue in life – whether the joy of playing an instrument or playing a sport, of chipping a sculpture from stone or building a business from the ground up – is the joy of knowing that there is a silence, a void, a space that waits for us to fill it? And could it be that God, the creator of both us and that void, is the witness, the audience, the Listener for whom we are always performing? And could it be that contemplation is the pause button that freezes time so that we listen to the Listening and witness the Witness?

Chapter 27

[...] Full Circle

[The words'] intent is to create space, to open up the possibility, to make available the moment – the now – for the in-breaking of the Holy. When our worship moves into this space, words and silence merge. Then, style, method, language, and format become inconsequential, and prayer dissolves into what the mystics so often experienced: a simple 'Ah!' before the mystery of it all.

Barbara Fiand[1]

To be effective over the long haul, to make a real and lasting difference, you need to have a secret life, rooted in a secret silence and calm stillness. In that stillness, you know there is a Listener, a Witness, holding you in loving attention. You know that what you are doing has value even if there are no visible results because the Witness has witnessed it. This is the unseen ice that buoys up the visible iceberg; this is the silence into and from which the music comes. This is the dark void into which creativity bursts like light.

A friend once described a dream to me that he felt God had given him on my behalf. He had been watching a television show about a huge dam being built in China. The reservoir was taking many years to fill up, but once full, it would provide electricity for millions of people for centuries. In the dream, he watched the water level slowly, slowly, slowly rising. This, he felt, was to be a picture for me of my life. During the long delays when nothing seems to be happening, when nothing seems to be working, when no power is being generated, in those silent times of waiting, potential energy is accumulating from which lasting power will flow in due time.

Which brings me back to the previous chapter, reflecting on music and musicians. Where does my impatience come from – my desire to get this and that done as soon as possible, my irrational desire to 'get finished' fast? I love the music and enjoy the making of each note, but yet I seem to want to get the song over with as soon as possible. Why? When I finish this song, what then? Hurry on to the next, to finish it as soon as possible? I feel like one of those contestants in an eating contest, jamming hot dogs in my mouth with one eye on the clock. My default mode of hurry tells me that I have so much more to learn from silence, from being still, from simply being, letting the reservoir slowly fill, storing up a deep but quiet power.

Many of us first experience this contemplative silence in the aftermath of tragedy. You've been rushed to the hospital with chest pains, put through a million hurried tests, then sped on a stretcher to your room and transferred to your bed. Another flurry of activity – monitors attached, blankets and bed adjusted, and then suddenly, the nurses are gone and you're alone. You look down at your left hand lying palm up on the sheet and suddenly you notice it. You move your fingers. You reach your right hand over and stroke the skin, notice the different sensations on palm, fingers, forehand. This hand has been yours for your whole life, but you have never really noticed it as you do now.

And then, as if by magic, the awareness of being alive spreads, as it were, up your hand and arm and across your chest, down your arm to your opposite fingertips, and then down your torso and legs to your toes, and up your neck to the top of your head. And for a few golden moments you are not only alive: you are aware you are alive, and whether or not you've been religious up to this moment, you suddenly know the meaning of the words *glory* and *holy*.

Or you're cutting the lawn and over the mower's growl you hear, behind you, the screeching of brakes out front. You remember your daughter was riding her tricycle in the driveway and your heart jumps a beat. You turn around and see her trike lying in the middle of the street, and a few yards away, you see a pick-up truck with the front door open, and by the front bumper, you see a teenage boy on his knees, leaning over something. And in that slow-motion moment as you break into a sprint across your front lawn toward the scene of the accident, you realise the full dimensions of your love for your little girl, scratched and bruised but OK, and you feel as never before the meaning of the word *love*.

You've been a half-day's drive away from home for a holiday with your family, but you get news that there's been a tornado, earthquake, landslide or fire in your town. Your heart is pounding as you rush back into your neighbourhood. You see devastation on all sides and neighbours picking through rubble. You turn the corner, and where your house should be, there's a void. But rather than feeling loss, you realise that the people who matter most to you are alive and with you, and that everything else can be replaced, and you feel, as never before, *blessed*.

The practice of contemplation puts us in a similar frame of mind, minus the triggering tragedy. It integrates awareness, aliveness, holiness, love, appreciation and blessedness, all in the presence of God in whom we live, move and have our being, all in the present timeless moment. We value or deem things more as God values and deems them, so for us, they become re-deemed, which is why the contemplative dimension of the spiritual life could also be called the redemptive dimension. It brings together all that we have learned, lost, gained and become through the previous seasons and practices of the spiritual life, and helps us simply *be* in holiness, love and blessedness ... a state of being that, once you've experienced it, gives meaning to the word *heaven*.

How do we practise contemplation? Of course, like many of life's best things, it's better shown than told, better experienced through practice than explained in words. If you were to meet with a spiritual director and ask to be introduced to contemplative practice, he or she might give the following directions:

First, get comfortable in your body. Sit or kneel in a comfortable position. Breathe deeply several times so your body feels at rest. Now for the harder part: bring your inner aliveness to a place of attentive quietness and rest in God's presence. Gradually put yourself in the posture of listening, of receptivity, waiting to hear rather than waiting to speak. Now realise that you are listening to God's perpetual listening; your openness and receptivity mirror God's openness and receptivity to you.

If unfinished business demands attention, you can attend to it, using the practices you have already learned – invocation, gratitude and worship; confession, petition and intercession; aspiration, refusal and lament; meditation and consecration. But there will always be unfinished business of some sort, so at some point, you'll simply need to let the unfinished business go. How to do that? Try imagining each worry, concern, or distraction that comes to mind as a pebble that forms in your hand. Name it, and then imagine letting the pebble fall. Or imagine it as a leaf floating toward you on a stream. Simply acknowledge it and let it pass. If you try to fight it, you'll increase its 'sticking power'. Just let it come and go. Let the internal narrative chatter, the whirring of the internal computer, be suspended ... and then return to a posture of quiet receptivity to God, in God's presence. This process may take several minutes.

It's not important that you feel anything, although you may. It's not important if you have a vision or feel you receive some message from God, although you may. It's not important that you receive some flash of insight or whisper of guidance, although you may. What is important is that you pull back from activity, from being driven by this or that need, impulse or compulsion that distract, you from who you already are and who God always is. Let the dust settle. Let the water clear. Let God be God to you, with you, in you. Just breathe. Just be. Listening, being listened to. Resting, in a greater Rest.

The spiritual director might help you see that this is the meaning of grace: the realisation that you are already loved, already accepted, already enough, without doing anything. You are loved nakedly, and grace is the warm blanket that enfolds you. You are loved not because you are good or because you do good, but because God is good, not because you must achieve and sustain being lovable, but because God is love. The surplus of God's loving goodness fills to overflowing every lack or vacuum you bring to the equation.

After this instruction, the spiritual director might read a psalm, perhaps like Psalm 131, ascribed to David as 'A Song of Ascents' – the kind of psalm one would sing on the final stages of a pilgrimage to Jerusalem:

> O Lord, my heart is not lifted up,
> my eyes are not raised too high;
> I do not occupy myself with things
> too great and too marvellous for me.
> But I have calmed and quieted my soul,
> like a weaned child with its mother;
> my soul is like the weaned child that is with me.
> O Israel, hope in the Lord
> from this time on and for evermore. (Ps. 131)

The spiritual director chooses such a psalm because it offers a wordless image: a child at rest in its mother's arms, not desiring milk but content to hear its mother's heartbeat. With that image, the spiritual director would leave you – not to think about the image, but to enter it and pass through it, and to be with God in the peaceful, intimate way it describes.

You may begin to learn contemplative prayer in a private session like this with a spiritual director, or perhaps on a retreat or in a special gathering with a church group. But these special times of practice are intended to make contemplation a regular and natural part of your daily life. You will gradually learn to take a little vacation spontaneously when needed, a few moments of Sabbath, times when you stop working, thinking, trying, striving, stressing. These mini-retreats can happen as you sit in a chair, take a slow walk, lie in bed in the middle of the night, ride on a crowded aeroplane or train or bus, wait in a doctor's office, lie down in a field or rest beside a stream. Nobody around you needs to know, but you are checking out of the mad rush and checking in with the living God.

Two streams in the Christian faith are converging, I think, to teach us about contemplation. First, there is the Pentecostal stream. Pentecostalism is, with little doubt, one of the most significant movements in Christian history, growing in a single century from a handful of people to six hundred million, constituting a quarter of the Christians in the world. What accounts for this phenomenal expansion? Many things, no doubt, but a renewed focus on the direct experience of the living God would be central to anyone's accounting, along with the expectation that the experience of God will ultimately bring, not fear and dread or self-loathing, nor a crushing weight of ceremonial propriety or tense reverence, but exuberant joy and liberation, effusive well-being and wholeness.

Pentecostalism has also provided means – practices – for experiencing God in this way: exuberant singing, passionate preaching, shouting, raising hands, even dancing. All of these practices both create and express a kind of breakthrough that allows participants to get beyond normal inhibitions and preoccupations and there, on the far side of our normal mode of semi-consciousness, we find God waiting for us or, as it is often expressed, we experience Spirit coming to us or upon us, visiting us, or baptising us in renewing joy, reviving peace and transforming power.

We might say that Pentecostalism teaches us to experience God on the far side of normalcy. If it's normal to sit and listen, then you stand and sing. If it's normal to stand and sing, then you raise your hands and shout. If it's normal to raise your hands and shout, then you jump for joy and dance. Like Peter, you step out of the familiar boat and find God as you walk on strange water, here and now.

At the opposite end of the spectrum, we might say, is the contemplative stream. It shares the same confidence that the living God can be joyfully experienced, and it too offers practices for experiencing God. But we might say it finds those practices in the opposite direction.[2] Instead of creating space for experiencing God through loud preaching and shouting and singing, it creates space in quietness and restful silence. Instead of preferring a huge crowd, it tends toward solitude. Instead of venturing boldly beyond the realm of normalcy, it dares acknowledge God at the very centre of normalcy. Instead of praying, 'Come to us, God, visit us, God,' it says, 'Let me realise, God, that you are already here, always here, here, now.'

Perhaps you see, in those words *here* and *now*, that we have come full circle. The last day of winter has become the first day of spring. We have arrived where we began: at a moment of invocation, awakening to the presence of God. Like a hawk or eagle soaring up on a thermal column of air, we have spiralled up in a widening arc. We have come full circle but at a higher altitude, from the first springtime of simplicity to a second and bigger simplicity. Soon we will also enter a second and deeper summer of complexity, and so on. We will experience all the seasons and their practices again, but at a higher altitude and with a loftier view and deeper vision, from invocation to thanksgiving to worship; from confession to petition to intercession; from aspiration to refusal to lamentation; from meditation to consecration and contemplation.

We have ascended into the experience described by another psalm, Psalm 46:

> God is our refuge and strength,
> a very present help in trouble.
> Therefore we will not fear, though the earth should
>   change,
> though the mountains shake in the heart of the sea;
> though its waters roar and foam,
> though the mountains tremble with its tumult. *Selah*.
>   (Ps. 46:1–3)

Whether in the Pentecostal way or the contemplative way, we have found a refuge, a safe and secure space where the terror of crumbling mountains and foaming waters can't touch us. As we've seen, that word *selah* probably signalled a musical interlude in the original public performance of this psalm, or perhaps a period of silence – either way, a time to practise contemplation, to experience what the poetry has pointed towards. In contrast to the shaking earth and raging sea, we now have the image of a powerful, peaceful river of joy:

> There is a river whose streams make glad the city of God,
> the holy habitation of the Most High.
> God is in the midst of the city; it shall not be moved;
> God will help it when the morning dawns. (vv. 4–5)

Jerusalem, of course, has no such river. This is a mystical river, the flow or current of the Spirit's presence in the centre of our lives. Through the night it ran while we slept, and now, at daybreak, we see it, we feel it, running strong and clear and

silent again today. And we are glad. That invisible river flows
with unimaginable power:

> The nations are in an uproar, the kingdoms totter;
> he utters his voice, the earth melts.
> The LORD of hosts is with us;
> the God of Jacob is our refuge. *Selah*. (vv. 6–7)

Suddenly, the tinny uproar and tottering chaos of 'the morning
news' seem trivial and old: the real headline isn't the latest
coup d'état or petty political scandal. The real news, the good
news, according to the psalm, is the 'with-us' presence of the
living God, a presence in which we learn to dwell as a refuge,
a place of security and safety. That realisation becomes the
refrain to which we return in the last lines of the song:

> Come, behold the works of the Lord;
> see what desolations he has brought on the earth:
> He makes wars cease to the end of the earth;
> he breaks the bow, and shatters the spear;
> he burns the shields with fire.
> 'Be still, and know that I am God!
> I am exalted among the nations,
> I am exalted in the earth.'
> The LORD of hosts is with us;
> the God of Jacob is our refuge. *Selah*. (vv. 8–11)

The inner peace of the river of God doesn't bring personal
calm to our individual lives alone. The Psalmist sees its ultimate effect, and invites us to behold it as well: violent empires
are reduced to ruins (desolations), bringing an end to war, a

destruction not *by* weapons but *of* weapons. In that post-war peace and eu-topian stillness we find God's self-revelation and God's true exaltation: *I am*, God says. *I am exalted*. It is a new day for all humanity, a new creation, everything made new. The ultimate cause of activism – the end of war – is intimately related to the personal practice of contemplation. The world changes as we are changed; peace comes to the world as peace flows in our innermost being and out through us to others. 'Let justice roll down like waters!' the prophet Amos said. 'And righteousness like an ever-flowing stream!'[3]

There is nothing more radically activist than a truly spiritual life, and there is nothing more truly spiritual than a radically activist life. If you fight for peace with an unpeaceful spirit, you guarantee that unintended consequences will trump your intended ones. If you struggle for a sustainable economy with unsustainable effort, you guarantee your own failure. Earth's outer ecology will, inevitably, mirror our inner ecology. So there can be no lasting poverty reduction in society unless we grapple with greed reduction in the soul. If we want loving relationships, joyful communities and peaceful nations in society, we must cultivate an inner fecundity of Spirit. That, of course, is no argument for passive pietism and quietism; it is, rather, a call to the most costly, radical activism, the one that calls us to be the change we want to see in the world. It is the call to *be* the light of the world – not merely to complain that the world is too dark. It is the call to *be* the salt of the earth – not merely to protest the world's rottenness. It's fruitless to argue being versus doing: you can't do what you won't be.

Do we dream of a more peaceful world? Then we nourish the vital connection with the Spirit of peace, and we live from that deep well. Do we thirst for a more verdant, green world? Then we nourish the vital connection with the Spirit of life, the breath of life, the living God of life, and we become seed-sowers and garden-growers at every turn. Do we burn for a message of justice to penetrate the hard hearts of the powerful and complacent? Then we nourish the vital connection with the Spirit of truth, and justice will flow from us like water, always seeking the lowest place where it is needed most.

There is a river that runs like a song through this world, a river of sacredness, a river of beauty, a river of reverence and justice and goodness. I know that some people have only rarely seen or barely sensed it. But I also know that you and I are learning to live like green trees along its shore, drawing its vitality into us, and passing it on for the healing of our world. Its waters are clear, refreshingly cool, and clean, and if you dare, you can strip naked, dive in, and swim.

Selah.

[...]

Afterword: The Sea Toward Which All Rivers Run

> When the soul is plunged into the fire of divine love, like iron, it first loses its [coldness and dullness], and then growing to white heat, it becomes like unto fire itself. And lastly it grows liquid, and, losing its nature, is transmuted into an utterly different quality of being... As the difference between iron that is cold, and iron that is hot, so is the difference between ... the tepid soul, and the soul made incandescent by divine love.
>
> Richard of St Victor[1]

Twelve simple words ... formative words that can help us grow an incandescent life with God, a life of vital connection with the whole regenerative community of creation.[2] You have probably anticipated where these twelve simple words must lead: to one word that enfolds them all, the final word, *love*.

Jesus was right. Paul was right. John was right. The Buddha was right. Even the Beatles were right.[3] It all comes down to love, or call it compassion if you prefer. Love is the vital connection. A life with God is a life of love.[4] You know God by loving God. You know God by loving others. You know your neighbour, a stranger or an enemy by loving him or her.

You know a tree or a bird or an ecosystem or a planet by loving it. Even yourself – you only know yourself by properly loving yourself. We are trained to see the universe in terms of fundamental forces – gravity, electromagnetism, weak and strong atomic forces, and so on. But might these physical forces serve as metaphors or scaffolding for the one ultimate fundamental force in the universe, love? Could love be the gravity that brings us together, the magnetism that attracts us, the electricity that makes us shine, the forces that hold us strongly together in community – but not so strongly as to fuse us?

Love begins with presence (Here). It appreciates (Thanks!). It adores (O!). It regrets all that wounds or obstructs love (Sorry!). It interprets need – in oneself or in the other – as an occasion for loving connection (Help! Please!). It sees delay or distance (When? Where?) as opportunities for intensifying desire. It dares hope in the beloved when all hope is gone (Why?). In the end, it sees without judgement (Behold), surrenders to tender proposals of the beloved (Yes), and finally finds no greater joy than simply being together in silence. Love is the last word.

Through love, all is re-ligamented, re-read and re-interpreted, re-joined, reconnected. Through love, at-one-ment triumphs, not in simple oneness where many beings are conquered by or assimilated into one being, but in the joyful one-anotherness of inter-being – the joyful relation that the language of the Trinity soars to celebrate. In that loving community of creation there is both unity and diversity, both melody and harmony, difference without division.

And so it is that the last simple word is the best and the biggest, comprising and fulfilling all others. Spirituality is love.

To hold nothing but naked love in your naked heart – not just the word *love*, but the reality – always, for all, that is the sea towards which all rivers run.

(For additional resources related to this book, you are invited to visit www.brianmclaren.net.)

Appendices

Appendix 1: Group Practice

All groups that gather regularly develop a liturgy – a protocol for meetings that embed certain patterns and practices into the group's life. Liturgy is often defined as the work of the people, but I like to define it as the work-out of the people.[1] The group's shared practices enable its members to bond with the meaning and values deemed important. In so doing, they build the group's inner strength much as physical exercise strengthens muscles. The twelve simple practices in this book are already being used in thousands of creative ways in faith communities around the world, as they have been for centuries. But even so, I believe we stand in great need of liturgical renewal. So many new possibilities await invention, rediscovery and development, and so many of our gatherings are criminally lacklustre and comatose.[2]

Too many gatherings run on a checklist mentality: *here are the things we have to do again this week, so let's get them done.* That mentality involves people in a series of practices without reference to the meanings or values they are intended to celebrate or strengthen. One could argue that this kind of mindless practice is worse than no practice at all in that it alienates and bores participants, turning them against the very practices they need. That's one reason so many people have turned away from organised religion – because the religious community they were part of maintained this well-organised checklist mentality, but forgot the purpose, mission and meaning of its practices.

Whether you're working in a traditional 'worship service' in a church or in an emergent faith community of some sort, you can help pioneer the kind of liturgical renewal we need, and I hope these twelve simple practices will assist you in that process.

William Temple (1881–1944), Anglican priest, Bishop of York, and Archbishop of Canterbury, famously defined public worship like this: 'To worship is to quicken the conscience by the holiness of God, to feed the mind with the truth of God, to purge the imagination by the beauty of God, to open the heart to the love of God, to devote the will to the purpose of God.' For those of us who want to explore, claim and expand the unfulfilled formative potential of public worship, Temple's definition is particularly useful because it links practices to specific faculties or powers of the human soul. We could easily expand Temple's five elements to include all twelve of the practices we have considered:

opening the heart to the presence and love of God
through invocation (Here)
awakening our attention to the generosity of God
through gratitude (Thanks!)
purging the imagination by the beauty of God through
worship (O!)

quickening (or invigorating) the conscience to the holiness of God through confession (Sorry!)

transforming our anxieties by the peace of God
through petition (Help!)

nurturing our empathy through the compassion of God
through intercession (Please!)

sustaining our endurance through the faithfulness of
God through aspiration (When?)

acknowledging our disappointments within the mercy
of God through refusal (No!)

exposing our wounds to the healing of God through
lament (Why?)

expanding our vision in the wisdom of God through
meditation (Behold)

devoting our will to the purpose (or mission) of God
through consecration (Yes)

resting our souls in the attention of God through
contemplation. (...)

How could these practices be integrated into a group experience? Here are some initial suggestions:

If your group reads this book together, you can naturally
gather to converse about some chapters and then experiment with the practices they introduce. Participants could
keep a prayer journal during the week, focusing on the
week's simple word. Then when you gather, each could
choose one or more entries to share. Nothing could be
simpler than starting a page with one simple word, and
then letting a prayer flow from that word.

The Twelve Simple Prayers (Appendix 3) could be used

in whole or in part during gathered worship.

I will host on my website (www.brianmclaren.net) some open-source space for sharing resources that can supplement 'holding the moment' – songs, litanies (interactive prayers), common prayers (written and read in unison), visual resources (clips from movies, great art, videos), sermon ideas, and so on. Drawing upon our God-given creativity, we can unleash a wave of needed liturgical renewal.

You could build a weekend retreat around the twelve practices, scheduling half-hour practice sessions for each practice, with time in between for quiet reflection, reading, sharing of experiences and fellowship. One person could lead all twelve practices, or twelve people could each practice – in private – with one, and then lead in public from their own experience.

You could plan a series of four sermons or teachings introducing each trio of practices, and then lead people in experiencing them, taking just two or three minutes per practice.

Each practice could be integrated with a body prayer, perhaps introducing one per week (see Appendix 2).

Appendix 2: Body Prayers

There are endless ways gesture and posture can be used to augment these simple practices. Here are a few possibilities:[3]

Here   Hold your palms open and facing down, saying, 'I am here in this place, now.' Then turn them upward, saying, 'I am here in this place, open to you, God.'

Thanks!   Raise your fists (in defiance against greed and the 'never-enough' system), and then open them as a gesture of thanksgiving to God, appreciating the abundance you already possess.

O!   Turn your open eyes towards the sky and open your hands upwards, gradually bringing your hands to your heart, lowering your head and closing your eyes, mirroring a glance toward the greatness of God leading to a humble, heartfelt response.

Sorry!   Cup your hands over your face as you name your wrongs, then open them as cups to receive God's mercy, finally splashing your face with mercy as with cold, clean water.

Help! Imagine your anxieties as a cloud above you, and clench your fists to express your anxiety. Then imagine the cloud condensing into a request and capture the request in cupped hands. Raise the request to God in open hands.

Please! Place your hands on your heart and call to mind a name of a person in need. As you lift that person into God's compassion, lift your hands to God as if you were lifting a baby into God's arms.

When? Stand at attention with head raised upward and hands at your side, as you name your aspirations and exasperations. Let your erect posture say, 'I am waiting.'

No! Cross your arms in an X, with your hands in fists, as you tell God what you will not do, accept, believe or settle for.

Why? Kneel with your hands open at your side, or lie prostrate with your hands open at your side, in an expression of not knowing and not understanding.

Behold Hold your hands outward as if welcoming or beckoning, as if to say, 'Let it come, let it be, let it be seen.'

Yes Interlace your fingers or lightly press your hands palm to palm, as if balancing God's *yes* to you and your *yes* to God.

[...] Rest your hands in your lap, one cradled in another, or fingers interlaced, expressing your rest in God's loving gaze.

Appendix 3: Twelve Simple Prayers

One simple word isn't intended to preclude other words. Rather, by using the one word, you create space for other words to arise. So you can create and tend soul-space with one word, but then let others flow as well. On my website (www.brianmclaren.net), I've posted twelve prayers associated with the twelve practices that have emerged from my own experience. But more important and helpful to you than reading my words will be to compose some of your own. The following prompts can serve that purpose. My suspicion is that if you were to use these prompts again a month, a year or a decade from now, very different responses would come, and you could trace the themes of your own spiritual story through subsequent responses to the same prompts.

Here

Here I am, Lord.
(Where are you? Physically? Emotionally? Personally?
   Socially? Spiritually?)
And here you are, Lord.

(Describe your experience of or feelings about God at this moment. How would you name God today?)

Here we are together.

(How would you describe your togetherness with God?)

Thanks!

Thank you, Lord, for ...

(Name gifts as they come to mind.)

If I stopped being grateful ...

(Tell God what would happen to you if you didn't give thanks....)

Thank you!

(Describe how you feel to be so blessed.)

O!

O, how _____ you are!

(Fill in the blank with a general quality that you associate with God, such as creative, mysterious, etc.)

You ....

(Complete the sentence with specific examples of the general quality you just named: 'You made the bird singing outside my window.')

O, how I _____ you!

(Fill in the blank with an appropriate verb such as love, honour, appreciate, etc.)

Sorry!

I'm sorry, Lord. I ...

(Confess what causes you regret – an action, an attitude, a flaw, a failure.)

I feel ...

(*Describe how you feel about what you have
   confessed.*)
Have mercy on me, gracious God, so that ...
(*Describe what you want to do or how you want to
   live as your move forward.*)

Help!

Today I am anxious about these little things ...
(*Name your minor concerns or anxieties.*)
And I am concerned about these big things...
(*Name your major concerns or anxieties.*)
Help me, Lord. To face these challenges, I need ...
(*Name what you need from God.*)

Please!

I carry a burden today for _____
(*Name a person or group for whom you feel compas-
   sion.*)
Please supply what they need, Lord ...
(*Name what they need.*)
I join you in your great compassion so that ...
(*Describe the outcome you desire.*)

When?

How long, Lord, until ...?
(*Describe what you are longing for.*)
I'm waiting, Lord, for you to ...
(*Describe what you need God to do or supply for you.*)
Until then, I trust you and reach out to you for ...
(*Describe the virtue or personal quality that you need
   to be sustained this day, this moment.*)

No!

I refuse to believe that ...
(Describe the doubt that you are struggling against.)
This is unacceptable to me because ...
(Name the beliefs and hopes that you are holding onto.)
No, Lord! May it never be that ...
(Describe the outcome you feel must be avoided.)

Why?

Why must it be that ...?
(Describe what has happened.)
I had hoped ...
(Articulate the hope that has been dashed or disappointed.)
In the middle of this pain, I affirm ...
(What good can you will with God?)

Behold

Behold! Now I see ...
(What previously resisted truth or insight do you now see in a new light?)
Behold! Now I feel ...
(Describe how you feel and how it differs from what you felt before.)
Spirit of God, now I know ...
(What new confidence has arisen within you?)

Yes

Living God, I feel you are offering me ...

(What do you feel God wants to give you? To what do you want to be receptive?)

I say Yes. Living God, I believe you are asking me ...

(What requests, invitations, or promptings do you feel arising in your soul?)

I say Yes. Living God, I offer myself to you.

(Describe what it means for you to surrender yourself to God.)

[...]

I am with you, Lord. As a ...

(In what ways are you with God?)

We are together, living God, as one.

(Silence.)

We. Amen.

(Silence.)

(For additional resources related to this book, you are invited to www.brianmclaren.net)

Notes

Preface

1. See 1 Samuel 19:23–24; Isaiah 20:3; Matthew 5:40.
2. See Mark 15:16–46.
3. See Genesis 2:25.

Introduction

1. In my previous book, *A New Kind of Christianity: Ten Questions That Are Transforming the Faith* (Hodder Faith, 2010, p. 305), I addressed the danger of focusing so much on the head that we forget the heart. 'In the end,' I said, 'if this quest leads only to a reformation in our thinking and talking, it is not a new kind of Christianity at all, but just a variation on an old kind ... So our quest calls us first and foremost to nurture a robust spiritual life ... a deep desire to know and love God.' Those sentences provide the bridge between that book and this.
2. The quote continues: 'As you know, the act of lovemaking requires some degree of nakedness, and perhaps sacred

silence to absorb the communion that is happening. The same is true in loving and being loved by God. We have to let go of our false self (as superior or as inferior) to be ready for real unity with God...' From Richard Rohr, *Simplicity: The Freedom of Letting Go* (Crossroad, 2004), p. 97.

3. This life characterised by naked encounter with God is what another Catholic thinker, Carl Rahner, meant by being a *mystic* in his famous quote: 'The Christian of the future will be a mystic or he [or she] will not exist at all.'

Chapter 1

1. Quoted in Jane Redmont, *When in Doubt, Sing* (Sorin, 2008), p. 312.

2. Nobody captures the embarrassments of growing up fundamentalist better than Frank Schaeffer in his sparkling fiction like *Portofino*, *Saving Grandma*, and *Zermatt* (DeCapo, 2004) and his disarmingly vulnerable non-fiction like *Crazy for God* (DeCapo, 2008).

3. Barbara Bradley Hagerty exemplifies a non-reductive, multi-perspective exploration of spiritual experience in *Fingerprints of God: The Search for the Science of Spirituality* (Riverhead, 2009).

4. Soon, the hope was that they would become Republicans too.

Chapter 2

1. Kenneth Leech, *True Prayer* (Morehouse, 1995), p. 39.

2. The adjective 'organised' deserves additional attention. Obviously, what people are looking for isn't disorganised

religion. But they sense that as religion becomes captive to an organisation or institution, something vital can easily be lost. That something vital includes many things: a mission of social transformation (as opposed to a regime of social control), a sense of dynamic community or fellowship (as opposed to static institutional membership), and the experience of vital spiritual connection that we're exploring in these pages (as opposed to ritual or conceptual conformity).

3. I'm using the word communion here as an alternative to the union of fusion on the one hand and the division of separation on the other. The two remain two but are intimately joined in love; there is difference without division.

4. According to Cicero (1st century BCE), the Latin root of the word was *re-legere* (the root of our words lectionary and lecture). So religion involved reading ancient texts again and again for new meaning. This meaning is related to re-interpreting – giving things a second thought. These two etymologies can be seen as mutually supportive. See Timothy Beal, *The Rise and Fall of the Bible* (Houghton Mifflin Harcourt, 2011), p. 184.

5. It's interesting that two of the key metaphors in the New Testament seek to capture this connection. Jesus' term *Kingdom of God* (which I explore at length in my book *The Secret Message of Jesus* [Thomas Nelson, 2007]) portrays a connection or community that includes God and creation. This beautiful whole, is, in this way, bigger than either God alone or creation alone, and comprises both. Similarly, Paul's term *body of Christ* connects God-in-Christ and humanity-in-creation, bringing them into a larger communion – again not a simple union or fusion where one is absorbed in or reduced to the other, but where one and

the other experience an at-one-ment, a one-anotherness, in which otherness remains but doesn't divide.

6. We might say that there are forms of deadly connection that contrast with vital connection. Colonialism, domination, assimilation, hostile takeover, conquest and lust, for example, all seek a deadly connection that degrades the identity of 'the other' into 'the one'. Vital connection, however, enhances, dignifies, celebrates and preserves 'otherness' in the sacred communion of 'one-anotherness'.

7. I'm leaving unaddressed the issue of clothing as an expression of personality, flair, style, class, and so on, although such a discussion would produce useful insights about religious life.

8. Because this is a book about spirituality rather than scholarship, I'm putting aside questions of authorship, source criticism, historicity, and so on, and taking the Gospel stories at face value, seeking meaning, guidance and insight for our lives today.

9. See John 4.

10. John 3:5.

11. Although powerful impersonal images are used to describe the Spirit – fire, wind, water and so on – we don't relate to the Spirit as an impersonal force or an 'it', but rather as a 'You'. That 'You' is not smaller or less than a force, but greater and more. The impersonal images help us avoid reducing the Spirit to a mere personification or projection of human personhood, but the You-ness of the Spirit helps us avoid reducing the Spirit to an impersonal force. In this dynamic tension, we encounter both You-ness and mystery, and that tension deserves to be preserved and celebrated rather than resolved one way or the other.

12. Some readers will say that Jesus too created an in-group that rendered others into an out-group. No doubt his followers were quick to do so (see, for example, Luke 9:54). But Jesus consistently rebukes his disciples when they use their affiliation with him as an exclusive barrier: he intends their identity as his disciples and apostles to be a bridge to others, not a barrier that excludes them.

13. For example, in healing a blind man (9:1–12), he moves from physical blindness to the deeper reality of spiritual blindness. In providing bread to a hungry crowd (6:1–14), he points to the deeper reality of spiritual nourishment. And in raising Lazarus from the dead (11:38–44), he points to a higher kind of life that transcends physical death.

14. John 2:1–11.

15. John the Baptist and Paul both use the term 'be baptised in (or with) the Spirit', which literally means be immersed into or plunged into or saturated with the Spirit. It's one of the under-appreciated purposes of Jesus' coming: to introduce or awaken humanity to the Spirit, not just as a concept but as an experience, a naked reality in which we live and move and breathe. See Mark 1:8, I Cor: 12:13, along with John 15:5 and John 3:5.

16. See Ephesians 5:18–19; John 15:5, 22; John 20:22; John 14:23.

17. See Romans 7:1–6 or Revelation 19:9; 21:2; 22:17.

Chapter 3

1. Quoted in Kenneth Leech, *True Prayer* (Morehouse, 1995), p. 39.

2. Thanks to the work of Dallas Willard and Richard Foster

for this approach to spiritual disciplines or practices. See
especially Willard, *Spirit of the Disciplines* (HarperOne,
1990) and Foster, *Celebration of Discipline*
(HarperSanFrancisco, 1988).

3. Some, like pragmatist philosopher William James, emphasise
    the personal dimension. Others, like sociologist Emile
    Durkheim, emphasise the social dimension (which he calls
    the cult). Similarly, some religious traditions – like
    Evangelicalism – emphasise the personal, while others, like
    Roman Catholicism, emphasise the social. But in the end,
    all agree both dimensions matter. See Jack Barbalet's dis-
    cussion in 'Classical Pragmatism, Classical Sociology:
    William James, Religion and Emotion', Patrick Baert and
    Bryan Turner (eds.), *Pragmatism and European Social
    Theory* (The Bardwell Press, 2007), pp. 17–45. Also available
    at http://www.jackbarbalet.com/uploads/CLASSICAL_
    PRAGMATISM.pdf.

4. A book like this one, in this light, has value in introducing
    you as an individual reader to personal practice. It can have
    greater value when a reading group uses it as a basis for
    social practice. Its greatest value comes, I think, when a
    group of practitioners finds and maintains a relationship to
    an ongoing faith community or tradition where the spiritual
    practices have been embodied over many generations. For
    more on this subject, see Michael Polanyi, *Personal
    Knowledge: Towards a Post-Critical Philosophy* (University
    of Chicago, 1974).

5. One of the most heart-breaking stories I hear from my spir-
    itual-but-not-religious friends again and again runs like this:
    When I tried to find a community where I could deepen my
    spirituality, I was judged and turned away because I wasn't

spiritual enough. Like banks that won't give you a loan unless you prove you don't need it, or health insurers that won't insure you unless you prove you're already healthy, these communities help give religion a bad name. Much of my life's work, first as a pastor and now as an author, is aimed at rectifying the sad reality that welcoming and transformative spiritual communities remain too few and too hard to find.

6. Those thinkers included William Blake (innocence, experience, higher innocence), Soren Kierkegaard (aesthetic, ethical, religious), William Perry (dualism, multiplicity, relativism, commitment), William Fowler (primal, mythical-literal, synthetic-conventional, individual-reflective, conjunctive, universalising), and Clare Graves, Don Beck and Ken Wilber (archaic/instinctive, animist/tribal, egocentric/exploitive, absolutist/authoritarian, scientific/strategic, relativistic/communitarian, systemic-integral, holistic), along with Sigmund Freud, Erik Erikson and Abraham Maslow.

7. Of course I don't intend these twelve to be an exhaustive list. Rather, they are a primer – a good start.

8. I've included traditional religious words like invocation and intercession, but I've tried to pair them with less explicitly religious words like presentation and compassion. This pairing will be of benefit to both religious and more-spiritual-than-religious people, providing a mixture of familiarity, freshness and accessibility.

9. In other words, harmony warms into a new simplicity, which leads to a new complexity, and so on. If, following the work of Alexander Shaia in *The Hidden Power of the Gospels* (HarperOne, 2010), you wanted to link one of the

four gospels to each season, I would suggest Mark/simplicity, Matthew/complexity, Luke/perplexity and John/harmony.

10. See 'Two Giant Fat People', in Daniel Ladinsky (translator), *The Gift: Poems by Hafiz, the Great Sufi Master* (Penguin Compass, 1999).

One: Simplicity

1. The phrase 'first love' evokes both the romantic experience of being 'in love' and the spiritual experience of lost love in Revelation 2:4.

2. My thinking here is especially indebted to William Perry, Jr, *Forms of Intellectual and Ethical Development in the College Years: A Scheme* (Holt, Rinehart and Winston, 1970), and 'Cognitive and Ethical Growth: The Making of Meaning', in Arthur W. Chickering and Associates, *The Modern American College* (Jossey-Bass, 1981), pp. 76–116.

3. It also may give us a few secret moments of great anxiety about the danger of being wrong – or just as bad, being *considered* wrong by our in-group with its strict standards.

Chapter 4

1. Quoted in Esther de Waal, *Seeking God* (Liturgical Press, 2001), p. 65.

2. I realise that Lewis himself would recoil from the implication that could be drawn from this line from the poem – that God is a 'thing'.

3. The Hebrew prophet Elijah mocked this idea that God requires a wake-up call (1 Kgs 18:27). When he confronted the prophets of Baal and witnessed their extravagant

attempts to get God to do their bidding, he taunted them along these lines: 'Shout louder! Maybe your god is deep in thought, or maybe he's busy, or away on a trip. Maybe he fell asleep!'

4. The refrain of an old hymn, the standard of Baptist altar calls, captures this here-ness beautifully: 'Just as I am, I come. I come.'

5. 'Isms' have been humorously defined as conceptual systems that try to convince us they contain all there is(m).

6. Richard Rohr, *The Naked Now: Learning to See as the Mystics See* (Crossroad, 2009).

Chapter 5

1. Sam Keen, *In the Absence of God* (Harmony, 2010), p. 74.

2. Exodus 3:1–6. Many readers will wonder if I believe these stories to be historically reliable. For some, Bible stories seem like fairy tales or silly legends because they contain supernatural elements, and so should be treated with suspicion, even condescension or mockery. For others, because the stories are in the Bible, they must be taken as factually, historically accurate in every detail. I'm not bothered by supernatural elements (although I am bothered by the modernist assumptions behind the watertight categories of natural and supernatural). Nor do I concern myself much with the historical accuracy of all these stories. Instead, whether these stories are journalistically accurate or literarily and imaginatively enhanced, I seek to plumb the profound, inspired meaning and wisdom they are intended to convey. If there was a man named Moses who saw a bush burning one day and said exactly the things we find in Exodus, that's wonderful. If the story instead is meant to convey through an artistic account a

crucial realisation that has arisen in human culture more generally about the God-human relationship, that's fine too. Either way, whether the story is historical or imaginative, I am free to receive it and savour it in all its revelatory fullness. I hope you feel the same freedom.

3. Ardent Bible readers may see a tension between this depiction of God as a non-consuming fire and the opposite depiction in Deuteronomy 4:24, echoed in Hebrews 12:29. I might suggest that the only thing God can 'consume' or destroy is evil. In that light, 'God is a consuming fire' would be better rendered, 'God is a purifying fire.' The bush, being a good element of God's good creation, has nothing evil to be purified of. Thanks to Shane Claiborne for this insight, via personal conversation.

4. The reference to Moses' father is fascinating, since Moses was separated from his true father and raised as an adopted son in Pharaoh's family as a consequence of Pharaoh's paranoid attempt at population control. So God could be saying, 'I am the God of your actual father – the slave, not your adoptive father – the slave-driver.' In other words, 'I am the God who names you with your true and original identity.'

5. This occurs, for example, when the patriarch Abraham argues and bargains with God in Genesis 18:22–32. Similarly, when the word of the Lord comes to Jeremiah, Jeremiah responds with an excuse: 'I'm not eloquent and I'm too young' (1:6). And when Mary receives an angelic visitor, she asks a question: 'How can this be?' (Luke 1:34).

6. The name Israel means *striver* or 'wrestler' with God (Gen. 38:28).

7. Here is St Francis' actual prayer: *Dio mio e mio tutto! Il*

Signor Iddio, io sono niente, ma tutto e la Vostra. (My God and my all. Lord God, I am nothing, but all is yours.)

8. Cynthia Bourgeault describes this idea of home beautifully in her book *The Wisdom Way of Knowing: Reclaiming an Ancient Tradition to Awaken the Heart* (Jossey-Bass, 2003), especially in the poem on pages 38–40.

Chapter 6

1. Quoted in Sam Keen, *In the Absence of God* (Harmony, 2010), p. 92.
2. Thanks to Josef Pieper for this insight, in *Happiness and Contemplation* (St Augustine, 1999).
3. This is an important theme in my book *Everything Must Change* (Thomas Nelson, 2008).

Chapter 7

1. Evelyn Underhill, Life as Prayer (Harrisburg, PA: Morehouse Publishing), p.186.
2. Sadly, under King Solomon, they did just that. Today's victims too easily become tomorrow's victimisers – a pattern repeated again and again in history.
3. This is, I believe, the core meaning of Matthew 6:33.
4. See James 1:2, Philippians 4:11 and 1 Thessalonians 5:18.

Chapter 8

1. John Muir, selected and adapted. See http://hummingbirdworld.com/spiritnature/muir.htm.
2. Like all good things, authentic Pentecostal worship is in many if not most places under assault by a kind of hyped-up bastardisation, useful in priming people for making big offerings to clever purveyors of the so-called prosperity

gospel, which seldom helps anyone achieve prosperity except the preacher.

3. Barbara Ehrenreich, *Dancing in the Streets: A History of Collective Joy* (Holt, 2007). Thanks to Ken Medema for recommending this book.

4. Kester Brewin, *Other: Loving Self, God and Neighbour in a World of Fractures* (HodderFaith, 2010).

5. Read again, in this light, the story of the sacred convocation in Nehemiah 8. Holiness demanded not solemnity but joy.

6. William Temple (1881–1944), Anglican priest, Bishop of York, and Archbishop of Canterbury, defined worship in terms thast comprise our spiritual practices of confession (quickening the conscience), meditation (feeding the mind), invocation (opening the heart), and surrender (devoting the will). Worship as explored in this chapter would correspond most specifically to his 'purging of the imagination by the beauty of God'. See Appendix 1 for more on Temple.

7. For more on this unitive way of seeing, see Richard Rohr's *The Naked Now* (Crossroad, 2009), and Jill Bolte Taylor's stroke of insight, available at: http://www.ted.com/talks/jill_bolte_taylor_s_powerful_stroke_of_insight.html.

8. Andrew Newberg and Mark Robert Waldman, *How God Changes Your Brain* (Ballantine, 2010). Michael Gerson's review can be found at http://www.washingtonpost.com/wp dyn/content/article/2009/04/14/AR2009041401879.html.

Chapter 9

1. From Jane Redmont, *When in Doubt, Sing* (Sorin, 2008), pp. 207–208. The original prayer in Hebrew is: '*Baruch ata*

Adonai, Elohenu, melech ha-olam shecheheyanu, v'ke-y'manu, v'higi'anu, la-z'man hazeh.'

2. From a song lyric by the author.

3. For a brief reading of Romans, see *A New Kind of Christianity* (Hodder Faith, 2010), ch. 15.

4. Here I am echoing an insight from Dallas Willard in *The Divine Conspiracy* (HarperSanFrancisco, 1998).

5. For more on fixed-hour prayer and related ancient practices, see the series for which Phyllis Tickle serves as general editor, which I had the privilege of introducing with *Finding Our Way Again: The Return of the Ancient Practices* (Thomas Nelson, 2007).

Two: Complexity

1. The world is still divided between good and evil, but now the good are identified less as the correct and more as the effective ... less as the ones who get things right and more as the ones who get things done.

Chapter 10

1. Fr Richard Rohr, *Falling Upward: A Spirituality for the Two Halves of Life* (Jossey-Bass, 2011), Ch 1.

2. Gareth Higgins wrote *How Movies Helped Save My Soul* (Relevant, 2003).

3. The Greek word for confession in the New Testament captures this idea beautifully. *Homologeo* literally means *say the same thing*. In confession, I try to say the same thing God would say about my behaviour.

4. See 2 Samuel 11–12.

5. Nobody I know has written more insightfully about the relationship between personage and person than Paul

Tournier, beginning with *The Meaning of Persons* (Harper & Row, 1982).

6. Of course, to modern ears, animal sacrifice sounds brutal as well. But in context, slaughter was the first stage in cooking a meal – as much a part of life as visiting the grocery store or opening the refrigerator are for us today.

7. By the use of the word 'possessed' here, I am echoing insights about the demonic in Scripture for which I am indebted to Walter Wink. See, for starters, *The Powers That Be* (Galilee, 1999).

Chapter 11

1. Quoted in Jane Redmont, *When in Doubt, Sing* (Sorin, 2008), p. 100.

2. This environment of grace, by the way, differs greatly from an imposter environment often labelled *accountability*. In groups built around a misguided sense of accountability, people often reinforce the sin-avoidance mindset. They share their secrets and failings at a weekly meeting under the assumption that they'll do better next week in order to avoid the shame of being exposed as a failure. In other words, accountability stops being about the grace of radical acceptance and becomes instead about the fear of shameful rejection.

3. You can imagine parallel dynamics being set in motion when we define ourselves in the opposite state, saying, 'I'm a bad person.'

4. We will deal further with the experience of being wronged in the practice of compassion and intercession.

5. The early church had a fascinating practice that has been lost in all but some Eastern Orthodox churches. At baptism,

new converts would spit toward the west. The land of the setting sun was seen as the home of the devil, and the new converts were in this way spitting in the face of the devil. At the beginning of their Christian life, they were switching sides and renouncing evil, ritually expressing that they now were members of a community that took evil seriously and positively despised it. Confession, seen in this light, allows us to maintain our hatred for evil, while simultaneously avoiding the temptation to pretend we are free from it. It allows us to simultaneously hold a high standard of behaviour while acknowledging that we fall far below it – all the while aspiring to elevate our behaviour rather than depress our high ideal.

6. The Big Kahuna (1999). Franchise Pictures. For more information, see www.imdb.com/title/tt0189584/.

7. In the Eastern Orthodox tradition, various versions of 'the Jesus prayer' have proven themselves deeply valuable to millions of people, including me. The version I have employed for years, 'Lord Jesus Christ, son of the living God, have mercy on me, a sinner,' can hold open space in the soul for confession, especially when the word *sinner* is emphasised. It serves as a sentence-long expression of *sorry*. The prayer can also be used less as a practice of confession/regret and more as a practice of invocation/awakening, functioning as a sentence-length expression of our first spiritual word, *here*.

8. This perfect integration explains why we humans are commanded not to judge. We aren't so good at shining a light on one another that is both just and merciful. Only God's light gets that integration right.

Chapter 12

1. Thomas à Kempis, *The Imitation of Christ*.
2. In his autobiography, Bob Dylan tells about being asked, '[~]"You a prayin' man, huh? What do you pray for? You pray for the world?": I never thought about praying for the world. I said, "I pray that I can be a kinder person."[~]' *From Chronicles, Volume One* (Simon & Schuster Pocket Books, 2004), p. 206.
3. Thanks to John Haught for this insight, in *God After Darwin: A Theology of Evolution* (Westview, 2007).
4. Some people's theology won't allow them to speak of Jesus growing. The New Testament has no such hesitancy, as Luke 2:52 and Hebrews 5:8–9 make clear.
5. Luke 22:42.

Chapter 13

1. *Mystically Wired* (Thomas Nelson, 2009), p. 6.
2. By Bruce Wilkinson (Multnomah, 2000).
3. Jesus speaks of the destructive power of anxiety in Matthew 6:25–34, as does Paul in Philippians 4:4–9.
4. Sometimes a fourth 'f' is added to the reptilian response repertoire: to fight, flee, freeze or … copulate, which may explain why powerful and stress-ridden people so often self-destruct through sexual misconduct.
5. Other reasons include the following: 1. I can re-read old prayer journals to get perspective on my spiritual journey. 2. The discipline of journaling my prayers helps me keep track of whether I have actually been praying or not. 3. Journaling helps me focus specific attention on each of the twelve different practices we're exploring in this book. 4. In a small group or with a spiritual director, I can share

various parts of my journal as a window into my spiritual life. 5. The act of writing prayers helps me slow down and go deeper, accessing deeper parts of me than I would if I were praying without writing. 6. Sometimes, written prayers become works of art – poems or songs or stories. For others with appropriate talent, they might also inspire drawings or paintings.

6. I originally learned this simple but helpful idea from John Maxwell. He is also the speaker who quoted Abraham Lincoln in the story shared in the previous chapter. For more on John's work, see http://www.johnmaxwell.com.

Chapter 14

1. Quoted in Kenneth Leech, *True Prayer* (Morehouse, 1995), p. 22.

2. Thanks to Parker Palmer for this beautiful image, from 'The Broken-Open Heart: Living with Faith and Hope in the Tragic Gap', available here: http://www.upperroom.org/weavings/pdf/PalmerReprint. Weavings.pdf.

3. This is described poignantly by the Apostle Paul (2 Cor. 1:3–11), who confesses to a spell of near-suicidal depression when he was 'so utterly, unbearably crushed that [he] despaired of life itself.' Eventually, he experienced God's comfort and was able to pass it on to others.

4. The technical word for attempted answers to these questions is *theodicy*.

5. A team led by Karen Armstrong has helped us move in this direction by drafting the Charter for Compassion (http://charterforcompassion.org), which reads as follows:

The principle of compassion lies at the heart of all

religious, ethical and spiritual traditions, calling us always to treat all others as we wish to be treated ourselves. Compassion impels us to work tirelessly to alleviate the suffering of our fellow creatures, to dethrone ourselves from the centre of our world and put another there, and to honour the inviolable sanctity of every single human being, treating everybody, without exception, with absolute justice, equity and respect.

It is also necessary in both public and private life to refrain consistently and empathically from inflicting pain. To act or speak violently out of spite, chauvinism or self-interest, to impoverish, exploit or deny basic rights to anybody, and to incite hatred by denigrating others – even our enemies – is a denial of our common humanity. We acknowledge that we have failed to live compassionately and that some have even increased the sum of human misery in the name of religion.

We therefore call upon all men and women – to restore compassion to the centre of morality and religion – to return to the ancient principle that any interpretation of scripture that breeds violence, hatred or disdain is illegitimate – to ensure that youth are given accurate and respectful information about other traditions, religions and cultures – to encourage a positive appreciation of cultural and religious diversity – to cultivate an informed empathy with the suffering of all human beings, even those regarded as enemies.

We urgently need to make compassion a clear, luminous and dynamic force in our polarised world. Rooted in a principled determination to transcend selfishness, compassion can break down political, dogmatic, ideological and religious boundaries. Born of our deep interdependence, compassion is essential to human relationships and to a fulfilled humanity. It is the path to enlightenment, and indispensable to the creation of a just economy and a peaceful global community.

6. See, for example, Matthew 9:36; 14:14; 15:32; Mark 6:34.

7. See John 7:48–49 in contrast to Matthew 9:36.

8. See John 8 and John 4 for the stories of these two women.

9. Compare Matthew 5:43–48 to Luke 6:32–36.

10. Since this is a primary theme of the paradigmatic biblical story of the Exodus, you might think such a point would not need to be made. But history – including contemporary religious history – proves otherwise.

11. See John 19:15.

Chapter 15

1. Philip Yancey, *Prayer: Does It Make Any Difference?* (Zondervan, 2006), p. 308.

2. See Romans 8:19–27.

3. A version of this story originally appeared in *Dreamseeker Magazine* (Autumn, 2001), and is available online here: http://www.cascadiapublishinghouse.com/dsm/autumn01/mcl abr.htm.

4. For more on this compassionate practice of blessing, which is closely related to intercession, see John O'Donohue's masterpiece, *To Bless the Space Between Us* (Doubleday, 2008).

5. In this regard, see the inspiring prayer by Serbian Orthodox bishop Nikolai Velimirovic, available at: http://brianm-claren.net/archives/prayer-regarding-critics-and-ene-1.html.

6. Two additional comments on this section of the Lord's prayer seem appropriate to add here. First, the word *debt*, used in

Matthew's version of the Lord's prayer (6:12), suggests *a failure to go far enough* in repaying an obligation. It might evoke the problem of indebtedness common in Galilee, where wealthy Judaeans from the south would give loans to their hard-pressed northern neighbours so they could pay their taxes to the Romans. Mutual forgiveness would signal reconciliation among people separated by class and political affiliation in Jesus' Jewish community. In contrast, the word *trespasses* is used in the commentary on the prayer (6:14). It suggests *going too far*, crossing a boundary of rightness or propriety. It may be a special reference to the Romans, whose occupation of Israel was an ultimate act of trespass. For the oppressed to forgive their foreign oppressors would be even more radical than for Galileans and Judeans to reconcile. Taken together, the words suggest radical reconciliation both among 'us' and with 'them'.

7. Not insignificantly, this teaching against revenge is one of the most frequently repeated imperatives in the New Testament.

8. See, for example, C. S. Lewis' classic *The Problem of Pain* (HarperOne, 2001), and Philip Yancey's *Prayer: Does It Make Any Difference?* (Zondervan, 2006).

9. The issues of suffering, God's agency, miracles and unanswered prayer come up in my book, *The Story We Find Ourselves In* (Jossey-Bass, 2008), *Finding Faith: A Search for What Makes Sense* (Zondervan, 2007), and *A New Kind of Christianity* (HarperOne, 2010).

10. A song, 'With Kindness', adapted from St Teresa, on my *Songs for a Revolution of Hope*, available at www.brian mclaren.net.

Chapter 16

1. Philip Yancey, *Prayer: Does It Make Any Difference?* (Zondervan, 2006), p. 32.

2. For more information on Kent Annan, see his first book *Following Jesus Through the Eye of the Needle* (IVP, 2009), and go to http://www.haitipartners.org. His new book, *After Shock* (IVP, 2011), recounts his experiences in Haiti since the earthquake.

3. Sadly, many, including some Wesleyans, interpreted entire sanctification to mean technical perfection, as if one could begin scoring a perfect ten morally day after day. This kind of immature scorekeeping sadly subverts Wesley's project, which aimed for something far greater and more challenging than avoiding a list of sins. His goal was maturity, a habitual state of living in love for God and others. The best description of Wesley's project that I've read is Thomas Oord and Michael Lodahi's *Relational Holiness: Responding to the Call of Love* (Beacon Hill, 2005).

4. These examples come from an old hymnal found by a friend in a second-hand bookshop in London: *The Methodist Hymn-Book* (Wesleyan Conference Office). Although the edition is undated, it was commissioned in 1901. They are found in a section entitled 'Aspiration and Hope,' in the subsections 'For Believers Praying' and 'For Believers Seeking Full Redemption'. However one may criticise the details of the Wesley's doctrine of entire sanctification, and putting aside the spiritual pathologies one can perhaps trace back to it, one can't deny the spiritual fervour – the anti-complacency and anti-apathy – evoked by these hymns. Nor can one deny their honesty. By expressing what they desire, the poets are frankly admitting what they do not yet have or

feel or experience. One can't help but lament how few hymns and songs in use today ring true with either this fervency or this honesty.

Chapter 17

1. Thanks to Erroll Narain for this reference.
2. Lucretius 'On the Nature of Things,' available online at: http://classics.mit.edu/Carus/nature_things.1.i.html.

Chapter 18

1. Quoted in Sam Keen, *In the Absence of God* (Harmony, 2010), p. 3.
2. Even faith communities that try to exclude doubters repeatedly have to acknowledge the place of sceptics among them. Biblical characters like Elijah, like Job can be saintly one day and sceptical the next. And today's true believers can have children who, when they come of age, raise tough questions in the community of faith.
3. C. S. Lewis, *The Problem of Pain* (HarperSanFrancisco, 2001).

Chapter 19

1. Quoted in Kenneth Leech, *True Prayer* (Morehouse, 1995), p. 84.
2. In this light, as Gustavo Gutierrez says (*On Job: God-Talk and the Suffering of the Innocent* [Maryknoll, 1987], p. 13), Job isn't primarily about explaining the existence of evil as is commonly assumed. Instead, it grapples with a far more practical question: *how can we wisely speak of and with God in the midst of evil?* See also Jane Redmont, *When in Doubt, Sing* (Sorin, 2008), p. 390.

3. It might be said that Palestinians face a related agony today. They repeatedly hear both Jewish and Christian Zionists minimise Palestinian anguish under Jewish occupation, and although they cry, 'No!', few seem to take notice, and things go from bad to worse.

4. http://blog.beliefnet.com/godspolitics/2008/05/never-again-by-duane-shank.html.

5. Richard Rohr captures it well in *Job and the Mystery of Suffering* (Crossroad, 1996) p. 20–21:

> An awful lot of religion is an excuse for not facing our fears, our self, and our doubts. True religion is not denial of doubt but a transformation of it; and often, to be honest, a temporary deepening of our doubt and darkness to get us there.
>
> God walks with us into our fears, to feel them, to own them, to let them teach us. During that time we are often in darkness and cannot uphold ourselves. It even feels like a loss of faith. It is then that we slowly learn to let Someone Else hold us, and we come out enlarged and more hopeful. As long as I have lived, I cannot explain the chemistry of this transformation, but those who have gone through *know* it to be true.

6. The questions, significantly, are about creation, which is God's original 'word' or self-expression. God's creation, in all its mystery, dynamism and complexity, deconstructs the feeble and simplistic moralisms and theological theories of Job's friends. And Job himself recognises that God's frame of reference is far bigger than his own, which reduces him to the same silence that his friends have been reduced to. Something similar seems to have happened, by the way, in recent years, where Darwin, Freud, Einstein, Hubble and others similarly

brought the 'logos' of creation to bear on many theological assumptions. The one once again deconstructed the other, much to the chagrin of many religious people.

7. Bruce Cockburn, from 'Understanding Nothing', on *Big Circumstance* (Golden Mountain Music Corp., 1988).

Chapter 20

1. Ruth Haley Barton, *Invitation to Solitude and Silence* (InterVarsity Press, 2004), p. 82.
2. One of the best definitions of orthodoxy I've read comes from Kenneth Leech: 'Orthodoxy is about being consumed by glory: the word means not "right belief" (as dictionaries tell us) but right *doxa,* right glory. To be orthodox is to be set alight by the fire of God.' Kenneth Leech, *True Prayer* (Morehouse, 1995), p. 11.
3. Walter Brueggemann, *Spirituality of the Psalms* (Augsburg Fortress, 2001).
4. Romans 8:18 (NIV).
5. Romans 8:22 (NIV).
6. Little is said about the possibility that the venom and violence of fundamentalists of various religions is a projection outward of their own inner turmoil and grief – turmoil and grief about a theology that is failing them individually and as a community.

Chapter 21

1. From my own song, 'Why God, Why?'
2. PFLAG: Parents, Friends (& Family) of Lesbians and Gays (see http://www.pflag.org.uk).
3. This is Matthew's wording (26:39). Luke's is similar (22:42). Mark's, which we might presume to be less edited, is even

stronger (14:36): 'Everything is possible for you. Take this cup from me.'

4. My Jewish friends might similarly say that during the holocaust, G-d was on the trains, in the camps, even in the gas chambers.

Four: Harmony

1. In *Finding Our Way Again* (Thomas Nelson, 2008), I expressed a similar idea with similar imagery: 'You can't take an epidural shot to ease the pain of giving birth to character. In a sense, every day of your life is labour: the rhythmic agony of producing the person who will wake up in your body tomorrow, creating your reputation, continuing your legacy, and influencing your family, friends, colleagues, neighbours and countless strangers, for better or worse' (p.11).

2. Paraphrased from Matthew 12:7; Matthew 6:33; Matthew 22:36-40; 1 Corinthians 13:13.

3. See Ecclesiastes 3:11; 1 Corinthians 13:12.

Chapter 22

1. Sam Keen *In the Absence of God* (Harmony, 2010), p. 85.

2. See Richard Rohr's *The Naked Now: Learning to See as the Mystics See* (Crossroad, 2009). Richard uses the term *contemplative* more broadly to include what I'm calling meditative seeing. I'm going to apply the word *contemplation* more narrowly in our last chapter.

3. Genesis 1:31. The word *behold* plays a fascinating structural role in the Genesis text in those translations that retain it (e.g. KJV, RSV). Note its significance in 1:29, 1:31, 3:22, 4:14 and 6:12.

4. This is not to deny that in simplicity, complexity and perplexity we were also seeing with God. When we learned to identify good and evil, we were seeing (imperfectly) moral realities that God sees. When we learned to cope with difficulty and complexity – to identify ways and means – we were seeing pragmatic realities that God sees. When we learned to deconstruct human constructions, we were seeing (and seeing through) social and conceptual realities that God sees (and sees through). Even when we learned to doubt human constructions about God, we were coming closer to what only G-d knows about G-d. But if G-d is love, as the New Testament affirms, then to see in love is to see most truly with G-d.

5. See John 8:1–11; Matthew 15:21–28; Acts 10:1–48; John 9:1–41.

6. Sadly, modern translations of 2 Cor. 5:17 for some reason tend to drop the *behold* (in Greek, *idou*, which means *Look! Open your eyes! See! Perceive! Be aware!*).

7. The word *holy* in the noted sentence deserves a brief additional comment here. In dual thinking, holiness suggests purity, according to which those who consider themselves pure judge, condemn and exclude the impure, often with remarkable harshness. Beyond dual thinking, *holiness* suggests *wholly otherness*, which means, among other things, *other-than-unkind* and *other-than-judgemental*. So this wholly otherness means holy otherliness, or perfect love. Non-dual holiness, then, is an even greater purity that includes being purified from harshness, rejection and exclusion. It is a purity that always includes and exudes pure compassion.

It is a holiness so holy that it loves the unholy, recalling

Matt. 5:43–48, especially as compared with Luke 6:27–36.

8. Roland Bainton, *Here I Stand: A Life of Martin Luther* (Mentor Books, 1955), p. 168.

9. Here are Steps 3 and 11 in their original form, as used by Alcoholics Anonymous:

    Step 3: Made a decision to turn our will and our lives over to the care of God *as we understood Him.*

    Step 11: Sought through prayer and meditation to improve our conscious contact with God *as we understood Him,* praying only for knowledge of His will for us and the power to carry that out.

10. The distinction can be felt in contrasting Isaiah 40:8–10 with 1 Kings 12:28. In the former, the people are invited to behold G-d, but in the latter, two politically-useful idols are proposed as a substitute. Isaiah 40, by the way, is certainly one of Scripture's most extravagant attempts at conveying the grandeur of God in words, employing vivid simile, metaphor, and rhetorical question. But even there, awe-inspiring words give way to awe-struck sight, as Isaiah points to the sky and says (40:25–26), finally: *take a look at that!*

11. Peter Rollins explores this theme energetically and brilliantly in his *How (Not) to Speak of God* (Paraclete, 2006).

Chapter 23

1. 'Out of the Question', by David Wilcox © 2003 Gizz Da Baboo (administered by Michelle Ma Soeur [SESAC], a division of Soroka Music Ltd.) Used by permission. All rights reserved.

2. Adapted from Bruce Cockburn's 1987 song, *Understanding*

Nothing. Two cinematic moments also capture this moment of beholding especially well. In *Jurassic Park*, two palaeontologists step out of a jeep to see a landscape in which brontosaurs, stegosaurs and other dinosaurs roam free. Creatures that were accessible to them only as fossils, traces of a lost past, have come to life here and now. In *Contact*, another scientist travels through a wormhole and sees a 'celestial event'; 'Indescribable,' she gasps. 'They should have sent a poet.' Beholding renders all of us dumbstruck, awe-struck. We are prose-bound scientists suddenly confronted by transcendent, poetic beauty.

3. I don't think I was reading Thomas Aquinas (1225–74) that day, but I arrived at the same conclusion he did. Years later I came across this quote: 'What God is always remains hidden from us. And this is the highest knowledge one can have of God in this life, that we know him to be above every thought we are able to think of him.' (Quoted in Kenneth Leech, *True Prayer* [Morehouse, 1995], p. 12).

Chapter 24

1. Quoted in Jane Redmont, *When in Doubt, Sing* (Sorin, 2008), p. 258.

2. Philippians 2:6–11. Interestingly, many translations add to verse six the word *although*, to say, 'Although he was in the form of God, he did not regard...' The text would more naturally read, 'Because he was in the form of God, he did not regard...' His descent reveals God's true nature – humble and self-giving, not detached and dominating.

3. 'Getting saved' or 'being born again' or 'praying the sinner's prayer' or 'making a decision for Christ' or 'accepting

Christ' are various terms Evangelicals use for the first 'yes' to God.

4. See John 15.

Chapter 25

1. From Jane Redmont, *When in Doubt, Sing* (Sorin, 2008), p. 371.

2. Adapted from Richard Rohr *Everything Belongs* (Crossroad, 2003), p. 31.

3. For a fascinating analysis of the four Gospels, see Alexander Shaia with Michelle Gaugy, *The Hidden Power of the Gospels: Four Questions, Four Paths, One Journey* (HarperOne, 2010).

4. Matthew agrees with John and locates the disciples' encounters with the risen Christ in Galilee. By contrast, in Luke's Gospel and in Acts, the disciples are explicitly told to stay in Jerusalem. Taken together, the accounts may suggest that the risen Chrust is to be encountered both at the margins and at the centre of society.

Chapter 26

1. Richard Rohr, *Simplicity: The Freedom of Letting Go* (Crossroad, 2004), p. 97.

2. Quoted in Jane Redmont, *When in Doubt, Sing* (Sorin, 2008), p. 76.

3. Mother Teresa's posthumously-published diaries reveal that she spent much time in Stage Three perplexity where God's presence seemed unavailable to her. That reality in no way undermines the validity and beauty of her life with God, but rather intensifies them.

4. Jim Wallis, *Faith Works: Lessons from the Life of an Activist Preacher* (Random House, 2000), pp. 254–255.

5. For more about Steve – and to order his music – please visit http://www.stevebell.com.

6. I believe it was my friend Jim Henderson from whom I first heard the word 'otherly'.

7. Mikhail Epstein, Alexander Genis and Slobodanka Vladiv-Glover, *Russian Postmodernism: New Perspectives on Post-Soviet Culture* (Berghahn, 1999), p. 169–170.

Chapter 27

1. Barbara Fiand, *Prayer and the Quest for Healing* (Crossroad, 1999), p. 20.

2. We might also say that contemplation is simply the next step beyond normalcy. Eventually all the Pentecostal noise and activity become normal – as do the normal routines of liturgy – and so we move beyond them to silence and rest.

3. Amos 5:24.

Afterword

1. Quoted in Kenneth Leech, *True Prayer* (Morehouse, 1995), p. 39.

2. This beautiful term, 'regenerative community of creation', is from a personal conversation with my friend Dr Randy Woodley, a native American Christian theologian who suggests that 'community of creation' is a good contemporary translation of 'kingdom of God'. 'Creation' in this case doesn't simply mean the thing – the created universe. It means the process of creation – a process in which God and creation collaborate. This term, like the term 'kingdom of God', encompasses both the infinite God and God's finite creation, and so is, if such a thing can be said, a reality bigger than God. However since God is said

to fill all things, it contains nothing that God does not also contain.

3. For Jesus, the greatest commandment was love (Matt. 22:37–40). For Paul, the only thing that matters is faith expressing itself through love (Gal. 5:6). For John, the age-old message we have heard from the beginning is to love one another (1 John 3:11). For the Buddha, each element of the eight-fold path is an expression of love or compassion. And the Beatles, of course, sang, 'All you need is love.'

4. In Jeremiah 22:16, God says that showing love to the poor and needy is what it means to know him.

Appendices

1. I explore this concept in some detail in *Finding Our Way Again: The Return of the Ancient Practices* (Thomas Nelson, 2008).

2. Ian S. Markham in *Liturgical Life Principles* (Morehouse, 2009) offers a needed primer in how liturgy works.

3. For much more on this subject see Doug Pagitt and Kathryn Prill's book *Body Prayer* (WaterBrook, 2005).